Made From Scratch

How to Start and Operate a Successful Organic Container Plant Business

Louise Placek

Acres U.S.A.
Austin, Texas

Made From Scratch

How to Start and Operate a Successful
Organic Container Plant Business

Louise Placek

Illustrations by John, Ruth and Louise Placek

Acres U.S.A.
Austin, Texas

Made From Scratch

How to Start and Operate a Successful
Organic Container Plant Business

Copyright © 2003 Louise Placek

Acres U.S.A.
P.O. Box 91299
Austin, Texas 78709 U.S.A.
(512) 892-4400 • fax (512) 892-4448
info@acresusa.com • www.acresusa.com

Printed in the United States of America

Publisher's Cataloging-in-Publication

Placek, Louise, 1952-
Made from scratch: how to start and operate a successful organic container plant business / Louise Placek
xiv, 288 pp., 23 cm.
Includes bibliographical references and index.
ISBN 0-911311-75-0 (trade)

1. Nurseries (horticulture) — Management — Handbooks, manuals, etc. 2. Potted plant industry — Handbooks, manuals, etc. 3. Ornamental plant industry — Handbooks, manuals, etc. 4. Greenhouse management — Handbook, manuals, etc. 5. Organic farming — Handbooks, manuals, etc. I. Placek, Louise, 1952- II. Title.

SB118.5.P65 2003   635.9/152 P

Acknowledgments

First, I am eternally grateful to my loving, supportive husband and soul mate, Chris, who gave me the courage to quit my nursing career and delve into the world of organic horticulture. He knew I had to do it and was always ready to play "devil's advocate" when I needed a reality check.

I am also indebted to my dad who spent uncounted hours with me in the greenhouse, assisting me with whatever needed doing, and helping me through the learning curve. His strong back and kind heart sustained me through the early years of my business. And to my mother, whose undying enthusiasm for whatever endeavor I have chosen to undertake in my life, has helped maintain my confidence and kinetic energy. Her strength, creativity, loyalty and unconditional love have nourished and inspired me through the years.

I am also thankful for the encouragement of my friends, Marilyn Abbott and Barbara "Bonnie" Lamar, who have helped me as employees and, more importantly, as friends and cheerleaders. Their ardent belief in the importance of what I was doing helped me maintain my focus during difficult times.

Contents

About Misty Hill Farm

In the early 1990s my husband Chris and I decided to buy a wonderful, hilly, 22-acre site that my dad had nabbed some years before. At first glance it didn't stand out much from other Central Texas land, but as we began to explore and watch, we found a magical place.

Beneath our feet, growing in the sandy-loam, are multitudes of ancient prairie grasses, bundles of gorgeous wildflowers and plants whose names and classifications have taken me years to find. The hills are dotted with oak, elm, juniper, prickly ash, hackberry, hickory, cedar, sugarberry, farkle-berry, flame-leaf sumac and pawpaw. The wild grapes, plums and dewberries have filled many a jar in my kitchen with their deep aromas and pungent flavors.

But the real magic was the view from the top of the highest hill where we put our house. From this place you can see storms dancing on the horizon 50 miles away. At night the skyline is freckled with the lights of large and small towns, too far away to see in the day. Many early mornings display placid pools of thick mist in low areas of the gently sloping land below our hill. It is not a surprise that the former owners called this stead Misty Hill.

There are many wonderful things about this special place besides the plethora of native flora, fauna and views. For one, there is a place on a mid-range hill where an oak and a cedar have grown together, literally fusing their trunks at intervals on their journey upward. It is awesome to realize that they are two completely different trees, each maintaining their individuality, yet they share a vascular system. The symbolism did not escape us and we were married under those trees in 1986.

Since we have been here I have observed the healing effect of this land on tired and stressed souls. Often people come here to shed the weight of their lives, meditate, sit, and ponder. Animals are drawn here as well, they seem to know this place is safe.

The plant "farm" was just a logical endeavor on a place like this. Misty Hill Farm was born in 1994 when I hung up my nursing hat and decided to take care of plants instead of people. I had been a registered nurse for almost 20 years and was ready for a new venue for nurturing. The transition was amazingly easy because many of the same principles I once applied to people also work with plants. My biggest challenge with plants was that they couldn't tell me where they hurt. I had to figure that out on my own.

The other challenge I faced was learning to grow container plants commercially without the use of all the industry-standard chemical fertilizers and pesticides. My mission was to prove to the industry that one can grow outstanding plants commercially using only natural, earth-made products. I had no manual or guide. I had no mentor. I had to figure it out and that I did. It was hard and even grueling at times, but very satisfying to accomplish what I set out to do.

Misty Hill Farm is the essence of a new approach to horticulture. It is part of a movement away from the standard use of the agricultural chemicals that are polluting our groundwater and aquifers. I am hopeful that soon all edible plants will be devoid of *any* pesticides and that all container plants will be grown in soil that supplies nourishment from nature, not a lab.

My prayer is that Misty Hill Farm can be an inspiration for those who desire to follow this same path, and that many torches will be lit in the years to come, causing critical mass, and a change in the foundation of the container-plant industry. It is a very worthy cause.

Louise Placek
Misty Hill Farm, 2002

Introduction

I know there are people who never read introductions because they are eager to get to the "real" content of the book. Although I am an introduction reader myself, I understand the temptation to pass it up and get on with the book; especially "how to" books. You just want to get the information and move along with your project.

I'm hoping that since you invested the time and space in your life to extract information from these pages, you will take a few minutes to understand why I wrote this book. It will help you understand more about my approach and my desire to help you become successful in your endeavor to "grow" your business. In this case it is better to take a path traveled by someone who's moccasins have holes from walking it before you.

When I started my container plant business I assumed it would be a piece of cake since I had been growing plants all of my life. I figured I knew all I needed to know about growing plants commercially using organic techniques since I had always eschewed chemicals. Boy was I wrong! No one should go through the learning curve I went through the first few years—the ecstasy and the agony, the *ah hah's* and the *oh no's*, the epiphanies and the really good cries, the kudos and the rejections—it was just plain hard.

There were issues that I had not dreamed were part of growing successfully. Who knew about the bugs, the heat, the freezing temperatures, the thermostats, the fans, the circulation, the soil mix, the fertilizer, the water quality, the bugs, the diseases, the cost, the supplies, the market, the space, the exhaustion, the time, the deliveries, the weeds, the seeds, the *needs* of all those plants? But I jumped in with the naive enthusiasm of any beginning entrepreneur and kept working through the disappointments, frustrations, failures, and puzzles. I had enough dumb-luck successes to keep me going and customers who were very supportive and happy to see my plants. (God bless them.)

After a few years, plants were bursting out of the greenhouse and onto dozens of benches outside. My father, who lives down the road, helped me daily, but I finally had to hire employees to keep up with demands. Eventually my plants were being delivered to over 25 different garden centers and grocery stores in five counties in the Central Texas area. Although primarily wholesale, we spent a couple of years doing farmer's markets, plant shows and herb festivals when we could find the time. While we have never encouraged on-site retail purchases since we are not set up for that, there have always been customers who met us at shows or bought our plants somewhere and felt the need to come out to see our place. We are quite a few miles away from most towns and cities in Central Texas, so I figured if they were that interested and determined, then they were welcome. It gave me an opportunity to show off plants in my demonstration garden and do some teaching on organic growing.

Through this experience I built a tangible foundation and reaped invaluable knowledge to pass along to those who want to grow plants without synthetic chemicals. This is not to say I have stopped learning. I am learning new things all the time that save me time, money and energy, and that improve quality and decrease plant attrition. It is just more about fine-tuning now. I am not blithe enough to assume that there won't be some mind-shattering discovery that changes the way I approach my work. As unlikely as it would be for that to occur, I know it could happen. But until then, I will use my hard-earned knowledge and a system that serves me well.

I also hope this book will help you understand that even though this is a wonderful business to be in, it is after all a *business*. There is much more to it than growing plants. As with any enterprise, there is the reality of financing, keeping books, marketing, selling, paying bills, and maintaining valuable employees. That's the other half of the horticulture business and cannot be shoved aside because it's not your "favorite" half. With solid perspective it can, and should, be integrated into the whole of your successful business.

So, welcome to my world. Use the information I give you as guidelines, not dogma. You will likely make mistakes along the way as you find the path that feels most comfortable to you. Know that stumbling, and even falling, is necessary in any business until you find your way. I just hope I can catch you a few times and help you avoid more bumps and bruises than necessary. Most of all, delight in your work—it is a joyful livelihood.

Chapter One

Start-Up

The Business Plan

As hard as it is for left-brain people to do, putting together a plan for your business will help you achieve your goals sooner. A good business plan can be the template for success. The act of putting your ideas, propositions and projections on paper makes your business come to life in an organized, sensible fashion that beats the heck out of random acts of energy and mental gymnastics. When the time comes to implement the plan it can be like the difference between driving a new car down a superhighway and driving an old farm truck down a pot-holed, gravel county road. If you've been there, you know the difference.

The plan should be like a story about your business. It should start with a description of what you want it to be. Where is it located? What does it look like? What product does it offer? What is your business philosophy? Why do you want to do this? This is your chance to take your ideas and invent the business you want from your vision. Put it all out there just as you conceive it. Create your reality.

When you have finished describing your vision, devise a plan for implementing it. Now the fun part is over and the work begins. The rest of the story is about how you get from the vision to actualization. The sections that follow will help you get a feel for how formidable the task of starting a business can be. The descriptions are related to the business of horticulture but can be applied to the start of any small business.

Getting to Know You...

Budding entrepreneurs often don't know what to do past the *idea* of the business. It is fun to daydream about what you want to do and how happy you will be owning your own business, being your own boss and doing something that you really love. Fantasizing and creating visual imagery about your dream business is indeed a big part of the beginning process, but now you have to imagine the work that goes into making that dream a reality. After you have filled your head with inspiration, it is time to get to work.

The first thing you want to do is *name your business*. The key to a good business name is to make it personal and memorable. Will customers be able to say it without twisting their tongues all about? Is there something in the name that gives customers a clue about what you do or what your product is? Is it distinct enough from other names that people won't confuse you with another company or business? The latter may take some investigation. You might be surprised to find your brilliantly unique name is being used by another business in the next county. If you think that does not matter, think again.

We have actually gotten calls for a business in California with the same name. Folks have instant access to all kinds of directories on the Internet now, and if your name is similar to, or exactly like, another business somewhere in the country, people will call you—or worse, people will call them instead of you.

So you've asked everybody you know what they think and you've settled on a name. Now you need to register the name as a DBA. (short for "Doing Business As"). The process for accomplishing this varies from state to state. In Texas, you run over to the county clerk's office, fill out a form recording the assumed name, and pay a fee. If you are unsure of the process in your area, ask a bank officer, your local chamber of commerce, the Small Business Association (SBA), the local library, or anyone you know who owns their own business.

Getting to Know All About You

We all know about the two inevitabilities of life: death and taxes. You become acutely aware of the "T" word when setting up a business. The IRS wants to know all about you and how much income you are generating, and the state comptroller wants to know if you are collecting sales taxes. Whether or not you owe Federal taxes at the end of the year, you will need to get an Employer Identification Number (EIN) from IRS. You fill out a form (currently the W-9) and return it to IRS, they will then assign your business a permanent ID number. This number will be on all correspondence with the Department of the Treasury, Internal Revenue Service.

If you plan to sell *anything* retail, you also need to get a tax ID number from the state comptroller. You will be required to report retail income monthly, quarterly or annually (depending on your taxable sales) and pay the taxes you collect based on rates in the counties or cities in which you sold taxable, retail product. Please remember that the sales tax you collect *is not yours*. This money should be kept separate from other income so it can be paid promptly when it is due.

Financing Your Business

Of all the start-up considerations that a business owner faces, financing is likely to be the most important one in terms of your survival the first few years. Unless you have years of experience, an established market, and the resources (including the human type) to begin production immediately and start selling within a few months, you might want to think hard about how you finance your business.

When I started my business, we had the cash to buy the greenhouse and supplies. Fortunately my husband Chris had a job to pay the bills until I figured out what I was going to do with this business. As it turned out, it took me several years of many costly mistakes and a negative cash flow to learn how to make organic horticulture work. My point is that even if you have the cash to buy your start-up necessities, do you have the money to maintain the business until it can sustain itself? Horticulture is a costly business no matter what aspect of it you choose to be involved in and no matter the level of experience with which you start. The old adage that it takes money to make money is never truer than in the plant growing industry. It may take you years to turn the cash flow from negative to positive.

This is not to discourage you. It is only to save you the grief of losing the business after several years because you did not foresee the financial burden created as the business is trying to get to a place where it supports itself. Thinking through the financing of the business means allowing yourself the freedom to learn how to make the business work without going bankrupt. Even if you pay cash for your initial investment of materials and structures, you still need to figure out how to finance the business in the time it takes to make it self-sufficient.

Granted, this time will vary depending on your experience, how steep your learning curve is, and how well your market supports the product. No matter how much time it takes, you need the financial safety net.

If you finance your business through a personal, bank or government loan, you will need to figure in operating capital. This is difficult because it is often based on speculation. At best you are guessing at costs and potential income. If you are wrong, you might need much more financial support than originally thought. Lending institutions do not look fondly on businesses that come back for more money because of inaccurate projections.

Experience helps a lot in this area. If you don't have the necessary experience, then go to people who do. Talk to as many horticulture business owners as you can to get the information you need. Some won't want to share, but many will. Allow yourself time to take notes on what is generally required to start and/or maintain a business of this kind. If you do this work thoroughly now, you won't have to keep rewriting your plan and plugging in the items that slipped your notice the first time around.

Once you have gathered as much information as you can, it is time to calculate projections (see *List of Considerations for Business Projections*). This means figuring your costs versus income on a monthly, quarterly or annual basis. One of the biggest considerations is the seasonality of this business. Your greatest costs (and income) will occur in spring and, to a lesser degree, fall. If you plan well enough, you might be able to produce something to sell in the summer and winter, but that depends on your market and where you reside. Here in Texas, nurseries do very little business in the middle of summer—it's just too hot. All over the country nurseries close down in the winter unless they are involved with Christmas selling or their climate is so mild they can do business year-round. Your projections must reflect seasonal variables in order to be accurate.

It might be helpful to use a computer program that assists you in putting these projections on a spreadsheet. Many business programs will help you see into the future by projecting cost/expense versus income over a three- to five-year period. You could, of course, do this by hand with a calculator and a grid sheet, but what a brain strain. Again, it depends on your resources. If you have lots of time and no computer, the choice is obvious. Either way, it must be done in order to have a realistic idea of what you are facing in the birth and growth of your business. I've provided a sample projection sheet for a business (see *One Year Projection—Well-Grown Plant Nursery*). It might help you see how important *all* the numbers are in the end.

If you are financing your business with a loan, you should be armed with reasonable expectations of what your business is capable of doing in a three- to five-year period. This is important to the lending institution because they want to know how the heck you are going to repay their loan. Most won't lend money on projections alone. This is where it gets sticky. You may have to prove that you have income outside the business that will support loan payments until the business is able to sustain that financial burden on its own. No doubt you also will have to have some pretty fancy collateral. Horticultural businesses are notorious for being bad risks to moneylenders. A failed nursery business isn't worth much in the open market and broken down into pieces is worth even less.

Again, I am not trying to dissuade you. I am just trying to help you see the challenges you face if you choose one path over the other. Any way you go, breaking down your costs is a very healthy exercise and reality check. Unfortunately people who get into the plant business are generally not number-oriented folks, but it really is an important step in implementing your plan. I think it is a good idea to educate yourself on building and maintaining a small business by reading books on the subject or attending workshops or classes (many are held by IRS, the SBA, and local business associations). Some community colleges offer evening classes by local business people on small business management, but many offered by government or small businesses associations are free. The more you learn ahead of time about profit and loss statements (P&Ls), a chart of accounts (breaking down income and expenses into meaningful categories), and creating financial statements, the better vision you will have for the future of your business.

List of Considerations for Business Projections

Income

In order to determine your income you must know what it costs you to produce your product (see next page). When you know this, you can figure what you will charge your retail and/or wholesale customers. Then you have to *realistically* calculate how much product you will be able to generate in a year, given your resources. When you know this, you can estimate your potential income with the assumption that you will sell what you produce. The only advice I can offer here is to try to be as pragmatic as possible. It is rare that a horticulture business sells everything it produces, but this may have more to do with the whims of the nursery business than with the quality of your product. Don't take it personally if, in the end, your income projections are a wee bit lofty.

Production Costs/Cost of Goods Sold

Note: This is the calculation of how much it costs you to produce each unit (6-pack, 4-inch, 6-inch, quart, gallon, hanging basket, etc.) so you truly know how much to charge your customers in order to make a profit. It is imperative to know this so your bottom line is not a surprise at the end of the year.

Soil. Whether you buy pre-mixed soil or make your own with individual components, you must calculate the cost of soil per unit. In other words, how much does the soil cost you per each container (6-pack, 4-inch, 6-inch, gallon, etc.).

Containers. You need to know the cost of each container (6-pack, 4-inch, 6-inch, gallon, etc.) in order to know (along with the cost of soil) what each unit costs you to produce.

Labels. Calculate the cost of each label and apply it to each unit to be produced for sale.

Seed. If you plan to grow any plants from seed you must assess a value and apply it to the overall cost. At best it is estimation because there is no way to calculate the cost of individual seeds unless they are big and pricey.

Plant Material. If you plan to buy starter plants (plugs, rooted cuttings, stock plants, etc.) this outlay needs to be added to the cost you calculate for plant production. These starter plants may be convenient, but they will drive up your costs.

Plant Losses. You will have plant losses. If you are just starting out you might want to plug in a generous allowance (say 20-30 percent). Plants can be lost to lack of experience, insects, disease and acts of God (try a hail storm). Your losses may be more or less than average, but it is better, when doing cost projections, to err on the side of higher projections. Then, if you do better than you projected, you will have a more accurate percentage to work with the next year.

Ancillary Costs. This can be anything from holiday nursery pics and pot covers to container sleeves. Anything you plan to send out with your plants, even if it is seasonal, should be counted here.

Expenses

Note: These are *ongoing* expenses (monthly, quarterly or annual) *not* one-time expenses. You can decide either on an annual budget amount that is pro-rated monthly, or a variable expense that fluctuates with the time of the year or season.

Utilities. You must estimate electricity, water, heating fuel (propane, natural gas, etc.) based on average expected cost during different times of the year. For instance, in Texas heating fuel will likely only be used three or four months out of the year unless you have a water heater in addition to a heating unit. Electricity will, on average, be higher during warmer months if you have exhaust fans or a water wall in your greenhouse. Water will be two to three times higher during the warmer months, not only because of increased evaporation, but you will likely have the most plants during the warmer months and therefore be watering more.

License/Permit Fees. Any fees you pay your state department of agriculture (or health department) for your nursery/floral, market, food handling, or organic certification.

Office Expenses. Any *ongoing* expense related to operating your business from your office. Postage, paper, pens, paperclips, business telephone, long distance business charges, Internet services, business equipment rental, etc. In this category you also want to budget notebooks and clipboards for record keeping in the production area, and marking pens for writing on pot tags.

Advertising. This covers expected costs of business cards, fliers, publication ads, help-wanted ads, etc.

Dues and Subscriptions. Annual membership dues and fees for industry-related organizations or publications.

Professional Development. Anticipated budget for industry-related conferences, trade shows or other educational opportunities to further your knowledge of the business.

Insurance. Anticipated cost of insurance related to business liability, health, automobile, trailer or workman's comp.

Vehicle. Budget amount set aside to pay for repairs, maintenance and fuel for your business vehicle(s). You might want to budget a monthly allowance that reflects higher usage at certain times of the year.

Sales Tax. If you plan to do any retail sales, you will have to estimate how much you will be selling in "non-food" plants. Texas, for example, has a very narrow definition of food plants, so you will have to check the laws in your region. In many places, herbs in pots are taxable.

Bank Fees. Any service charges or check printing costs applied to your business account by the bank.

Interest Expenses. This is your estimated budget on any business related interest (loans, vehicle payments, credit cards) you will owe during the projected time frame. Generally you can get this information from your loan amortization schedule.

Loan Principal. This is the estimated budget for principal costs associated with loans related to the business. Again, you can get this information from your amortization schedule.

Auxiliary Production Materials. This will include fertilizers, pesticides, or other pest control costs such as beneficial insects, sticky traps, pheromone traps, etc.

Employee Expenses. You will need to estimate your payroll expenses, which includes Social Security and Medicare taxes. These expenses will fluctuate a great deal as you add and subtract employee hours from peak production times like spring and fall to slower times like mid-summer and winter.

Professional Fees. For a business this will usually be service by a CPA. It could also be for attorneys or business consultants if you foresee using either during the projected period.

Market/Stall/Booth Fees. If you plan to do retail sales at plant shows, flea markets, farmers markets, etc., you will need to estimate your expenses for booth/stall rental and associated fees (electricity, water, chairs, tables).

Building Rental. This is any expense for rental of a structure necessary to the business such as a retail shop, storage building or office space.

Travel Expenses. Business-related overnight lodging and meal expenses for conferences, trade shows, plant shows, obtaining supplies, etc. If you know ahead of time what out-of-town excursions you will be taking, it should be relatively easy to budget these expenses.

Tools/Equipment. Budget an amount that covers any of the anticipated supplies in this area that would be necessary for production. These might include garden tools, pruners, trowels, pumps, sprayers, carts, hand trucks, hoses, cut-off valves, hose-end sprayers, etc.

Miscellaneous Supplies. This category might include things like dish soap, hand soap, bleach (for disinfection), mops, towels, scrub brushes, brooms, trash containers, plastic tubs or anything that you can think of that will be used regularly in the work area.

Owner Pay. If you plan to give yourself an income from the business, then put this in the budget. If there is not enough projected income to allow for your salary, then you had better have another way to pay your *personal* bills because they should not come out of the business income.

Your Bottom Line:

Total Income minus Production Costs and
Cost of Goods Sold = Gross Profit
Gross Profit minus Total Expense = Net Income

The spreadsheet provided is a mock projection sheet for a fictitious business to give you an idea of how to plan and implement one for your own business. This exercise is the most important one you can do to determine if you are indeed ready to take on the responsibility of a business. Simply plug in your own items and numbers, and do the math.

The numbers tell the truth about the viability of this business.

Market Research

If you are getting financial assistance from someone, whether it is your uncle, a banker, or an investor, one of the first questions they will ask you is, "Who is your market?" It is a good question. There is no point in manufacturing widgets if they are not needed anywhere. If no one wants your widgets then you either have to forget about producing them, or make whatsis instead.

Before I grew my first plant commercially, Chris and I visited business owners around Texas who were growing the *kinds* of plants I wanted to grow, but who all had a different way of growing and marketing them. Some grew in containers, some in raised beds, some organic, some conventional, etc. By looking at all the different ways people grew and marketed their products, I was able to get a better idea in my mind of which direction I wanted to go with my business. You have to start somewhere.

If you have an idea of what your product is going to be, you can begin narrowing down who your potential market is. If you are growing container plants for wholesale, then the obvious markets would be the retail nurseries in your area. Other outlets might be farmers markets, grocery store chains, florists, landscapers . . . basically anyone who buys plants for retail sales or commercial use. If you are growing to sell retail yourself, you still have to figure out who is going to come to your place to buy your plants. Especially if there is an established nursery a couple of miles down the road or a home improvement center in town that has an extensive garden center.

This brings up the question of competition. When you go to talk to your potential customers, see if they will tell you from whom they buy regularly and if they are happy with what they are getting. Get the phone book out and look up wholesale plant nurseries in your area, look at plant tags for identification, or ask your state department of agriculture for a listing of all the wholesale plant nurseries within 50 or so miles of your target market. Inevitably there will be some wholesale nurseries that have been chugging away, selling plants to all the nurseries for years, comfortable in their niche. If this is the case, then you have some work to do to set yourself apart.

Once again, go back to your plan-in-the-making. You have identified *what* you want to grow, *how* you want to grow it, *who* you want to sell it to, and *who* your major competitors are. The next step is to ask yourself if you want to grow and sell the same product as your established competitors and to the same outlets, or do you want to do something a little different and/or

One-Year Projection–Well-Grown Plant Nursery

Income	Jan	Feb	Mar	Apr	May	Jun	Jul	Aug	Sep	Oct	Nov	Dec	Grand Totals
Plants Sold Wholesale:													
Vegetable Transplants	500	1,000	3,000	6,000	3,000	1,000	2,000	2,000	3,000	4,500	3,000	1,000	
Culinary Herbs	1,000	3,000	6,000	9,000	6,000	3,000	3,000	2,000	6,000	4,000	2,000	1,000	
Native Ornamentals	2,000	5,000	7,000	10,000	9,000	7,000	5,000	5,000	7,000	10,000	7,000	3,000	
Succulents	300	800	1,000	2,000	3,000	3,000	1,000	1,000	1,000	500	500	2,000	
Subtotal:	3,800	9,800	17,000	27,000	21,000	14,000	11,000	10,000	17,000	19,000	12,500	7,000	169,100
Retail sales:													
Farmers Market	0	0	0	500	1,500	2,000	0	0	2,000	1,500	0	0	
Plant Shows	0	4,000	0	6,000	3,000	0	0	0	5,000	3,000	0	0	
Total Income:	3,800	13,800	17,000	33,500	25,500	16,000	11,000	10,000	24,000	23,500	12,500	7,000	197,600
Production Costs/Cost of Goods Sold													
Potting Soil	2,360	3,400	5,400	4,200	2,800	2,200	2,000	3,400	3,800	2,500	3,400	1,520	
Containers	295	425	675	525	350	275	250	425	475	313	425	190	
Labels	118	170	270	210	140	110	100	170	190	125	170	76	
Seed	0	0	0	0	0	800	0	0	0	0	0	1,800	
Plant Liners	1,200	1,200	0	0	0	0	0	0	1,200	1,200	0	0	
Holiday Pics/Covers	0	100	0	200	0	0	0	0	0	0	0	200	
Product Attrition 20%	790	1,780	1,269	1,027	658	677	470	799	1,853	1,548	799	757	
Total COGS:	4,763	7,075	7,614	6,162	3,948	4,062	2,820	4,794	7,518	5,686	4,794	4,543	63,779
Gross Profit:	-963	6,725	9,386	27,338	21,552	11,938	8,180	5,206	16,482	17,814	7,706	2,457	133,821

Expenses

Expenses													Total
Utilities - Electric	200	200	300	300	300	400	400	400	300	200	200	200	
Utilities - Propane	1,000	800	800	400	400	0	0	0	0	400	800	1,000	
Utilities - Water	60	60	60	120	120	120	120	100	100	60	60	60	
License/Certification Fees	0	0	0	0	0	0	0	0	0	0	0	200	
Office Supplies	50	50	50	50	50	50	50	50	50	50	50	50	
Advertising	50	50	50	0	0	0	0	50	50	0	0	0	
Dues & Subscriptions	25	25	25	25	25	25	25	25	25	25	25	25	
Insurance	650	650	650	650	650	650	650	650	650	650	650	650	
Truck Maintenance	150	250	400	400	250	250	150	120	150	300	250	150	
Sales Tax	0	280	0	455	315	140	0	0	0	315	0	0	
Bank Fees	15	15	15	15	15	15	15	15	15	15	15	15	
Interest Expense	0	0	0	0	0	0	0	0	0	0	0	0	
Loan Principle	0	0	0	0	0	0	0	0	0	0	0	0	
Auxiliary Production Materials	200	400	600	800	600	400	400	400	600	600	400	200	
Payroll + Taxes	2,154	3,067	3,524	3,981	3,981	3,067	2,611	2,611	3,067	3,067	2,154	2,154	
CPA	0	0	0	250	0	0	0	0	0	0	0	0	
Market/Stall/Booth Fees	0	350	400	25	700	200	0	0	500	250	0	0	
Business Travel Expenses	0	300	0	400	300	100	0	0	300	300	0	0	
Tools/Equipment	75	75	75	75	75	75	75	75	75	75	75	75	
Misc. Supplies	25	25	25	25	25	25	25	25	25	25	25	25	
Owner Pay	570	2,070	2,550	5,025	3,825	2,400	1,650	1,500	3,600	3,525	1,875	1,050	
Total Expense:	5,224	8,667	9,524	12,996	11,331	7,917	6,171	6,041	9,997	9,857	6,579	5,854	100,158
Gross Profit	-963	6,725	9,386	27,338	21,552	11,938	8,180	5,206	16,482	17,814	7,706	2,457	133,821
minus TOTAL EXPENSE:	5,224	8,667	9,524	12,996	11,331	7,917	6,171	6,041	9,997	9,857	6,579	5,854	100,158
Net Income	-6,187	-1,942	-138	14,342	10,221	4,021	2,009	-835	6,485	7,957	1,127	-3,397	33,663

find an alternative market? If the latter is what you choose, then you have some more planning and investigating to do.

Nursery/Floral License

Every state has regulations through its department of agriculture regarding the inter- and intrastate sales of container plants. These laws reasonably protect the end consumer from encountering diseased or insect infested plants at the point of purchase, whether it is from the wholesale grower, retail nursery, florist, flea market, or farmers market. Therefore, anyone growing container plants for sale must comply with these regulations. Generally this means filling out some paperwork, paying a fee (which depends on how much you are growing), and having your growing operation inspected by a department of agriculture regional inspector in your state. If there are no problems, you give them money and receive a nursery/floral certificate with your registration number on the front. This will have to be displayed anytime you are selling plants from your place of business. Annual renewal and inspection keeps you in business.

Market Certification

In Texas, and probably other states as well, if you plan to go to markets, shows, or other temporary locations to sell your plants, then you will need to get a market certificate. The Texas Department of Agriculture issues a certificate with 30 market opportunities at $5.00 each. This means you pay $150.00 whether you use one or 25. To use the certificate you call your regional office each time, before any market, to get a number that is recorded on the back of your certificate. If you use them all up before the end of one year and you want to do more markets, you have to purchase another market certificate. If you go to only one location outside your place of business (like a farmers market), but you go every week, it could be considered an alternate, permanent location (other than your primary place of business). Then you might have to just get a regular Nursery/Floral license for that location. I doubt if the department of agriculture cares as long as they know where you are selling your plants to the public. Just be sure to check with your own state agency to find out what the requirements are for retail sales outside of a permanent retail location.

Organic Certification

You might wonder what it means to be a certified organic grower. Simply put it implies that you do not use anything that is manufactured in a chemistry lab on your plants or soil. Most organic pesticides are botanical in origin, which means that, although they may be extremely toxic to the insect, they don't linger around on the plant surface; *i.e.,* they break down quickly, often within 24 hours. Some organic pest controls are actually beneficial bacteria, fungi or nematodes that are harmless to animals (humans included), but deadly to target pests. Plant nutrients in an organic program are obtained from earth-based products such as fish, seaweed, compost, composted manure, igneous rock, mined minerals, etc. Seed must come from organically grown plants, or at least be untreated with fungicides. Cuttings or other plant material purchased to use in your production must come from organically grown stock and not be fed with chemical fertilizers. The rules have varied somewhat from state to state because of inconsistencies in guidelines by certifying agencies, but the general idea is that everything you use and grow must have natural, chemically untainted origins.

I have been asked by many people, mostly conventional growers, why I have chosen to go through the "trouble" of growing plants this way. When I started out, even the garden centers told me that it didn't make any difference to them whether something was organic or not. In our area, no one had consistently sold plants that were grown without chemicals, so buyers and consumers could not attach any value to the concept. I began the journey into organic container plant growing to give consumers an alternative to chemical-laden commercially grown herbs. To me, this was especially important with herbs since people—and their children—would be putting the plants directly into their bodies.

As my experience evolved and I began growing vegetable bedding plants and then non-edible garden plants, I noticed that they were incredibly healthy and had a vitality that was apparent to anyone comparing my plants to others. They also had an outstanding track record in people's gardens. People who bought my plants would call me (our phone number is on the pot tag) just to tell me how exceptionally well my plants did in their gardens. I have gotten so much unsolicited positive feedback from buyers and consumers that I realized that growing organically was not just about giving people plants that are grown without petroleum-based pesticides and laboratory-formulated fertilizers; it was, in addition, giving people a high-quality plant that is virtually guaranteed to do well in their gardens or containers. If those aren't reasons enough, I don't know what else there is.

Eventually, the garden centers and grocery stores that consistently bought my plants began to see an expanding market for plants that are not only grown organically, but that were certified organic. In time there was more demand than I was able to fill. My mission now is to encourage more growers to join the crusade to offer quality alternatives to consumers, and to become certified in their state in order to show how committed they are to a horticultural future that does not poison our bodies and our planet.

At the time of printing, the National Organic Standards are newly enacted. I know there are many people who don't cotton to the government telling them they cannot use the term "organic" on their product unless they join the "organic standards" club. The problem that a lot of consumers of organic products do not comprehend is that growers, producers, and manufacturers in this country have many different interpretations of what the word organic means (see *organic* in the glossary).

In Texas, the organic standards set and maintained by the Texas Department of Agriculture are pretty strict. The program is voluntary and it gives the consumer "reasonable assurance" that growers, producers and manufacturers who go through the trouble of adhering to the certification process are following guidelines that uphold basic, organic standards. Because the vast majority of folks who are growing in this manner are concerned about the earth and are generally good people, "cheating" is ludicrous. I know there are always people who try to get away with as little work as possible and may be tempted to bend the rules for a quick fix to problems. But chances are, in this business they aren't going to last long anyway. In order for organic growing to work, you have to put sweat into the process.

With that said, here is the simple version of how it's done in Texas: Paperwork, paperwork, paperwork. The biggest problem with the system is that in trying to get all the information they need to measure compliance, intentions and plans, you have to fill out a lot of forms, draw a lot of diagrams, and do a lot of explaining—no big deal to an old nurse like me, but it can be downright intimidating to people who aren't used to pushing a lot of tree pulp around. Plus, if you are going to be growing primarily in containers, most of the forms are not even appropriate to your operation because the organic standards were created for agriculture (crops and animals), not horticulture. Just be creative. Give them the exact information they need in your own words on your own paper in an easy-to-read format. You could even make up your own form that gives you something to work from, based on the information they are asking for. Most importantly, don't leave anything out—be brutally honest.

Aside from the paper, for initial certification they will need the exact location (on a map) of your business, drawings of where and what you are growing, buffer zones (25-50 feet) around the growing area (including greenhouses), soil samples from areas where plants will be grown in-ground (sent off to an independent lab), water samples if you are not using community or city water, and plant samples from the growing area(s) that go into a blender and are analyzed for various naughty chemicals. All these things are done along with an inspection from an agriculture department field representative. We have had two different inspectors and they have been very supportive.

If you have a brand new greenhouse, you will likely be certified right away. But if you are growing in a greenhouse that has used restricted chemicals, there might be a delay in outright certification. In Texas there is a transition period for growers that are changing from chemical to organic methods. Traditionally it is three years, but may be more or less depending on the evaluation of the environment and how "clean" the plant material is when tested by the inspectors.

When you are approved, you pay a fee and receive your certification. This certificate shows your registration number and states what growing area on your premises has been approved for organic certification. Then, every year, your business is inspected, you fill out some more paperwork, and you pay a fee to stay certified. Almost all my inspections, whether nursery/floral or organic certification, have been unannounced.

It's worth noting that every year there are changes in the system and you will likely have something new to deal with at least every year or so. I wrote a letter to the agriculture commissioner one time regarding how I felt about a particularly senseless change. I received a phone call about a week later from an "assistant" to the commissioner and we had some rather heated words for about 30 minutes. I don't think to this day, she really understood how absurd the new system was. And my opinion obviously had no weight despite the fact that I am a grower and the new ruling had a direct impact on my business.

States that don't involve themselves in organic standards sometimes have independent certifying agencies. These regulatory agencies are better than no supervision but, again, there have been some significant differences in the interpretation of what constitutes an organically grown plant or animal. This is why the National Organic Standards were written. It gives everyone a level playing field.

The bottom line is that organic standards have varied from place to place and the best idea is to learn about organic growing and regulations in your particular area. Again, it is always an excellent idea to meet like-minded growers in your region. Often there are organic organizations—both community-based and government-sponsored—as well as meetings that will be helpful to anyone interested in organic growing.

Transportation Options

If you plan for your business to make deliveries, one of the hardest things is seeing far enough into the future to make decisions about vehicles of transport. Some people may be conservative in this area and might choose a vehicle with large enough capacity to get them through the first couple of years, if left to their own devices. On the other hand, others are more forward thinking and will get what seems like a whole lotta' too much space, but in the end they will be right. It's hard to comprehend in the beginning how fast that shelf space fills up when the business begins to cook.

If you really do not have a clue, you might start out by renting a vehicle from a commercial rental place. You can try all sorts of vehicles including vans, trucks and trailers. Many of these places will lease the vehicle to you for one month to a year. During that time you can work with different shelving options and evaluate space requirements. One real advantage of using a rented or leased vehicle is that you are not locked into payments on a vehicle that you will not be meeting your needs six months down the road.

There are several types of trucks commonly used by small businesses in the plant industry. One is the large cargo or utility-type van. These heavy-duty vehicles (up to one ton) may be purchased completely stripped so you can put in shelving brackets for adjustable shelving or permanent structures. These vehicles hold an amazing amount of cargo and, with a trailer, can give you tremendous flexibility. An advantage to the van/trailer arrangement is that the van can be used for running errands, picking up supplies, carrying equipment, etc., without hauling around the extra cargo space. The disadvantage is that when you need the extra space, you have to hook up the trailer.

The other option is the (truck) cab with a "box." This is the classic delivery truck you see around town. They come in many sizes and shapes with options like roll-up or swing-out

doors. One very big advantage is accessibility to the shelving. Generally you can walk through the middle of the box to pull flats or plants from the shelving on either side. This can be really nice if you have a day or two of deliveries to make. The one main disadvantage is that these are cumbersome vehicles and, practically speaking, can only be used for one purpose—carrying your plants. I guess you could throw the soccer team back there when it's your time to pick them up, but I think they might be a little uncomfortable.

Some folks just use a trailer for all their deliveries and hook it up to their pick-up truck on delivery day. You might have figured this out already, but the open or flatbed trailers are totally impractical for plant deliveries unless you want to share pieces of your plants with the cars behind you on the highway. The box or closed trailers come in many heights and lengths and can be purchased stripped down or custom designed by the dealers to meet your needs. Options include stone guards, nose cones, insulation, paneling, shelving brackets, flooring, special braking systems, one-axle/two-axle, suspension, ventilation, wiring, lighting, etc. An advantage of the double axle (tandem) is that it has a much smoother (less bouncy) ride. No matter what trailer you choose, be sure

Single Axle

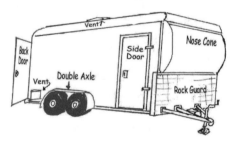

Vent

Back Door

Side Door

Nose Cone

Vent   Double Axle

Rock Guard

you have a vehicle powerful enough to pull one of these things when it is loaded.

Purchased new, these trailers are not cheap, but it is worth your while, if you go this avenue, to get the best quality you can afford. Most trailer dealerships offer financing, but it might be in your best interest (assuming you can't pay cash) to just get a loan through the bank where you have your business account. Down the road those regular trailer payments might give you an advantage if you need further financing on something else.

Whatever you choose for transportation, just make sure you are giving yourself ample delivery capacity. Base your decision on what you would need if you meet or exceed your production and sales projections. You may not fill it up in the beginning, but eventually the extra space will be used.

Following these suggestions for starting a new business is a lot of work, but it pays dividends by giving you a viable template to work with and a clear idea of where to start. Inevitably you will make changes along the way as you gain experience growing your plants and learning what sells, what doesn't, and what just isn't worth your time and energy. Those changes will make your business stronger if they are the result of hard-earned knowledge. After a few years, your business will stand out because of your careful attention to the creation of your own unique cubbyhole.

Chapter Two
Greenhouse Options

There are so many reasons why people put up greenhouse structures that the industry has given businesses a dizzying number of options to meet all the different needs. I could not begin to cover all the available choices, so I will just go over the basic concepts to try and help you understand which (if any) of these greenhouse options might meet your needs.

There are some questions you need to ask yourself to determine what kind of structure you should get. The object is to both keep you from getting more than you need or from not getting enough.

1. What kind of climate do you have? Are you going to try to grow in winter? Are your winters long and bitterly cold? Are your concerns more in the area of protecting plants from extreme heat? Do you have high winds or frequent storms with hail? Is your climate predominantly humid or dry?

2. What kinds of plants are you going to grow? Are you going to grow plants that need a controlled climate, or tough natives that need no pampering? Will you be doing your own plant propagation from seed or cuttings?

3. Will you be producing plants year-round or only a specific number of months out of the year?

The idea is to consider what kind of protection you will need. If you live in a harsh climate (hot or cold) then you may need a more climate-controlled structure to grow stress-free plants. For some growers, shade structures are the primary concern because of the relentless sun. For many, plastic and heat are only needed for a short time in winter to keep stock plants or early spring seedlings from freezing. In the warmer months, the plastic can be replaced with screening or shade cloth. In hot, dry climates a cooling system may be needed to keep plants from being oven-baked. And if you live in the "grasshopper belt" or "deer haven" you may need a completely screened structure just to keep the bugs and other creatures from devouring your precious inventory.

As a rule, greenhouse structures alone are not very expensive. It is when you add the covering, shade cloth, screening, exhaust fans, shutters, circulation fans, wiring, thermostats, heating and/or cooling, plumbing, water walls, pumps, gravel, weed cloth, etc., that you get into the real expense. This is why it is pretty important to know what your real needs are before you jump into a $45,000, high-tech greenhouse.

When I started out, I knew nothing about greenhouses except what I was able to see on visits to other growers. Some were rather primitive, wooden, home-built structures and some were steel structures with sturdy cross-members and support beams. Some were covered in plastic, some in fiberglass, and some in glass. They all had exhaust or circulation fans, and they all had some kind of gas/propane heating systems. The greenhouse floors sported anything from hard-packed dirt, to gravel, to concrete, to black weed-cloth. Most were hard-wired for electrical power. Most were plumbed with functional sinks and at least had inside stub-ups with cut-off valves for hoses. I saw every manner of plant bench from wooden planks and cinder blocks to metal frames with wire mesh grating. A few places just had the plants lined up on the floor.

The reason I am recounting all of this is because I believe that in order to make intelligent choices, one needs to know what those choices are. A little common sense thrown in doesn't hurt. If you only listen to your horticultural supplier or the greenhouse manufacturer, you may end up with something on the other end of the spectrum. I mean way out there. It does-n't hurt to listen to what they have to say, as they often have valuable insight and knowledge, but talk to other growers too. Go and see every greenhouse you can, including university or botanical garden greenhouses. Pay attention and take notes. The more you see, the more knowledge you will possess.

Once you have a pretty good idea of what is available, you can begin your hunt for the greenhouse you want. There are nursery trade shows going on around the country all the time where you can always find greenhouse manufacturers who can supply you with catalogs and prices. You can look for ads in nursery trade journals or contact your state nursery/land-scape association for information. There is always the Internet. If you have access to this amazing research tool, all you have to do is type in "greenhouses" and you will get tons of infor-mation on manufacturers. Of course you will get a lot of other stuff you don't think you want, but it is all information.

I have tried to provide general information on structures and equipment most commonly used, (see *Greenhouse Structures Defined* and *Greenhouse Equipment Defined*). You might also be able to get a free publication from your state department of agriculture (or, as in Texas, from the agricultur-al extension office) on greenhouse management, which will furnish you with lots of diagrams and suggestions for operat-ing a plant nursery in your part of the country. I can't tell you enough, the more you know ahead of time, the fewer costly mistakes you will make. Research beforehand is time well spent.

Greenhouse Structures Defined

Detached or Freestanding Greenhouse. This is a house that stands alone; *i.e.,* not attached to another structure.

Gutter Connected or Ridge and Furrow Connected Greenhouses. These are houses that are connected to each other at the eve of the side wall. Generally the wall does not extend below the eve (inside) so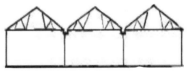

there is greater space efficiency inside the house. Several greenhouses connected in this way are called a *range* of houses.

Quonset-Style Greenhouse. Sometimes called a *cold* frame when small (10-20 feet wide). This style is the most inexpensive to build, but will likely require solid-structure end walls for stability. 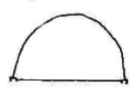 Growers who need minimal protection for their plants use this ground-to-ground, arched structure most often. It can either be covered with plastic in winter or screen/shade-cloth in the summer. This is a good choice for those on a tight budget, but has the disadvantage of reduced efficiency of space along the side walls.

 **Round Topped or Arched Greenhouse.** This house has an arched roof like the Quonset, but instead of the arch going ground-to-ground, it connects to a side wall that can range from two to 10 feet tall. Generally the side wall is solid, but they can also (instead) be covered with plastic that can be rolled up in warmer weather for good air circulation. The side walls increase efficiency of space and allow you to gutter connect the houses if you desire.

Gabled Greenhouse. This house also has side walls, but instead of an arch across the top, it has a pitched or double-sided roof (like a house). This is generally one of the most expensive houses to build, but also the sturdiest. This 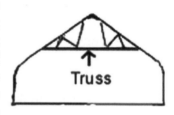 kind of frame can take the weight of heavier coverings such as glass or fiberglass and has the advantage of being well suited for placement of roof vents to get rid of hot air in summer. These houses are also good in climates that get heavy snowfall in winter. Most are supported across the top with a sturdy truss.

Rafters. These are the "ribs" of the greenhouse that produce the arch or the triangular shape of the roof. They are placed anywhere from two feet to six feet apart depending on the strength requirements. In the arched or gabled houses they are attached to side posts.

Side Posts. These are the vertical supports (sometimes called "stubs") of the side walls to which the rafters are attached. They are spaced between two to six feet, as are the rafters, and are set about two to three feet deep in concrete.

Purlins. This is the horizontal support attached to the rafters that runs the length of the greenhouse and generally spaced four to eight feet apart.

Truss. A reinforced structure generally required for stability in greenhouses that are more that 30-feet wide (see *Gabled Greenhouse*).

Cross Tie. This is a cable-wire or solid cross-structure attached to the purlins or the rafters from one side of the upper wall or lower roof to the other. It may be necessary in areas where high winds are a problem.

Gable End or End Walls. These are the walls at either end of the greenhouse. They have vertical, structural posts spaced two to six feet apart and cross-braces or "girts" placed in various patterns that best suit the wall material to be attached. This is often where doors, exhaust fans and windows are placed unless you have tall, rigid side walls.

Framing Materials. Most greenhouses are constructed from galvanized (zinc-coated) aluminum or steel. Wood may be used, but deteriorates rapidly in the wet, humid environment of a greenhouse. In addition, the chemicals used to treat wood for decay prevention may give off harmful gases or drip chemicals (like copper arsenate) onto your plants.

Covering Materials. If you have an endless supply of money, you might want to go with glass. It lets in optimum light levels, lasts indefinitely and can be louvered with vents to allow hot air to escape. Fiberglass is another rigid option, but generally breaks down and becomes brittle from UV rays in a few years. Polycarbonate and other acrylic polymer materials are being used as a clear, sturdy substitute for glass but still tend to be expensive. The advantage over glass is that these polymers are less likely to break in a bad hailstorm. The least expensive way to go is with plastic (polyethylene) film. Many companies are now offering UV-resistant plastic that can last up to five years if well cared for. Most growers use a double layer of plastic with a small fan at one end that blows air between the layers forming an air pillow. This increases insulation from cold and heat and works well for almost any climate.

Floor Covering. Black weed mat is by far the least complicated and most effective covering on the floor of the greenhouse. It can be swept and mopped and it keeps the weeds out. Gravel is nice to walk on and drains well, but it cannot be cleaned easily, and things will grow in it if you don't stay on top of your weeding. I've heard cedar flakes are good because they repel insects and mold, but they are a bit messy. Plain dirt floors are muddy and weedy. To me the best (although most expensive) option is concrete. With strategically placed drains or a sloping angle on the floor, all you would have to do to clean is blast it with a high-pressure hose. Concrete is also the best on which to roll carts.

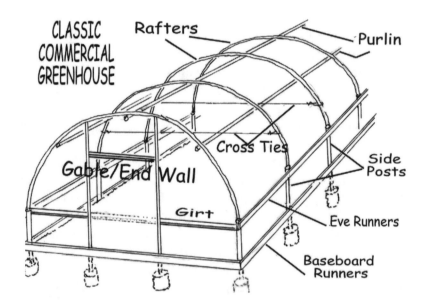

Eave and Baseboard Runners. This is the two-by-six to two-by-twelve wood that runs the entire length of the greenhouse at the base and at the eaves. It is fastened to the side posts and used to attach the side wall material whether it is fiberglass, polycarbonate or sheet plastic. There are many ingenious locking devices for any covering or side wall material you decide to use.

Greenhouse Equipment Defined

Heating

Among growers, heating a greenhouse is probably the most challenging, and possibly the most expensive, consideration in the business. There is a lot of discussion about whether to heat the air of the greenhouse or to heat the *root zone* of the plants. (By root zone I mean heating the bench itself or the air under the bench.) My understanding of current recommendations is that unless you have a really well-sealed greenhouse, with a good system for keeping the warm air from rising above the level of the plants, your best bet would be to find an alternative to heating the air. It just makes sense that it is going to cost you more in the end to warm the enormous square footage of the inside of a greenhouse than it would to just warm the root zone of the plants.

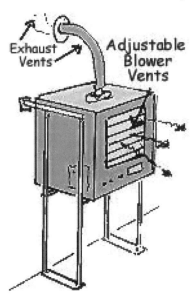

The biggest difference in the beginning would be the initial cost of setting up one system over the other. The traditional industrial gas heaters used most in greenhouses are easy to find, easy to install, and are not terribly expensive in the grander scheme of initial business set-up costs. They are, however, very expensive to run in the middle of winter when the cold north winds are blowing your warm air out the smoke hole. Even if you maintain a "cool" house, winter temperatures and winds can cause fuel costs to skyrocket.

The primary alternative is setting up a system that brings heat to the place that is most important in winter, the roots of the plant. I can't begin to describe all the methods I have heard about (some I never did understand). My suggestion is to research all the newest and most energy-efficient systems available in order to decide if this is what you want to do.

There are systems that provide warmth with heated water (from specially designed circulating water heaters) running through pipes either directly under the bench, on top of the bench between the containers, or imbedded in sand, rock or even perlite.

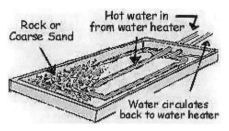

Rock or Coarse Sand

Hot water in from water heater

Water circulates back to water heater

There are also rubber mats that roll out on top of the bench with thermostatically-controlled heating wires inside. I have even read about black barrels full of water placed under the benches that absorb radiant warmth from the sun during the day, and these in turn heat the benches at night as the heat rises from the barrels. After the initial (sometimes formidable) cost of setting up these systems, the cost to run them in the middle of winter is generally much less than the cost of fuel to run gas heaters.

Other heating methods include things like radiant heat from specially designed electric heaters (that only heat the plant, not the air), wood heat from a wood-burning stove, and kerosene heaters. The last two should, of course, be vented to the outside with standard metal vent pipes (as might be used to vent a gas water heater or furnace) in order to avoid toxic fumes.

Heating Mat

Thermostat

Ventilation (Air Circulation)

Proper air movement in a greenhouse is one of the most critical considerations for a grower. Good air circulation is important for the prevention of fungus and some species of bacteria that thrive on damp, stale conditions. It also helps dry out soggy soil during certain times of the year when evaporation is low due to cool temperatures or high humidity.

The most common air circulation methods in commercially sized greenhouses are from fans. Two specific types of fans are commonly used. There are many companies that produce them and many options beyond these two types, but when setting up your greenhouse these two should be considered first.

HAF (horizontal airflow) fans are generally 12- to 20-inch circular, heavy-duty fans hung in strategic positions around the house to move the air close to the plants. In a standard 30-by-100-foot greenhouse, there are usually four positioned so that the air actually circles the inside of the house. They are generally left on at all times when the big wall fans are off. These fans are very important. If you have no other equipment, you should have HAF fans.

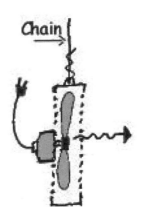

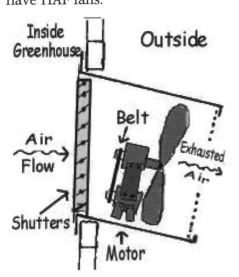

Wall (exhaust) fans are not unlike the old attic fans you used to see in houses before air conditioning became so widespread. These large, usually belt-driven fans are placed on one end of the greenhouse to pull large volumes of outside air from one end of the house to the other. When they come on, they exhaust the accumulated hot air and replace it with a continuous flow of fresh air from outside. The opposite end of the big fans must have windows that open automatically when the fans come on. These can be shutters that open from the pull of air or from motor-mounted shutters that open the vents when the fans are operating. We simply mounted Plexiglas with top hinges that swing open when the fans come on. Then the panes come completely off in the summer.

Thermostats

The kind of thermostat(s) you use in the greenhouse will depend on what you are regulating. You will frequently have a separate control for your heating mechanism, fans, water walls, and/or the root zone heating system. If you have exhaust fans, you will need one thermostat per fan unless you want them to always come on simultaneously. Most 30-by-100-foot greenhouses have two exhaust fans, each regulated by one thermostat. They will have different temperature

settings so that they come on as needed when a little or a lot of air movement is needed. The gas heaters are easily controlled by an ordinary household thermostat. Water walls are regulated by the same thermostats that control the exhaust fans.

Many high-tech greenhouses have master control panels that are digitally operated and often coordinate with timing mechanisms or sensors. Some of them even set off alarms if the power fails. Don't forget to ask about thermostats when setting up your heating, cooling and ventilation systems. A reminder: For thermostats to work correctly they need to be protected from direct sunlight, radiant heat and water, and should have good air flow around them in order to accurately sense the temperature. Don't be surprised if you have to move them a few times to find the best location.

Benches

Unless you plan to set flats and containers directly on the floor, you will need benches on which to put your plants. I have never recommended putting plants on the floor because they do not get as much air circulation and do not drain well. Both situations set you up for root rot and other fungal problems. Although good benches can set you back a bit moneywise, they often last for many years once you have made the investment.

The bench dimensions you decide to use depend on how you want to set up the interior of your greenhouse and what kind of containers or flats you are going to use. For instance, if you choose to use the 10-by-20-inch flats, then the width of your bench should be wide enough to hold two flats end to end. The length of the bench should be a factor on the width of the flats, for instance 60 or 80 inches, with at least a quarter of an inch allowed between flats to make it easier to slide them on and off.

Cinder blocks or concrete blocks have been the foundation for many commercial greenhouse benches. They are durable, sturdy and relatively easy to set up. They also give you multiple choices in height and width with single or double blocks set up together in various patterns to give you the base you need.

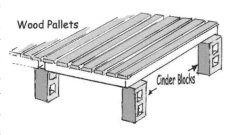

Wood Pallets

Cinder Blocks

Bench tops can be made from an assortment of materials including lattice, snow fencing, wood or plastic pallets, and metal or wood frames with wire mesh. Whatever you decide to use, keep in mind economy of space. For instance, the wood pallets are cheap and sturdy but they come in odd sizes and it is generally hard to fit web trays and individual containers onto them without wasting valuable space. It's better to make your own with carefully measured width and length that works well in the space you have, and with the flats and containers you plan to use.

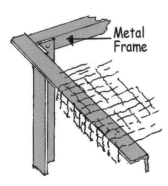

Metal Frame

Commercial benches can be purchased in plastic or metal and are usually very well made and long lasting. They are also pretty expensive. If you have more money than time, these are the ticket.

Wood benches can be built out of inexpensive pine wood but tend to decay, bow and rack. If you go this route, find a really good design that gives your benches adequate stability with plenty of cross bracing.

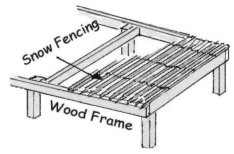

Snow Fencing

Wood Frame

Unfortunately, this also makes them heavy and cumbersome. Avoid chemically treated wood as the chemicals may leach into your pots when the wood is wet (which it will be a lot of the time). Cedar or redwood are good decay-resistant alternative choices to pine. Painting with a wood sealer would also increase the life span of your creation.

Wire mesh is often used to cover the top of benches. If you use wire be sure to use *welded wire* with fairly small holes (one-half to one inch). Anything larger or with a looser weave (like chicken wire) tends to bow and bend with the weight of plants, even with good cross bracing. If the wire holes are too big, it is difficult to set individual pots on the bench without having to place them on a tray first. It is a real pain to have your plants

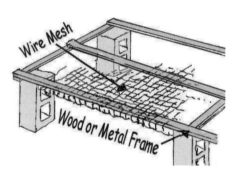

falling over due to "dips" in the wire or because the bottom of your pots do not sit right on the mesh. And keep in mind, if you are using wooden pallets for benches, even a cheap wire covering would make the spaces between the slats more usable.

Soil Bin

Whether you decide to mix your soil by hand, in a machine, or buy it by the bag, you need a place to put it for easy access when you are potting plants. The height of the bin depends on how you set up your work area and how the soil gets to the bin. For instance, we mix the soil by hand so our bin must be at a height that is easy to get into to mix the soil components, and have a volume capacity that allows us to get a good bit of work done before we have to fill it again. The bin I use is about thigh high and holds 15-20 square feet of soil. On the other hand, if you mix the soil in a machine or buy it by the bag, you could use a bin that is hip or waist high which is a better working height. Consider also the depth of the bin. It should not be so deep that you can't easily get to the bottom. If you are bending double to reach that last cup or two of soil, it's too deep.

Although I have seen soil in plastic and galvanized tubs, the vast majority of work areas have bins made out of wood. A simple rectangle or square bin is easy to 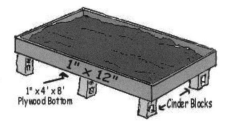 design and build. Four sides of one-foot by 12-foot wood on top of a piece of plywood, glued and screwed together make a very good soil hopper. If you use pine, it should be painted or sealed to make it last a bit longer. I also recommend using an interior grade wood to avoid splinters in all those hands reaching in there to dip out soil. The bin can be built onto permanent metal or wooden legs or can be placed on cinder blocks or sawhorses.

Sink

For some, a sink may be considered a luxury in the greenhouse or work area but I deem it a necessity. I use the sink for washing my hands, washing pots or buckets, washing plants (to de-bug them), washing tangled root systems, etc. My "sink" consists of a fiberglass washtub with a flexible pipe attached that drains the water outside to an 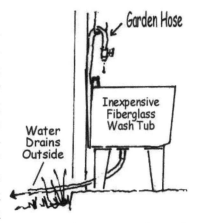 unused grassy area. My water source is a hose over the tub (looped over a pot hanger) with a cut-off valve. Simple but indispensable. Of course you could actually put in a permanent sink with real plumbing, but it would cost more and you could not move it as easily if you decided to rearrange your work area.

Water Source

By this I mean how you get the water to your plants inside the greenhouse. You could, of course, drag a hose in and out of the greenhouse but that would get real old real fast. You might as well plan to plumb a cut-off valve into the greenhouse near the center for convenience. Attach your hose and you are set to go.

Auxiliary Greenhouse Equipment

Cooling

In Texas and other hot climates, keeping your greenhouse from becoming an oven in summer takes some forethought and, in some cases, a bit of extra money. The easiest way to keep temperatures from getting out of hand is to remove the greenhouse covering (usually plastic) and replace it with shade cloth. End walls also should be removed and replaced with screen or left open to allow free flow of air. With circulating fans it will be about five to ten degrees lower than the outside air. If you leave the plastic on, even with shade cloth, the inside temperatures can rise to 120 degrees or higher during the hottest part of the day. That is too hot for most plants to thrive. Forget trying to get anything to germinate in those temperatures.

Evaporative cooling systems can be used during the hottest times of the year if the relative humidity is not too high. The higher the humidity, the less cooling will be accomplished with this type of system. One way is to spray an ultra-fine water mist into the flow of air in the greenhouse. This can be accomplished by running tubes or pipe above the circulation fans with super-fine fogger attached at intervals. These pipes are attached to a pump that is connected to a timer. The mist is released at designated intervals and the fans carry the cooled air through the house.

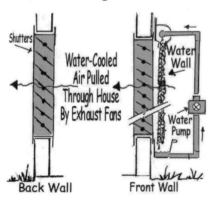

Shutters
Water-Cooled Air Pulled Through House By Exhaust Fans
Back Wall

Water Wall
Water Pump
Front Wall

Another type of evaporative cooling system is more common and definitely more costly. The idea is to develop a *water wall* (a porous-type wall that has water trickling down it) through which air is pulled by large fans at the opposite side (end) of the greenhouse. A simple pump is used to reclaim the water as it falls into a reservoir at the bottom of the wall and the water is re-routed to the top of the wall to be released to trickle down again. The air is cooled as it is pulled through the wall. Most are thermostatically controlled and have shutters that open and close either as a result of the air being pulled through the wall or via small, mounted motors that open the shutters when the pump is activated. These systems can be ordered as kits or can be designed and built by your own hands. Instructions for building your own can be found on the Internet, in books on greenhouses, by asking other growers, or from agricultural extension service publications on greenhouse management.

Misting Systems for Propagation

If you plan to do a lot of propagating from cuttings, then you should consider setting up a designated area for this activity. Whether it is one bench or half a greenhouse of benches, there are some things you need to consider. First, do you have plumbing to that area? Availability of water is, of course, imperative to setting up a misting system. Second, is there good air flow and good drainage below the benches or flats? This needs to be determined ahead of time to avoid fungal problems from stagnant air or puddling water. The type of cuttings you want to work with will also be a factor in what kind of system you choose. For in-

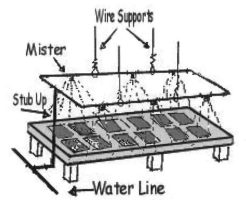

stance, if you are doing nothing but cuttings from dormant wood in winter, then you probably do not need anything more than a bit of vigilance and a spritz with a hand-held mister now and again. However, if you are doing a lot of softwood or semi-ripe cuttings with actively growing stems, you will need to set up a system that maintains the right humidity/moisture level to prevent the cuttings from drying out.

The design of the system is determined by the size of the benches or area that needs humidity. The idea is to release a fine mist to the plants that moistens rather than wets the leaves. The system has a water pipe or pipes connected to a pump and timer, with intermittently placed nozzles that spray a mist at a pre-set time interval. Generally, there are two timers: one to turn the system on in the morning and off at night, and one to release the flow of water at shorter intervals during the day to provide even moisture levels. There are also systems that operate from a pad sensor (on a balance arm) that lies on the soil surface to determine soil level moisture. When the pad dries out, it lifts and triggers the misting system by opening a solenoid valve (and therefore the flow of water), which gets the pad wet and heavy, making it lay on the soil surface until it dries out to trigger the system again.

Most of the components are pretty standard, but there are quite a few options for nozzles. Each choice has a different spray pattern and volume, so you want something that works best for the area with which you are working. The biggest problem with any of them is the tendency to clog with mineral deposits; therefore, get nozzles that you can remove easily to clean (soaking in vinegar works well), or that can be inexpensively replaced. Instead of providing a fine mist, clogged nozzles only drip.

Misting systems are vital to successful commercial propagation of leafy cuttings, but there are flaws in the timer systems. The one most often observed is the problem with fluctuating temperatures during the day. During the cooler times of the day, the plants may get too much moisture due to decreased evaporation levels, and during the heat of the day when evaporation increases, if adjustments are not made in the timers, the plants may dry out between mist releases. Additionally, rainy weather or overcast skies increase humidity levels and/or decrease temperature which may lead to a fungal crisis if your plants are getting moisture they do not need.

Shade Cloth

This woven (usually polyethylene) fabric comes in white, green and black and blocks varying amounts of solar light from 10 percent to 100 percent, depending on the weave.

Shade cloth is used whenever solar radiation threatens the health of your plants. When heat and light are too intense, as is the case with summers in the South, shade can get the plants through a stressful time with minimal or no damage. The depth of shade needed depends on the level of solar intensity, which varies vastly depending on what part of the world you live in, and the tolerance of the individual plants to heat and light. For example, orchids would be much more sensitive to these extreme conditions than a native Texas shrub.

Most growers in Texas use cloth in the 46- to 73-percent range in summer. At that range, shade cloth can bring mid-afternoon temperatures down 10 to 15 degrees. Some shade cloth is made with aluminum fibers to deflect the harsh solar rays away from the growing area. Just remember, increased shade means decreased light to your plants. It is a balance between heat and light in our brutal summers. In hot weather, many growers pull the plastic off the house and leave the shade cloth on. This provides cooler inside temperatures because the plastic is not trapping the heat. This lowers electric bills (no big exhaust fans necessary) and keeps your plants much happier.

You can also just set up a shade area outside if insects or hungry herbivores are not an issue. A simple wood or metal

Outdoor Shade Area

structure with a cloth thrown over it can give your plants some much needed relief from the scorching summer sun.

Obviously, there are a lot of choices to be made here. Only you can decide where to begin based on the size of your business. Some people have the resources to start big and grow into their operation. Others prefer to grow along with the business, adding greenhouses as money allows. My advice is always to start with the best that you can afford, an inferior greenhouse will only frustrate you as time moves on and your business grows.

Chapter Three

Botany 101

First Things First

If you are going to grow plants successfully, then you need to understand some elementary things about them. After all, you couldn't raise a baby, or even a puppy, if you didn't grasp the fundamental needs of each. You have to know what to expect as they mature, what nutrients they need in order to be healthy, and how to protect them from harm. The same applies to plants. By understanding the nature of these organisms, you will increase your chances of raising them right.

In this chapter, we will explore plant anatomy, physiology and reproduction. I want you to be able to talk the language of plants with other people who are knowledgeable about plants; to speak fluent "botanese." Learning the fundamentals makes the process of growing plants so much easier.

The anatomy of plants will be broken into digestible sections. The order in which they are presented is simply my interpretation of the most logical way to do that. The important thing is to understand how all the parts are connected. When we are through defining and examining plant parts, we will then look at some of the most common horticultural terms you will encounter.

Seeds

No red-blooded, pathologically enthusiastic gardener can deny the awesome power, potential and wonder of seeds. Watching a small seed germinate, grow, and become an enormous plant is awesome. I never get tired of watching this miracle. Even though I see the process all the time in commercial production, it has never ceased to amaze me.

By beginning the description of reproduction of flowering plants with the egg instead of the chicken, I realize I have made a choice between the two. But it has to start somewhere, and the seed seems like the most logical choice to me, because it is the source of many of the plants you will be growing.

There are two major categories of seed-producing plants that growers are most familiar with: *angiosperms* and *gymnosperms*. Once these two categories are explained, we will explore the anatomy and physiology of seeds and how germination takes place.

Angiosperms

This is the class of flowering/seeding plants that most of us grow in our gardens and landscapes. The name comes from the Greek words *angion* meaning vessel, and s*perma* meaning seed. The seeds are formed inside a container called a fruit, (sometimes called an ovule). Flowering evolved as a result of plants needing to find new ways to reproduce and survive. The variations in color, size, shape and fragrance of blooms was the individual plant's attempt to attract the specific pollinator needed to do the job most efficiently.

You will find that most of the seed-producing plants you grow develop their seeds inside some kind of pod. The pod can be very small, as in some wildflowers, or quite big, as in something like a watermelon. Sometimes we are not even aware of the vessel in wild plants because they dry and split open quickly to disperse the tiny seeds. Often by the time we think to look for them, the fruit and seed are long gone. So whenever you hear someone refer to the "seed pod" of a plant, remember that the botanic term is the "fruit." Even vegetables are really, technically, the fruit of the plant, although we have tried to classify edible fruits into either the vegetable or fruit category in order to make a reasonable distinction between them.

Gymnosperms

These are the other group of seeding plants that we are most familiar with. The name comes from the Greek words *gymnos* meaning naked and again the word *sperma* meaning seed. Very literally, these are seeds that develop out in the open. Actually they are usually snuggled in between the (often) woody, flaps of cones (as in pinecone), so they have some protection. This category of plants are primarily made up of conifers, which are trees like cedar, pine, redwood, fir, juniper and sequoias (some of which are the largest plants on earth). Gymnosperms are more primitive in origin than the angiosperms.

Size

Seeds come in an incredible number of sizes. Some are the size of dust, as are the seeds of orchids and many wildflowers, and some are very large as is the seed of the coconut palm (the seed is the coconut that we eat).

Shape and Outside Structure

Shapes vary almost as widely as size. Shape and structure often tell you how the seed is dispersed or how it stabilizes itself once it reaches a place it can germinate. For instance, the seeds of many angiosperm trees have a light, papery "wing" covering that allows the  seed to float in the wind, giving it an opportunity to disperse itself far from the parent plant. Some seeds have sharp burrs which allow them to attach themselves to passing animals (or humans). Think about that the next time you remove one of those blasted sand burrs and throw it onto the ground. You are doing exactly what they want you to do. You have also seen seeds that have puffy, fluffy parachutes that allow them to sail away on a breeze. And some seeds have unique shapes like thin, sharp and narrow; smooth, flat and slick; crescent shaped, or round like a pebble. Each has a reason to be shaped that way, whether it is to allow them to catch easily onto surface debris, lodge between rocks, or to nestle easily into loose soil. Each shape and structure gives the seed a chance at successful germination in the wild.

Anatomy of a Seed

Seed Coat: This is the protective "skin" covering the seed. It varies in thickness, color and texture and determines how fast water is able to enter the seed to begin the process of germination. Some seed coats are very thin and light which enables the seed to germinate quickly. These seeds are usually produced in abundance by the parent plants because the thin coat also makes them susceptible to fungal or bacterial infection, which, in nature, takes out a fair percentage of the seeds produced. Some seeds have thick, hard seed coats that must be worn down in order for water to finally be able to enter and allow the seed to germinate.

One theory about why some seeds have such resistant outer coverings is that it allows the seed to survive severe environmental or climatic stresses, which gives the seed time (often years) to find a time when conditions are perfect for germination to take place. During the wait, the seed coat is slowly worn down by fungi, bacteria and by mechanical means such as the grinding action of coarse soil, enhanced by heavy rains and wind. Since variable conditions make it possible that seeds might not be produced in abundance in any given year by these plants, it is to their advantage to have seeds that can wait a few years for germination to take place, until they have a better chance of growing into a sturdy, healthy plantling.

Seed coats, whether thin or thick, can protect the precious contents for a long time if they remain dry, cool and clean. I am sure you have heard stories of intact seeds found buried with people in tombs for thousands of years, or that were found in frozen tundra or in glacial ice. Some of these seed discoveries have even germinated. The environments kept the seeds safe from conditions that would destroy them. Pretty amazing.

Embryo: Inside each seed is a complete, miniature (often microscopic) plant. This tiny plant has everything needed to begin life: a root (called a radicle from Latin *radicula* meaning small root), a short stem, and a pair of leaves. These tiny plants have all the genetic material needed to grow into a plant similar to that of the parent plant. But just like people and their children, the genes of seeds may vary some in characteristics from the parent plant, producing progeny that generally look like the parent, but may result in a small percentage of the "children" sporting a slightly different bloom color, or leaves with a somewhat different texture, or fruit that is a bit bigger or smaller, etc. These are the random characteristics that create the opportunity for new selections of a particular variety of plants. With time some recessive genes may be brought into dominance.

Cotyledon: Cotyledons are the mother's milk for the tiny new plant. Upon germination these leaf-looking storage systems supply the growing embryo with food until the real leaves, called true leaves, are developed enough to begin creating food for the plant through photosynthesis (see *chloroplasts* under the heading *Leaves*). When the seedling plant has used up all the stored nutrients in the cotyledon, these "milk leaves" wither and fall off. The cotyledons contain everything needed for new life to grow including amino acids (proteins), starches (converted into sugars), and fatty acids.

Angiosperms are divided into two major groups, producing two different types of cotyledons—*dicots* (*di-* meaning two and *cot* meaning cotyledon), and *monocots* (*mono-* meaning one and *cot* meaning cotyledon). So, obviously the 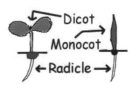 dicotyledons have two milk leaves and monocotyledons have only one. When you plant seeds in the ground or in a germination tray, you will see the cotyledon come up first, pushing either one or two milk leaves out of the soil.

Endosperm: Some groups of seeds have an additional starchy food source for the developing embryo called the endosperm (*endo-* meaning within). This is most frequently represented in grains, which are mostly members of the grass family. The white flour commonly used in baking is primarily the endosperm of the wheat grain (which is the wheat seed).

Germination

The process of germination is truly one of the great miracles of nature. Against many formidable odds, these packets of genetic material and potential have covered the earth with new life year in and year out, century by century, millennium by millennium. The progression from seed to seedling to mature plant is nothing short of magic.

Only when the time is right does the seed begin the process of growth and development. The first thing that happens to start germination is the taking in of water by the seed. The seed coat is softened; easily in the case of a thin skin, or more slowly in a seed with a thick coat that needs mechanical or chemical help. Either way, there is eventually a break in the seed coat, allowing the internal components of the seed to soak up water and swell. This process is called *imbibition* (Pronounced: em bi bish' yun) and is not unlike what happens when you put a dry sponge in a pan of water. The seed will usually swell to about twice its original size by the time the embryo begins to respond and grow.

Along with water, oxygen is needed by the seed to begin the conversion of all the stored nutrients (in the cotyledon) into usable form by the embryo. That is why a loose soil is best for germination, as it has plenty of air space to supply needed oxygen. The following are terms that are used to describe various aspects of germination:

Viability: This is a term describing the probability of a seed to germinate or not. If a seed is *viable*, then it is likely that it will germinate successfully if all the environmental factors necessary for this to happen are also in place. A small amount of moisture is needed inside the seed at all times (less than two percent of its weight) to maintain its state of viability. A seed can become non-viable (essentially dead) if it is allowed to dry out completely. Also, some seeds actually need extreme temperatures (either cold or hot) to make the embryo fully viable (developed) and ready for germination.

Dormancy: This is the suspended, non-active state of a viable seed before germination takes place. Many viable seeds can stay dormant for an indefinite amount of time as long as the seed coat remains intact. Seed banks around the world keep supplies of valuable and potentially threatened (almost extinct) seeds in cold, dry storage to maintain their genetic heritage. In nature, viable, undamaged seeds will stay dormant in the soil until conditions are perfect for germination.

After-Ripening: This is something that happens in many seeds after they leave the fruit vessel. It is sort of like the process an infant goes through in the womb. In animals, if a baby is born before it is developed enough, it will likely not survive. In some seeds, if the after-ripening process is not finished, then the seed may not germinate. After-ripening can be very fast or very slow, depending on the plant and environmental circumstances. Often, in a batch of seeds dropping from the parent plant, the after-ripening process happens at different times for each seed. This is an evolutionary precaution developed by plants to ensure that all their seeds will not germinate simultaneously, which could end in extinction if something happens to kill all those plants at once. In some cases, the after-ripening process can take years.

Scarification: This is the process of thinning the thick, tough seed coats of some seeds. As mentioned before, the layer can be removed over time via decomposition from bacteria and fungi, or mechanically by having it ground off by coarse soil granules, assisted by rain and wind. It can also occur when the seed travels through the gut of a bird or mammal. By being exposed to digestive enzymes as it travels through the alimentary tract, it softens and thins the seed coat, making it perfect for germination, leaving the body in a pile of ready-made fertilizer. Some plants have this planned out perfectly by offering their seeds in bright colored, delicious berries, irresistible to birds or other foraging animals.

Scarification can also be done manually by growers trying to germinate these seeds. Tough seed coats can be scored with a knife, sanded with sand paper or a nail file, boiled in water and even soaked briefly (one to five minutes) in sulfuric acid. Another method is to paint the inside of a jar with glue and pour sand into the jar, rotating it until all the surfaces are covered with a layer of sand (this can be repeated to give you a good thick layer of sand). When this dries thoroughly, put your seeds into the jar with a lid and shake the jar until the surface of each seed is sufficiently scratched. Horticulturists all have their favorite, foolproof way to break down the skin of these seeds.

Some seeds have an inhibiting chemical attached to their seed coat that must be washed off before they can germinate. This is often coordinated by the plant so that a specific amount of water (rain) is needed to wash away the chemical, which incidentally is the same amount needed to germinate the seed, and usually occurs at the optimum time of year (fall through winter). This is to prevent the seed from germinating after a brief shower at times like the middle of summer, when high temperatures and mostly dry conditions would quickly diminish the seedling's chances of survival.

Stratification: Many seeds from native plants require specific conditioning called *stratification*, to be ready for germination. In the temperate part of the world (where hot and cold temperatures are generally not extreme), scores of native plants shed their seeds in late summer or early to mid-autumn to allow them to go through this conditioning process before spring. The seeds are moistened by the usually ample rains of fall, seasoned by the cold winter temperatures (a sort of after-ripening that helps them develop), so when spring brings warming conditions, they are ready to germinate.

Conversely, many desert seeds fall in the spring so they can be conditioned by the very hot temperatures of the desert floor (up to 120° F or 50° C) through summer, before germinating in late summer or fall when the autumn rains come. A rare few desert seeds actually need the scorching of fire to ready them for germination when the monsoons come. They grow in areas where wildfires from lightning are not uncommon. The parent plants burn to the ground, raining their nutrient-rich ashes onto the desert floor giving the scorched, ready seeds a perfect environment to come to life.

If you want to germinate native seeds artificially, then you have to mimic the conditions they require to ripen. In the first case, they can be placed in a moisture-proof bag between moistened paper towels, or mixed into moist vermiculite (peat moss may be too acidic) and kept in a refrigerator or freezer (depending on the type of seed) for a month or two before attempting to germinate. In the case of the desert seeds, they may be heated in an oven (for up to a week at 120° F) before attempts at germination will be successful.

If you are going to germinate wild, native seeds, it is a good idea to find information on the stratification needs of the individual seeds before embarking on this method of growing. There are now good books available on native plants and information about specific plants can often be obtained on the Internet, from the USDA, or from universities that have strong botany or horticulture departments. Most U.S. states and Canadian provinces now have native plant societies that present a wealth of information about the needs of endemic plants. It is a fascinating and challenging endeavor.

Light Requirements: To germinate, most seeds have specific requirements for light. Some need light, some need darkness, and some are not particularly picky either way. A general rule of thumb for planting seeds is to cover them with an amount of soil that does not exceed the size of the seed. Basically (although there are exceptions), the bigger the seed, the deeper it should be planted. Very tiny seeds (the ones that look like grains of fine soil) need only be sprinkled on top of the soil and gently misted with water to settle them in. Covering them with any soil would be too much. Most seed packets have planting depth on the label so there is no mistake what the light requirements are.

Soil Temperature Requirements: Seeds are also fairly picky about soil temperature in order for germination to begin. Commercial growers of bedding plants often have heating mats on large benches where seeds are germinated early, to be sure plants will be ready when people want them in the spring. In the wild or in the garden, seeds will only begin germinating when they are good and ready. For the most part they can't be fooled. The soil temperature is either right or it's not. In Texas people are obsessed with tomatoes, and they always try to put them in the ground too early in the spring. I have told people repeatedly that tomatoes will not actually grow until the soil is warm enough, so they might as well wait until the time is really right.

Moisture Requirements: Seeds need water to germinate. The amount may vary, but a general rule is to keep the soil moist (like a wrung out sponge), but never soggy. Once germination has begun, do not let the seeds dry out. This is death for a tiny seedling. Even wilting can cause too much stress in the emerging plantling, causing it to die or become stunted. Read the directions on the seed packet for any special moisture requirements.

Initial Growth and Development: When the seed imbibes enough water, the embryo begins to grow. The tiny stem between the embryonic root and leaves starts to lengthen, pushing the cotyledon out of the soil. As the cotyledon makes its way out, it stays folded to protect the tiny, undeveloped leaves from being damaged by the gritty soil. Once out, the cotyledons spread, the leaves are pumped with the stored nutrients, and they begin to grow—sort of like a butterfly emerging from its cocoon. Often the embryonic leaves are so tiny that you can't see them until they are well into development. Once you do see them, you will notice that they are a darker green than the cotyledon. That is because they have *chlorophyll* (see *chloroplasts* under *Leaves*) which is going to allow them to manufacture food for the plant. When the leaves have devel-

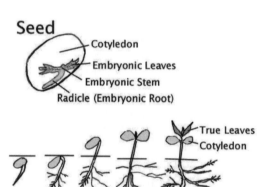

oped enough to begin capturing light with the chlorophyll (the light is converted into energy for plant metabolism), and manufacturing their own food, then they have probably used up all the food in the cotyledon(s). Having given the plant all they can, these "milk leaves" wither and fall away.

As the stem and leaves are growing, the embryonic root is developing below ground. It lengthens and works its way into the soil creating fuzzy looking root hairs that enhance the plant's ability to absorb water. As the root grows, special cells within the baby root push out and form branches into the sur-

rounding soil that anchor the plant pro-
portionally to the development of the stem
above the ground. At the end of each of
these branches is a tough root cap that is
sort of like a war helmet, protecting the
branching root from damage by coarse soil
granules as it lengthens and spreads.

As the root system develops, it begins
to take up nutrients from the soil that are
pumped (via the water) up the stem to the
waiting leaves. The leaves capture light
with the chlorophyll, giving the plant the energy it needs to
convert the nutrients that are brought up from the roots into
food. As the root system grows, more nutrients are available.
The more nutrients that are available, the more growth can
take place in the stem, leaves and roots.

Damping Off: A term referring to seedlings dying of a systemic infection from pathogenic (harmful) soil fungi such as
Pithium, Fusarium and Rhizoctonia. The seedling stem
becomes "boggy" and will wilt, drop over onto the soil and die.
Not all fungi cause the death of seedlings. Many are beneficial
and are actually an integral part of a healthy root system (see
mycorrhizae under *Roots*).

Plant Parts and Function

One can spend four years obtaining a botany degree at a
university and not know everything there is to know about
plants. But many commercial growers know very little of even
basic botany. Understanding how plants grow, the names and
functions of each part of a plant's anatomy, and how they are
different from each other and yet the same, is a way of increas-
ing your appreciation for the miracle of plant life. My goal is
not to make you a botanist, but to give you a fundamental
understanding of the anatomy and physiology of plants. This
knowledge not only makes it easier to speak intelligently with
other growers and nursery people, but it helps you understand
why things go wrong or why your plants are responding to
their environment in a particular way. Plants can't talk to you
or cry or smile, so it is a good idea to know what makes them

tick. The following presents a simple explanation of how plants are put together in order to clarify how the parts relate to each other.

Roots

Roots are the underground part of a plant. Their purpose is to anchor the plant in place and to absorb water and nutrients from the soil. The following are all the simple, basic aspects of roots.

Osmosis: This is the way water and nutrients get from the soil into the root. It is the passive movement of water and minerals from outside the root (the soil) to the inside of the root via peripheral cells with pores that let the water and minerals in. It is kind of like a siphon. Once the passage of these substances gets started a positive pressure is created that forces the water and minerals through the cells to the middle of the root where they enter tubes called the *xylem* and *phloem*. Upon entering these tubes that run the length of the center of the root, the water and dissolved minerals move up into the stem and ultimately to the leaves where they are needed for growth and development of the plant.

Osmosis happens because nature wants water pressure to be equal everywhere. Water molecules are attracted to places that have less water, or that have water with a high concentration of minerals. Water will be pulled into these areas to try to dilute the solution, or equalize the pressure. The cells in plant roots have the kind of chemical make up (*i.e.,* mineral concentration) that attracts water molecules. As the water enters the first cells and fills them up, then the next cells over attract the water and fill up, then the next cells, etc., until the water begins to spill into the xylem tubes, to be transferred where it needs to go in the plant.

Root Pressure: This is the pressure created by the osmotic siphoning action described above. It is like there is someone pushing the water into the cells which pumps it up the xylem and phloem. Water molecules don't like to be broken and will form a kind of chain that creates the continuous pressure, forcing the water into the roots and up the plant. If you have ever watched water droplets on a car window when it is raining you will remember how the water drops, as they travel down the window, are attracted to each other and will form bigger and bigger drops until they stream down the window together. This is essentially what happens when the water from the soil enters the roots.

Xylem (*zy'lum*): These are bundles of individual tubes that run through the center of the root and stem that provide water and minerals to the plant. The water and dissolved minerals work upward through the xylem from the roots. It branches off when necessary to provide water to new shoots and stems.

Phloem (*flow'um*): These individual tubes also run in bundles between the bundles of xylem and carry food that has been manufactured by the leaves to the plant.

Root Hairs: These are the tiny projections near the ends of roots that absorb most of the water. They are there to increase the surface area of the root so more water is available to the plant. These tiny (often microscopic) projections are easily damaged if a plant is disturbed, or dug up and moved. That is why plants that have been transplanted often wilt. They have temporarily lost the efficient absorption of water from the root hairs. Watering these plants thoroughly before and after moving helps get them by until new root hairs can become established.

Root Cap: The tip of the root often has to work itself through some pretty tough soil particles, so plants have adapted the root tip to contain a protective "cap." I always think of it as a helmet, as one of those hats worn by construction workers to avoid being hit on the head by falling debris. These specialized cells are constantly worn off and regenerated like the skin on our bodies.

Epidermis: These are the cells covering the entire outer layer of the root. One cell deep, these epidermal cells (from the Greek *epi* meaning upon and *derma* meaning skin) are the ones that begin the process of water absorption and from which root hairs develop. As in humans, the epidermis protects the inner layers of the root and, if broken, may result in infection and water loss.

Root Cortex: The area between the epidermis and the vascular tissues (*i.e.*, the xylem and phloem) is called the root cortex. It is loosely packed to allow easy movement of oxygen (O_2)

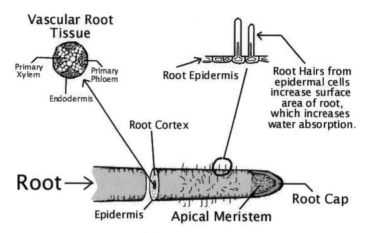

Vascular Root Tissue

Primary Xylem

Primary Phloem

Endodermis

Root Epidermis

Root Hairs from epidermal cells increase surface area of root, which increases water absorption.

Root Cortex

Root→

Epidermis

Apical Meristem

Root Cap

and water (H_2O) molecules, and contains food stores in the form of starch granules.

Endodermis: As the epidermis covers the outside of the root, the *endodermis* is a layer of cells that encases the xylem and phloem.

Root Branch: These are extensions that grow out at right angles (usually) from the older root sections, and are there to augment the search into the surrounding soil for water and nutrients. All branches are functional copies of the original, parent root.

Root Growth: To be most effective, roots need to work their way out into the soil, away from the center of the plant. The farther they can go, the more water and nutrients they can bring back. The cells responsible for the lengthening of roots sit right behind the root cap and are called the *apical meristems* (apical from Latin *apex, apic-* meaning top or tip, and meristem from Greek *meristos* meaning divided). These cells divide rapidly and then lengthen causing the tip of the root to move further out into the soil, sometimes with significant force. This type of growth is called *primary growth* because it is the formation of all the cells involved in the primary workings of a root system (*i.e.*, the epidermis, cortex, and vascular tissue).

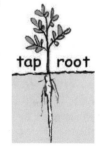

tap root

Tap Root: This is a thick, sparsely branched root that grows straight down. This type of root is good for anchoring plants in places with high winds or soft, shifting soils. Because it goes deeper than other types of root systems, it is able to "tap" into water and minerals that lie in the deep subsoil. Tap roots are well designed for storing food, which gives the plant plenty of reserves in leaner times. They are also nutritious for animals and humans as evidenced by one of our favorite tap root vegetables, the carrot.

Diffuse (Fibrous) Root: These thin, profusely branched roots are closer to the soil surface and, for that reason, are good for controlling soil erosion. Because they are shallow, they absorb water quickly as it percolates into the soil, and are able to absorb nutrients near the surface. Plants with diffuse root systems are tough, and often able to survive drought when other plants are struggling. Most grasses have this kind of root.

Tuberous Root (root tuber): These are thick, food storage roots that contain places where new shoots form, growing new tuberous roots that grow new shoots, etc. The sweet potato is a tuberous root, but a white (Irish) potato is a fleshy underground stem (see *stem tuber* under *Shoot System*). Sometimes things that look similar are actually quite different.

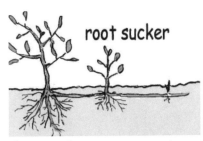

Sucker: A vegetative shoot arising from an underground root, attached to a parent plant. These are often found popping out of the ground all around the base of trees and shrubs that have this kind of root. It is beneficial to remove these as they sap energy (nutrients and water) from the primary plant.

Root Nodule: These are knobby nodules on the roots of some plants that are the result of the bacteria *Rhizobium*, which pulls nitrogen gas from the air and fixes it into the root. In return, the plant supplies the bacterium with food in the form of carbohydrates. Most of the nitrogen-fixing plants are legumes.

Mycorrhizae: A specific group of soil fungi that constructs a beneficial relationship with the young root systems of many species of plants. The fungi invade and surround the roots, extending themselves into the soil, picking up and sharing nutrients with the plant, while the plant shares photosynthesized foods with the fungus. These beneficial soil fungi are part of most healthy, native soils and, if used in commercial plant production, can increase resistance to pathologic fungi and generate plants that withstand transplant and environmental stress better than plants grown without them.

Shoot System

The stem, its branches and attached leaves make up what is called the *aerial* part of the plant, or in other words, the part that is above ground. First we will go through the anatomy of a stem and its shoots, dissecting all the parts that are readily identifiable. Then we will examine the structure, physiology, and different types of leaves, looking at what their role is in the health and wealth of the plant. Later, we will look at the reproductive system of plants.

Apical Bud: Remember *apical* means top or tip. The apical bud is the tiny package (about 1 mm) at the tip of the primary shoot (the main stem) and any of the secondary shoots (branches). This bud has all the cells and genetic instructions for making the plant grow, mature, and branch. The very tip is the *apical meristem* which, like the root tip, is where cells are actively dividing and

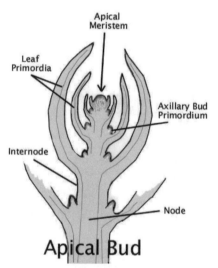

elongating causing the plant to lengthen. But the meristem on an apical bud does not have a cap to protect it as the root does. Instead, it is protected by tiny, undeveloped leaves that fold themselves up and around the tip (see illustration), shielding the meristem from elements, such as sun and wind, that might damage the delicate tissue. These miniature protrusions are called *leaf primordia* (from the Latin *primordius* meaning first) and are the early stages of leaf formation.

The angular place where the leaf primordia are attached to the stem is called the *axil.* Snuggled in this axil is a primitive, apical bud called the *axillary bud primordium.* This bud stays dormant until the plant sends a message to the bud that it is time to begin growing into a new shoot or branch. Then, using its own apical bud—previously the axillary bud primordium—it will begin growing and developing identical characteristics of the original apical bud. Snipping the top off a plant causes it to activate the primordial buds because it has lost its original mechanism for continued growth; *i.e.,* the primary apical bud. The plant will also activate the primordial buds if it begins to need the support of more leaves, which would produce more food to maintain growth.

Primary Growth: This is initial growth in the tip of stems (and roots) created by the division of cells in the apical meristem. It forms all the primary structures of the plant (*i.e.,* the epidermis, cortex, xylem, phloem, pith, etc.).

Stem: The main supporting structure of a plant that connects all the other parts such as the leaves, branches and flowers.

Node/Internode: The place on the stem that the leaf primordia and the axillary bud primordium develop is called the *node.* The node is genetically predetermined and spaced distinctly in different varieties of plants. For example, some are placed opposite each other on the stem, some are placed alternately around the stem, and others are placed in a whorl (circle) around the stem. The placement of nodes, and therefore the leaves, is a distinguishing characteristic of plants that helps growers identify the species and the variety.

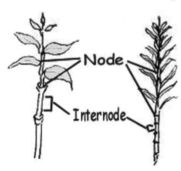

The space between the nodes is called the *internode.* As the cells in the apical bud meristem divide, the cells in the stem lengthen to create a space between the nodes that separates the leaves allowing better air circulation and exposure to the sun. As with the placement of the nodes, the internode space is genetically predetermined, although environmental conditions can alter this growth. For instance, if a plant is growing in low light, it may lengthen the internode space to make the plant taller so it can reach for more light. This is called *stretching.* Conversely, plants that are constantly being snipped, mowed or nibbled, may shorten the internode space in order to make sure there are plenty of leaves to compensate for the constant loss of food production.

Runner: Stem growing along the surface of the soil (horizontally) planting itself as it goes by producing roots at nodes or at the growing tip.

Stolons: Often called "runners", these are stems that originate near the parent plant and root easily when the growing tip touches the soil. The new rooted shoot then sends out more horizontal stems to root, spreading in increments outward from the original plant.

Rhizome: Horizontal stems growing *below* the soil level which are capable of developing roots and new shoots from nodes and axillary buds. (Note: Runners, stolons and rhizomes are all associated with plants that are considered "invasive.")

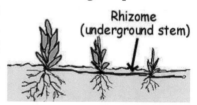

Stem Tuber: A swollen rhizome, the most common example being a white (Irish-type) potato. The "eyes" are the axillary buds and the area between is the internode space. Each eye will form a shoot from which roots and ultimately more tuberous rhizomes will develop.

Leaf Scar: The healed scar left on the stem where a leaf has been broken off or has fallen off from age. The area is sealed by the plant with a layer of cork to prevent invasion by disease-causing organisms.

Callus: The tough, hardened tissue that covers a wounded area of a plant. Some stem cuttings must be allowed to *callus* to prevent rotting when placed in soil to root.

Latex: Latin for fluid. This is the sticky, most often white (but may be opaque or clear) substance that oozes from breaks along the stems and roots of certain plants (most notably *Euphorbias*). Contains resins, gums and particles of rubber that create a seal at the site of injury.

Lenticel: Often looking like scale insects or scars, these are actually pores seen on the smooth stems of woody plants that allow the movement of gases (including oxygen) between living cells of the inner bark.

Axillary Bud: This is simply the term used for the dormant buds (formerly primordial) on the leaf axils of mature stems and branches. Many of these buds can stay dormant for the life of the plant, never being called into use because they weren't needed. Remember, the primordial axillary buds are called that because they are the beginning stages of those buds. As the plant matures these structures are simply called axillary buds.

Leaf Axil: As mentioned previously, this is the space between the stem and the leaf where the axillary bud is located.

Cuticle: This refers to the surface of the stem which is covered in a waxy substance called *cutin* (pronounced *kyoot'n*, from the Latin *cutis* meaning skin). This layer keeps the plants from losing too much water and dehydrating. In some plants it is thick enough that it also gives some protection from bacterial, viral and fungal invasions.

Epidermis: Below the stem cuticle is a single row of epidermal cells. As with our skin, the epidermal layer protects everything inside. If it is broken, infection and loss of fluids can occur. Some plant stems have a dense, light-colored mat of epidermal "hairs" that give the pant a fuzzy appearance (called *pubescence*). These hairs are a deterrent to some chewing insects.

Vascular Tissue: The xylem and phloem from the root travel up the stem in bundles of tubes called vascular tissue (from the Latin *vasculum* meaning little vessel). Although it is arranged a little differently in the stem than it is in the root, the basic function of this tissue is the same; *i.e.*, the xylem carries water and minerals, and the phloem carries food to the entire plant that has been manufactured by the leaves.

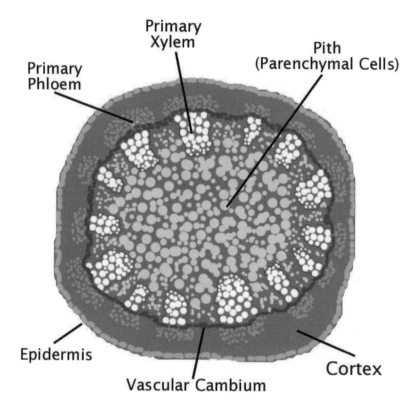

Stem Cross Section

Vascular Plants: Plants that have evolved over millions of years and that contain water and food conducting tissue (vascular tissue).

Cortex: Just inside the epidermis—between the epidermis and the vascular tissue—are several layers of cells called the cortex. This is where the cells that carry the green pigment chlorophyll, which makes young stems green in the herbaceous stage, are located.

Herbaceous: This refers to the stage in plants when the stem is soft, supple and green and containing little or no woody tissue. Some plants remain herbaceous throughout their entire lives, but many, like mature shrubs, vines and trees, are only herbaceous when young and later only at the growing tips.

Pith: The area filling the center of a stem and some of the area around the vascular bundles.

Parenchyma (*pa ring' ka ma*): These are large, thin-walled cells sometimes referred to as the fundamental cells of plants because they are basic and undifferentiated (*i.e.,* they have no specific function). All new plant cells begin as parenchymal cells before eventually changing into a specific type of cell. The cells making up the pith in stems are parenchymal cells. The word parenchyma comes from the Greek word *parenkhein* meaning to pour in beside. At first this didn't make any sense to me as a root word, but as I thought about it, parenchymal cells are often cells that fill in areas between other groups or layers of cells. If you look at it that way, it has a bit more meaning.

Primary Tissues: These are all the tissues described in herbaceous stems; *i.e.,* the epidermis, cortex, vascular bundles (xylem and phloem), vascular cambium, and the pith. They are all formed in the primary growth that takes place in the apical meristem.

Vascular Cambium: The word *cambium* is Latin for barrier. The *vascular cambium* is a single layer of cells that divides the xylem bundles from the phloem bundles, and also runs between the pith and the cortex of the stem. The interesting thing about these cells is that they are meristematic (*i.e.,* they divide). However, instead of creating primary tissue like the apical meristem, they produce three other kinds of tissue that are involved in the thickening of plant stems, and ultimately in the formation of wood and bark (cork) in perennial plants (those that have an indefinite lifespan).

The vascular cambium grows in three different directions: toward the inside of the stem; toward the outside of the stem; and sideways (around the circumference). The inside growth produces secondary xylem, the outside growth produces secondary phloem, the sideways growth adds more (meristem) cambium cells to keep up with the outward growth of the stem. All of these tissues together are called *secondary tissue.*

Turgid: The state of a plant when cells are adequately hydrated and are therefore fully "inflated." The plant appears upright, firm and perky.

Secondary Growth: As the shoot and roots develop, *secondary growth* takes place. This is the division of cells within the stem (and to a lesser degree the root) that's needed to thicken and strengthen the plant. As the stem grows taller (in upright plants) or longer (in vines or climbing plants), it needs structural reinforcement to keep it from falling over or bending and breaking. This is most noticeable in older stems of herbaceous plants where the stem has hardened and become somewhat thicker. It often will develop an outer bark or at least a darker, rougher surface. Tree trunks are the most obvious example of secondary growth. The diameter of the trunk expands as the tree grows taller. Bark is simply a coarse, corky, outer layer of protection that cracks as the girth of the tree expands. Secondary growth comes from the vascular cambium which produces the secondary tissue.

Secondary Xylem: The cells laid down on the inner side of the vascular cambium have thick walls and eventually the protoplasm (the living part of the cell) dies leaving a rigid structure that becomes water-conducting cells called *secondary xylem.* This is the part of a stem we know as wood. The rings on a tree observed on a cross-section of a tree trunk, are mostly the secondary xylem.

Secondary Phloem: The outer side of the vascular cambium forms thin-walled cells that become food conductors. Many of these cells live on, some developing thick walls to give structural support to the other relatively fragile cells of the *secondary phloem.*

Lateral Meristem: The area of cell division in a stem that creates the secondary xylem and phloem and that increases the girth of the stem to stabilize the plant.

Wood: This is the dense, internal tissue developed by mature plants that aids in supporting the trunk, stem and/or branch as it lengthens and expands. With age it thickens, and the corky outer layer cracks to allow expansion as the plant increases in diameter. Although the word *wood* is used loosely to describe all the parts of a mature stem, it is actually made up primarily of the secondary xylem, and constitutes the majority of material in the "rings" found inside older perennial plants.

Prickle: Sharp, pointed and sometimes curved woody outgrowths developing from the internodal, epidermal tissue of stems, leaves and some fruits.

Spines: Sharp, pointed, woody projections are modified leaves or sections of leaves (like the outer margins).

Thorns: These sharp, hard points are actually modified short branches developing from axillary buds.

Twiners: Stems that spiral around upright objects or other plants nearby, giving it added support. The higher they go, the tighter the grip is on the support object.

Hormone: Organic chemicals (containing carbon) produced by all parts of plants that "excite" or catalyze biochemical activities affecting growth and development of the plant. Many growers use chemically extracted hormones to regulate or control growth in container plants.

Phytotoxin: Poisonous chemicals (predominantly alkaloids) produced and stored by plants, causing symptoms in humans from mild rashes to death. There are vast differences in plants from the entirely toxic Rhododendron, to the tomato, whose fruit is edible but has toxic leaves and stems.

Shrub: Generally, a woody plant with many, branching stems close to the ground. Some shrubs are so big that they might be called small trees.

Tree: As a rule, this is a plant with one or two main stems or "trunks" supporting a large crown of foliage. As with shrubs, the distinction between tree and shrub is sometimes fuzzy.

Leaves

Leaves play the most dominant role in the survival of plants. Their species-specific structure, arrangement, texture, color, and thickness all play vital roles in how well a plant adapts to its environment, and how it captures light and manufactures food.

First we will discuss the anatomy of leaves, and how they differ from plant to plant. Looking at leaves is one of the easiest ways to identify a plant species and can even be used to distinguish varieties among the same species. Then we will look at the physiology of plants and what role leaves play in the production of food and in the exchange of gases, both of which directly effect the well being of all living creatures on earth.

Petiole: Most leaves are attached to the stem by a thin, sturdy stalk called a *petiole* (from the Latin *pediculus* meaning little foot). This plant adaptation, sometimes called a leaf stalk, evolved to allow the leaf some flexibility in wind and heavy rain, and allows the leaf to turn or "track" the sun as it changes position in the sky during the day. It also allows the leaf to stand out away from the stem and from other leaves to give it the best advantage for exposure to light. A leaf that has this structure is called a *petiolate leaf.*

Stipule: A usually small outgrowth at the base of the petiole; look like small leaves and sometimes are modified into protective, thorn-like structures.

Sessile Leaf: This is a leaf that is attached directly to the stem; *i.e.,* it has no petiole.

Leaf Blade: This is the leaf itself which is generally a thin, often translucent (lets some light through), blade-like structure, whose primary purpose is to capture light and manufacture food.

Midrib: The food and water carrying tubes from the stem (xylem and phloem) branch into the petiole and merge into the leaf via the midrib. It looks like a vein and travels up the middle of the leaf blade.

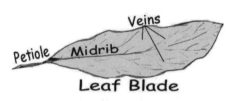

Veins: The midrib branches off on both sides of the leaf blade into what are called *veins.* These carry water and nutrients to and from the leaf.

The most recognizable pattern is *pinnate venation* where all the veins branch off the midrib.

The second most recognizable pattern is the *palmate venation* where, like a palm leaf, the midrib spreads into several fingering branches before the veins start branching off of that.

Sessile leaves have veins that run in parallel lines from the stem to the tip of the leaf. This is called *parallel venation.*

Note: When a leaf has been nibbled or broken, the part that has been severed from the rest of the leaf, will not regenerate. That is because the growing part of the plant (the meristem, where cell division occurs) is far away from the leaf blade. However, you no doubt have noticed that when you cut or

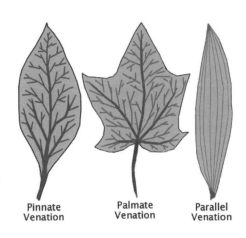

Pinnate Venation   Palmate Venation   Parallel Venation

trim grass (the blades of grass are the leaves), it continues to grow. This is because the meristem in grass is near the ground so if the top of the leaf (grass blade) is cut, it continues to grow from the bottom, pushing the severed leaf up. The meristem in grass is called an *intercalary* meristem. The word intercalary means "to insert between other parts" so an intercalary meristem is one that is inserted between the stem and the leaf blade.

Simple Leaf: A leaf as an individual unit on the plant is referred to as a *simple leaf.* There may be thousands of them on a plant, but each one is attached singularly to the stem or branching shoot.

Compound Leaves: Groups of smaller leaves in a specific pattern are called *compound leaves.* The word *compound* in botany means "composed of more than one part." The leaves in this compound group are called leaflets. There are advantages to the plant to have groups of smaller leaves instead of many individual leaves. First of all, light passes around smaller leaves more easily so the lower branches get more illumination than they might otherwise. Also, compound leaves tend to weigh less meaning they don't need as much support from the stem.

Pinnately Compound Leaves: Pinnate (from the Latin *pinnatus* meaning feathered) groups are those that have single leaflets arranged along one central stalk. If there are dissecting branches on the central stalk then the leaflets would be arranged in a grouping called bi-pinnately compound (*bi-* referring to two dissecting branches). If those second branches were further dissected, it would be called tri-pinnately compound, etc. The more dissected the grouping is, the more feathery it looks.

Palmately Compound Leaves: If you think about what a palm leaf looks like, this one will be easy to remember. The leaves are arranged so that they are all attached to the stalk at one spot at the tip of the petiole. They look like fingers spread out.

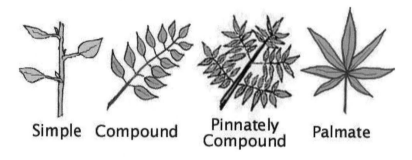

Simple Compound   Pinnately   Palmate
                    Compound

Leaf Margins: Looking at the outside edge of leaves (the margin) can help you identify plants because the leaf margin is very specific in different species and varieties. The following are the most common labels for leaf margins:

Entire–Smooth, regular; no breaks or bumps.

Sinuate–Slightly wavy.

Crenate–Sort of scalloped around the edge.

Serrate–Several pointed "teeth" on each side, generally aimed toward the tip of the leaf, which is also pointed.

Dentate–Shallow, sharp "teeth"; looks like someone took pinking shears to it.

Lobed–Deeply wavy on both sides; *i.e.,* the indentation goes deeper into the leaf.

Double Serrate–Like serrate only smaller "teeth" around the larger ones.

Leaf Arrangements: In order to reduce competition for light on a stem, leaves are arranged so that optimum light levels are achieved, based on the need of the plant. The following are the three primary arrangements of leaves on a stem:

Alternate–Arranged so that each developing leaf is placed in alternate positions up the stem, often like the steps of a circular ladder.

Opposite–Paired on opposite sides of the stem, but each pair in alternate locations from the others.

Whorled–Smaller leaves arranged in a circle around the stem, from a central point.

Cuticle: This refers to the leaf surface, top and bottom, in most plants which is covered in a waxy substance called cutin. This layer keeps the plants from losing too much water and dehydrating to its death. As in the stem, sometimes it is thick enough that it also gives some protection from bacterial, viral and fungal invasions.

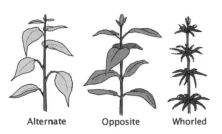

Alternate   Opposite   Whorled

Epidermis: Just below the cuticle in a leaf is a single row of cells called epidermal cells. As with our skin, the epidermal layer protects everything inside. If it is broken, then infection and loss of fluids can occur.

Some plants have a dense, light-colored mat of epidermal hairs that give the plant a fuzzy appearance (called *pubescence*). These hairs–often found on desert plants–are a deterrent to some insects, and reflect sunlight off the surface to keep the leaf from baking in a very hot sun. It also keeps dust and dirt from getting into the stomata and (see *stoma*) clogging them up.

Mesophyll: If you think of a leaf blade as if it were a sandwich, then the epidermis is the bread and the *mesophyll* is the filling in between. The mesophyll (from the Greek *meso*- meaning middle and *phyll* meaning leaf) has all the cells that contain the pigment chlorophyll which captures light and converts it into energy for food production. There are two different parts to the mesophyll:

1. Directly below the upper epidermis are the *palisade* cells which are long and tightly packed. These are the first to trap light as the sun hits the surface of the leaf blade.
2. Below the palisade cells are the irregularly shaped *spongy* cells, which are much more loosely packed to allow the free flow of carbon dioxide, oxygen and water vapor. These cells catch the light that gets past the palisade cells.

The xylem and phloem bundles carried by the leaf veins run through the mesophyll, supplying water and carrying newly made food to other parts of the plant.

Chloroplasts: These are the cells that contain the green pigment *chlorophyll*. In a fraction of a second, these cells take the energy of light (captured by the chlorophyll) plus water and carbon dioxide, and produce food in the form of various sugar compounds. The process called *photosynthesis* yields extra oxygen molecules as a waste product. These bond together (O_2) and are released into the atmosphere via small openings in the leaf surface called stoma.

Leaf, Cross Section

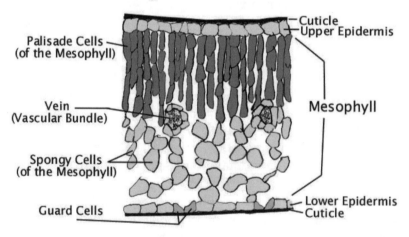

Palisade Cells (of the Mesophyll)

Vein (Vascular Bundle)

Spongy Cells (of the Mesophyll)

Guard Cells

Cuticle
Upper Epidermis

Mesophyll

Lower Epidermis
Cuticle

Stoma: These are special, tiny cells, usually located on the underside of leaves, that allow the plant to absorb carbon dioxide (CO_2) needed for the manufacture of food. They also give the plant a way to get rid of excess water (H_2O) in the form of water vapor and oxygen (O_2), which is a byproduct of plant metabolism. There are many thousands of these openings per cubic centimeter of leaf surface.

These cells play an important role in assisting the water pressure which is started at the roots. As the water fills the root cells and is pushed up the plant, it is simultaneously being released by the stomal openings in the leaves, which increases the efficiency of the water pump. This is what completes the siphoning action.

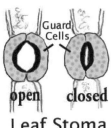

Leaf Stoma

The *stomata* (from the Greek *stoma* meaning mouth) are very good at regulating water and gas exchanges. At night, since the plant does not need CO_2 for photosynthesis (because it's dark), the stomal openings in most plants close. They also close if the soil is too dry, if the weather is hot with low humidity, or if it is excessively windy, because all these conditions might otherwise cause the release of more water than is being taken in by the roots, causing a deficit very quickly.

Stomata are surrounded by cells called *guard cells* that are actually what make the stoma open and close. When the guard cells are full of water, they form a crescent-like shape (()) and make the stoma open. When they are slightly depleted and relaxed they sit side by side (II), which makes the stoma close. The guard cells respond very quickly to changes in the environment in order to protect plant hydration.

Transpiration: Water vapor lost from stomatal openings during normal metabolic processes. *Transpiration pull* refers to the drawing (siphoning) action of water from the roots to the leaves that occurs when water vapor is lost.

Phototropism: Caused by the plant hormone *auxin*. This is the growth movement by plants to a source of light. The most obvious example is how some plants will turn their leaves toward and follow light from a window or lamp.

Foliage: The collection of leaves associated with above-ground stems/branches of a plant.

Bud Scales: Modified leaves that form around the growing tips of deciduous plants to protect the apical buds from the ravages of winter. Looking like armor, these scaly leaves are pushed aside in spring when the bud begins new growth.

Tendrils: Modified leaves or stems growing out of apical buds, that coil around objects with which they come into close contact, anchoring the stem as it grows. *Leaf tendrils* come from the small leaflets of compound leaves, stipules or petioles. All evolved as a way to elevate the plant giving it more exposure to light.

Flowers and Reproduction

To aficionados of flowering plants, whether they be short-lived annuals or flowering perennials, the primary reason for growing them is pure enjoyment of the shape, color, and scent they provide to a garden. Flowers fill our souls with delight, and as an added benefit, attract hummingbirds, butterflies and bees to our little Eden. Without flowers, a garden is simply a palette of greens and browns, fine for some, but not nearly as fun for the majority of gardeners.

However, to the plant, flowers are simply the route to survival. As I mentioned before, flowers evolved as a way for the plant to ensure that it will be visited by certain insects or other animals which sets reproduction in motion by spreading pollen from one plant to another, and for the purpose of dispersal of the seeds, which are the genetic packages created by the reproductive process. The different shapes, sizes, scents and colors were perfected over time to attract the exact type of pollinator needed to do the job. Many are so specific that only one type of insect can get deep enough into the flower to reach the reproductive organs. In a case like that, the insect is native to the same environment as the plant, so the plant is assured of survival as long as that insect is around, and/or the plant remains in its native habitat. This type of close relationship of plants to specific insects and animals can easily be threatened if something causes an imbalance in the ecosystem. Something like poisons, alien predators or significant climatic changes.

The information in this section is not designed to diminish your appreciation for the aesthetic value of flowers, but to increase your appreciation and awe of them as tools developed by these plants over millennia to assure the survival of the species. It is nothing short of miraculous.

Structure

Pedicel: As with the petiole of the leaf, the pedicel is the stalk that carries the flower bud. Pedicel comes from the same root word as petiole (Latin: pediculus meaning "little foot").

Flower Bud: A flower bud is formed when the apical meristem of a shoot or axillary bud changes its cellular template from stem or leaf production to one designed to begin the reproductive process. Instead of leaves and all the associated vascular tissue, the parenchyma, (remember they are the non-differentiated, fundamental cells), begins to form the structures

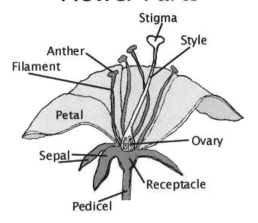

Flower Parts

Ovary + Style + Stigma = PISTIL
Anther + Filament = STAMEN

necessary for this function. The floral structures are arranged in a pattern of circles called whorls. So instead of seeing new leaves burst from the bud, one witnesses the unfolding of a complex, multi-layered flower.

Receptacle: The very end of the shoot or stem where the flower bud is forming is called the *receptacle*. The Latin root word *recipere* means to receive. The flower organs are there to "receive" the visitors needed to fertilize eggs.

Calyx and Sepals: The first thing you notice on a flower bud is the tight, (usually green) outside covering that is protecting the developing flower parts before opening. The covering is called the *calyx* and is made up of several individual leaf-like parts called *sepals*, arranged in a whorl around the base of the flower. (Apparently the root words of both calyx and sepal mean covering.) When the flower opens, the sepals either curl back or become unnoticeable underneath the bloom, often shriveling and falling off, as they are no longer needed.

Corolla and Petals: The corolla is the sum total of all the individual petals either arranged singly in a whorl, or layered and overlapping. The word *corolla* is Latin meaning little crown and *petal* is Greek meaning thin plate.

Perianth: The calyx and corolla together are called the *perianth*, (from the Greek *peri-* meaning around and *anthos* meaning flower). So perianth literally means "around the flower."

Tepal: Some flowers have something that is not quite a sepal and not quite a petal. It is a sort of combination of the two, but after opening, has much of the classic coloring of other flowers. The word *tepal* comes from the French word *tepale* meaning alteration. Tulips and lilies are typical examples of tepal flowers.

Bract: Some flowers are so insignificant that they would go unnoticed if they were not surrounded by the sometimes brightly colored, modified leaves called *bracts*. Two clear examples of this are the poinsettia and the bougainvillea.

Whorl: Flowers, petals (or leaves) arranged in a ring around the stalk or stem. An example of flowers arranged this way is the Monarda family (Horse Mint, Bee Balm).

Stamen: The male part of the reproductive system consisting of the following:

> *Stalk*–Also called a *filament*, this is the long, thread-like structure that holds the anther upright in a position surrounding the female structure, the *pistil*.

> *Anther*–The anther is the small structure at the tip of the stalk or filament that produces (and is covered with) pollen.

> *Pollen*–Microscopic structures containing two cells that are involved in fertilizing the plant eggs. Pollen granules have unusual shapes that are unique to the plant. Seen only by microscope, these tiny structures often look knobby or barbed, giving them a rather other-worldly appearance. The outer covering on pollen is so durable and tough that ancient pollen grains have been found intact, giving scientists a good idea of what kind of flora was present during a specific time in the history of the earth.

Pistil: The female part of the reproductive system consisting of the following:

> *Stigma*–This a knobby-shaped structure at the very top of the pistil that is sticky so that pollen adheres to its surface.

> *Style*–The *style* is the stalk of the pistil that holds the stigma up into the most advantageous position for pollination.

> *Ovary*–Located at the base of the pistil, this structure contains the eggs which are nested inside *ovules* (undeveloped seeds). As the eggs are fertilized by the sperm from the pollen, the walls of the ovary thicken and eventually becomes the fruit.

Inflorescences: Flowers that form in clusters on the plant, (as opposed to a single flower on a single stalk), are referred to as *inflorescences*. The following are the most typical types of these flower clusters:

> *Spike*–The flowers are attached directly to the main stem of the plant without a stalk. Examples might be many of the wild Orchids, Monardas (the Bee Balm family), many Salvias, Mullein, etc.

> *Raceme*–The individual flowers are attached to the main stem via a short stalk. Flowers in this category include Snapdragons, Foxglove, Lupines, Penstemon, etc.

> *Panicle*–Flowers that are attached to the main stem via multi-branched stalks. Panicles are well demonstrated in Begonias, Borage, Baby's Breath, Forget-Me-Not, Four-O'clocks, etc.

> *Umbel*–Like an inverted umbrella, these flowers are attached to multiple flower stalks that are connected at one spot at the tip or end of a stem. Examples are Queen Anne's Lace, fennel, dill and members of the garlic and onion families.

> *Composite*–This type of inflorescence is tricky. It looks like one flower but is really a bunch of tiny, tightly packed, individual flowers called *disc flowers*, surrounded by flat, thin, blade-like petals belonging to what are called ray flowers. Typical composite flowers are sunflowers, daisies, asters and dandelions.

Spadix—In this inflorescence the spike is a tall column-like structure containing miniscule male and female flowers surrounded by a sheath-like leaf bract called a *spathe*. Flowers of this type are found on plants like Calla Lilies, Jack-in-the-Pulpit, Dieffenbachia, and Philodendron.

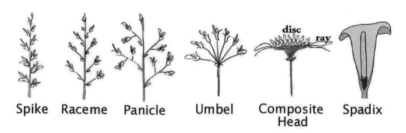

Spike   Raceme   Panicle   Umbel   Composite   Spadix
Head

Photoperiodism: Refers to the day length required by certain plants for the development of flowers. For some plants the day length is very critical. An example would be the "Christmas Cactus" which needs short days (or long nights) to stimulate bud formation.

Day-Neutral Plant: A plant whose flowering response does not depend on maximum or minimum day length.

Reproduction: A Miraculous Process

There is nothing quite as awe inspiring as the process of reproduction, whether it is animal or plant. Although many plants have alternate ways of replicating themselves, the process of making seeds (embryos) is the most common form of reproduction in Angiosperms and Gymnosperms. The "sexual" method used by plants is not significantly different from humans and other animals, making it more obvious to the close observer that all living things on earth are more similar than many would like to admit. It should make us all feel more connected to our phenomenal planet.

We have discussed the morphology of seeds and how they germinate, and I have described the structures involved in reproduction. Now I will take you through the actual progression of events that leads to the creation of the seed—that amazing little packet of genetic heritage that keeps our world filled with the beauty and benefit of plants.

Pollination

Pollen is the host container for the male set of genes. Fertilization can only occur when pollen from the stamen of a plant lands on the pistil of a plant of the same species. The sticky pistil can be pasted with pollen from other species of plants, and fertilization will not occur. The pistil is able to discriminate shape and chemical makeup of the pollen that lands on it, and will only be receptive to a genetic match.

To further the complexity of the situation, most flowering plants are designed to only be receptive to the pollen of another plant of the same species, (this is called *cross-pollination*). In other words, each plant does not want to be fertilized by its own pollen. This is nature's way of ensuring genetic diversity. The plant considers its own pollen to be "alien." However, some plant species have evolved a sort of backup system that allows the flower to be pollinated with its own pollen if none other is available at the time it is needed. For instance, if the plant relies on wind or insects to carry pollen, there may be times when there is no wind, or insect activity is low due to cold temperatures or cloudy, rainy weather. The plant will sacrifice genetic diversity for a simple chance at survival.

Flowering plants have several ways of making sure their own pollen will not interact with the pistil from the same plant. First, as mentioned, there is an actual chemical incompatibility that makes the plant consider its own pollen to be foreign. Another method is to have the stigma and pistil develop some distance from each other inside the corolla so that chances of them coming into contact with each other is diminished. A third way is to have the pollen release timed so that it happens before the pistil is ready to receive it. The most extreme way to protect genetic diversity is for the pollen to come from a completely separate "male" plant, and for the flower with the ovaries develop only in a "female" plant.

Part of what makes this so amazing is that many flowers are only open for a matter of hours in the course of a day. Everything has to happen exactly right or fertilization will not occur. This is why sometimes a "fruit" will only have a couple of seeds, and sometimes it will be loaded. Also, the fertilization of seeds causes the development of the ovary wall to occur, which means if eggs in one side of the ovary somehow miss being fertilized, it can mean irregular or stunted development of the fruit. There are many factors involved in the success or failure of this process.

Pollen is carried from one plant to another by wind, by water (in the case of bog-type plants), by insects and by certain animals like hummingbirds or bats. These insects, birds and other animals that visit flowers are there primarily for one reason—*nectar*. This sugary liquid sustains many creatures on earth and is produced by plants in specific places inside the flower called *nectaries*. The plants with nectaries often place them strategically so that the pollinator has to go deep into the flower to get at it, thereby passing through the pollen patch, taking a bit of it with them to the next flower. Pollen, however, is quite nutritious and some insects like bees and some beetles actually collect the pollen and take it back the nest or hive to feed the masses. Along the way, of course, they enjoy the energy boost of nectar as they work their way through the flowers.

Flowers that need the assistance of pollinators have developed intricate color patterns that attract and maneuver the insect or animal to the place where the nectar is hidden. These *nectar guides* are rows of dots, circles, contrasting colors and iridescence, or special pigments that emit specific wavelengths reflected by the ultraviolet light of the sun, and that attract, and virtually provide a runway for, the interested party. Nothing is left to chance, especially if the flower needs a very specific pollinator.

Fertilization

So, how does the pollen grain, with its accompanying genetic material, enter the pistil to fertilize the eggs? It starts with the chemical recognition that I talked about earlier. The pistil and pollen grain are matched like two pieces of a puzzle. Once they are snapped into place, the pollen grain does something amazing. One of the two cells (remember each pollen grain has two cells), begins to tunnel into the pistil and down into the style, creating a structure called a *pollen tube*. The tube continues down until it locates and attaches itself to a tiny opening in a single ovule. Once the tube is established, the second cell in the pollen grain releases a couple of sperm into the tube which travel all the way down, entering the ovule, locating the egg, and fertilizing it.

The ovary in each species of flowering plant has a set number of ovules with eggs waiting to be fertilized. Apparently this happens very quickly and how the pollen grains with their pollen tubes are so efficiently able to find the tiny openings to each ovule without getting in each other's way is still a mystery to botanists. One amazing example of this is an ear of corn. Each kernel is a separate ovule which must be fertilized by an individual grain of pollen.

But, you ask, there are two sperm? One fertilizes the egg, so what happens to the other one? The second sperm hitches itself to another cell in the ovule to make temporary food tissue for the developing zygote (the fertilized egg). The food tissue is called *endosperm* which you will recall is the name of the stored food in some seeds. The endosperm is used for food as the zygote develops into an *embryo* (the miniature plant inside a seed). Most embryos use it up by the time they are fully developed, but some seeds retain a significant amount of endosperm to assist the embryo develop into a plant during germination. Again, the corn seed (the kernel) is a perfect example of this.

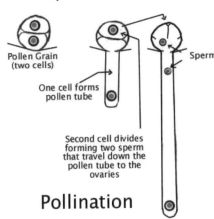

Pollen Grain
(two cells)

One cell forms
pollen tube

Second cell divides
forming two sperm
that travel down the
pollen tube to the
ovaries

Sperm

Pollination

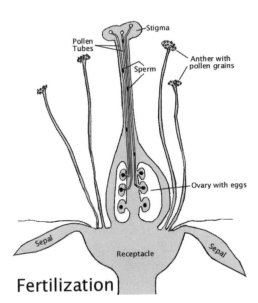

Stigma

Pollen
Tubes

Sperm

Anther with
pollen grains

Ovary with eggs

Sepal

Sepal

Receptacle

Fertilization

Once the eggs have been fertilized, the ovary enlarges around the ovules which contain the developing seeds. Although the vast majority of mature ovaries (fruit) are simply a pod of some kind which eventually dries and splits open to disperse the seeds, some maturing ovaries ripen with a thickening of the *pericarp* (the ovary/fruit wall) which becomes fleshy, soft and sweet. Examples are peaches, plums and cherries. These examples have one seed per fruit surrounded by a hard "pit" which is part of the pericarp. Apples and pears have the distinction of having the walls of the fruit develop from the base of the perianth (actually part of the calyx) which thickens around the ovary. When you cut open an apple, you can actually see where the wall of the ovary fused with the perianth on the inside, near the seeds. Strawberries, blackberries and raspberries develop from a receptacle that has numerous individual pistils packed tightly together and containing one ovary with one ovule, each. So the fruit of these plants are in actuality a conglomeration of many fruits, each with their own seed.

As always, botanists feel the need to distinguish one plant from another using specific criteria to do so. Fruiting habits of plants is one important way to distinguish one from another. Remember that "fruit" does not imply the edibility of a plant. It is referring to the way it develops the seed package. The following are the three characteristics that can be applied to flowering/fruiting plants.

> *Simple Fruit*–This is the result of a flower having only one ovary. The ovary may have different numbers of ovules, but there is only *one* ovary. Examples are peaches, plums, grapes, apples, pears, tomatoes, citrus fruit, squash, melons, etc., as well as many other ornamental, flowering plants.
>
> *Aggregate Fruit*–This comes from a single flower with multiple ovaries, as in the case of blackberries, raspberries, strawberries, etc. The juice sac around each seed is the mature pericarp. An ornamental example of this would be the native Texas lantana.
>
> *Multiple Fruit*–These are plants that develop what look like aggregate fruits, but instead of individual ovaries on one flower, they are the result of *multi-*

ple flowers with pericarps from ovaries that have fused together as they ripen. Pineapples are an example of this kind of fruit.

Full Circle

We now have come full circle from the seed, to germination, to growth and development, to food production, to reproduction, and back to the seed. As muddled as your head might be at this point, I have tried to make this as easy to understand as possible. Botany is not an easy subject and I have had to learn and relearn over the years to make it stick. But I maintain that it adds a dimension to growing plants that is unattainable otherwise.

Horticultural Terms

The following are more general terms relating to plants and growing. Some are actual botanical terms and some are simply descriptive words you will likely hear in the plant trade.

General

Horticulture: In the strictest sense *horticulture* might be defined as the activity of growing flowers, fruits, vegetables, tropical, native and other ornamental plants, or the science or art of cultivating a garden. This covers a wide range of involvement with plants whether leisure or professional. For the purpose of this book, horticulture will be referring to the businesses involved in the propagation, growing and selling of plant material in containers. (Note: Although licensing relating to commercial horticulture is under the department of agriculture, there is a distinct difference between the two. Agriculture is the process of cultivating field crops and/or production of livestock.)

Organic: Broad term referring to anything on earth (or beyond) containing carbon (and hydrogen), the inference being "living organisms." All living beings from humans to plants to protozoans are carbon based. When the term *organic* is used to describe a method of growing, it is referring to the avoidance of laboratory-produced chemical fertilizers and pesticides and emphasis on earth-generated ("organic") fertilizers and plant-based pesticides. The method also emphasizes the importance of encouraging a natural, environmental balance through the use of beneficial insects, trap crops, companion planting, sanitation, beneficial soil microorganisms and a healthy dose of patience and common sense.

Organic Horticulture: The business of commercially growing plants in containers without the use of synthetic fertilizers, pesticides, fungicides or herbicides.

Xeriscape: A form of landscaping using *xeric plants* (those needing little water to survive) to conserve dwindling ground water and aquifers in regions where this is a concern. In these areas of water shortage and drought the use of non-native plants can substantially reduce the overall availability of water because of their greater need, and consequently their higher uptake from the soil. This means less water for humans and other animals as well as native flora. Native plants are adaptable to water shortages and will survive by going into dormancy to conserve available resources.

Hardiness Zone: These are the geographical (zonal) guidelines set up by the U.S. Department of Agriculture that indicate average winter and, in some cases, summer temperatures. These extreme temperatures are important in deciding what kinds of plants will grow in your area. The problem with these "official" zones is that there are in reality many gradations of these temperatures to the point of being zones within zones. And when you factor in average rainfall and soil variations, there may be significant differences in growing conditions within 50 miles of your local region. The USDA maps are great as general guidelines, but you need to dig a bit deeper when you are growing plants for an area, to make sure you understand what unique conditions your customers are living under.

Descriptive Terms

Allelopathy: This is where a plant inhibits growth and/or germination of other plants by releasing chemicals from twigs, leaves and sometimes roots into the surrounding soil. The word allelopathy means "mutual suffering."

Annual: A plant whose entire life cycle (germination, growth, fruiting, death) is completed in the time-span of one growing season. These cycles vary in length with the species of plant, from only a few weeks to nearly a year.

Biennial: Plants that complete their life cycle in the span of two growing seasons. The first season is usually spent on foliar growth and the second season it blooms, fruits and dies. Some biennials may live longer in frost-free climates, but will lose vigor with time.

Bolting: Unusually rapid growth of an annual plant resulting in premature flowering, often due to unusually warm weather, especially with plants that need cooler temperatures for growth and development.

Cold Hardening: In preparation of freezing winter temperatures, the cells of deciduous plants change structure and function slightly to prevent the fatal formation of ice crystals.

Deciduous: Refers to perennial plants that lose their leaves due to a quickened, hormonally induced aging process in the leaves, triggered by lower temperatures and shorter days. The process includes dormancy in which the roots and/or stems slow metabolism and store food. New growth will be stimulated by warming and longer days and will be sustained by the stored nutrients until the foliage actively begins photosynthesis.

Determinate Growth: Generally refers to fruiting annuals that produce only one or two (often large) flushes of fruit and/or that have a predetermined growth pattern. Most determinate plants are hybrid vegetables or flowers that are bred for very specific (desirable) characteristics.

Dormancy: The state of a plant when growing (cellular activity) has diminished due to heat and/or drought or cold temperatures. Any of these situations bring on leaf drop and temporary interruption in active growth. The plant survives on stored nutrients until it produces enough foliage to begin producing food again via photosynthesis.

Drip Zone (Drip Line): This is the area of soil directly under the outer tips of the branches of trees and shrubs (perimeter) that often has root tips waiting for water to drip off the leaves. When fertilizing or watering, it is important to attend to the entire area under the foliage, including the drip zone. But be aware (especially with trees) that often the roots extend out beyond the drip line.

Evergreen: Perennial plants that do not lose their leaves as a result of seasonal changes although growth often slows in times of drought, or extreme heat or cold. Leaves only drop as a result of normal aging or extreme stress and/or disease.

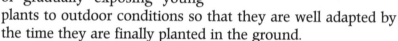

Hardening Off: The process of gradually exposing young plants to outdoor conditions so that they are well adapted by the time they are finally planted in the ground.

Hardy Plants: These are native or non-native plants that survive the challenging environmental stresses of your region. The stresses can be anything from extreme cold and/or heat to drought, humidity, rainfall and specific soil conditions.

Herbicide: Chemicals that have selective or broad-spectrum plant killing properties.

Host: Plants used by parasites (see *parasite*) as a source of nourishment. Depending on the parasite, the host plant may suffer from as little as minor metabolic disruption to (ultimately) death.

Indeterminate Growth: These are annual plants that fruit continuously and whose growth patterns and production are primarily influenced by soil, water and nutritional factors. Most heirloom vegetables are indeterminate. (In essence all non-hybrid plants are indeterminate, but the terms determinate and indeterminate are used to help gardeners understand what to expect of the seeds or plants they are purchasing for their home gardens.)

Native Plants: Generally speaking, these are plants that are indigenous to a specific region. That is, they have genetic traits similar, if not identical, to plants that grew in the region before the settlement (and ecological disturbance) of humans.

Naturalized Plants: These are non-native plants that have been introduced to a region by wind, animals, or humans and are uniquely suited to the area to the point of growing as well or better than the native plants. This can cause major problems for the survival of the native ecosystem if certain naturalized plants begin to dominate.

Necrosis: Death of a stem, roots and/or leaves often caused by calcium deficiency because of its importance in the synthesis of pectin, which is what holds cell walls together.

Parasite: From the Greek *parasitos,* meaning one who eats at another's table. In botanical terms these are specific fungi, bacteria, viruses and some plants that are unable to manufacture their own food and so must attach themselves to a host plant and invade the root or arial (above-ground) tissue in order to procure enough nourishment to live out its life cycle, which includes reproduction. It often leads to death of the host, but might only drain specific resources like water or minerals, which weakens the plant, making it more vulnerable to other disease or pest problems.

Perennial: Plants that have an indefinite lifespan. Some are short-lived (5-10 years) and some last for centuries. Some have continuous, above-ground growth and others have top growth that disappears (dies back) each year to return the following season. Some are deciduous (losing foliage in winter) and some are evergreen (maintaining foliage year-round). All have dormant periods where growth is slowed or temporarily suspended due to extreme heat, cold or simply genetically predetermined growth cycles.

Phytotoxcity: Refers to the damaging effect of chemicals applied to plants, resulting in stress or even death of the plant. Environmental toxins, herbicides and some pesticides may cause this effect.

Shade Tolerant: Plants that photosynthesize better in low light. Many of these plants will actually die if exposed to bright sunlight for too long.

Stunting: Plants with abnormally short stems, small, often deformed leaves, and overall poor color and performance. Caused by environmental stress such as water or nutrient deprivation, disease, pest insect infestation, or consistently harsh climatic conditions such as extreme cold, heat or wind.

Symbiosis: When plants have a mutually beneficial relationship with another species, such as insects that feed on the nectar and spread pollen, and birds that eat the fruit and drop the indigestible seed.

Xeric (pronounced *zeer′ ick):* Of or characterized by conditions requiring very little water to survive. The most obvious example would be the desert and its plants. Xeric plants are those that have adapted to very dry conditions, allowing them to survive extreme drought through a unique system of water and nutrient storage and the ability to become completely dormant during times of severe stress, conserving their resources and thereby allowing them to survive.

Genetics

Genes: The molecular-sized hereditary units attached to chromosomes in the nucleus of all cells that dictate the inheritable characteristics of an organism. Some genes are dominant and physically apparent, and some are present but tucked away in the chromosomes and passed on to later generations. When growing out non-hybrid seeds, it's always interesting to see recessive characteristics popping out occasionally in a few of the plants. This of course is where much of the commercial horticultural selection process begins.

Genotype: The gene composition of a plant.

Heirloom: Plant whose characteristics are the result of natural selection rather than hybrid gene mixing. Many heirlooms are essentially, genetically identical to the parent plant with only subtle, (evolutionary) genetic differences occurring over time. These plant varieties are often very old; the seeds or cuttings having been carefully (and lovingly) handed down through the generations to protect the genetic heritage.

Hybrid: Often designated in seed catalogs as F1 meaning the plant will be an offspring of two related species of plants, each of whom contribute specific, desirable characteristics to the genes of the hybrid plant. Successive seeds from these hybridized plants (after growing out and fruiting) will, if not sterile, eventually go back to the original parent plant characteristics.

Non-Hybrid: Although this category includes many heirlooms the term simply refers to plant species and varieties that have not endured genetic tampering. Many of these plants are tried and true, solid producers.

Open-Pollinated: Refers to non-hybrid plants that are wind-, insect- or self-pollinated and are capable of cross-pollinating with other plants of similar species. These plants carry the foundational genetic makeup of the species and pass it on to the next generation.

Phenotype: This is the apparent or visible expression of a genetic characteristic such as leaf shape, height, width, color, etc.

Selected Variety: Variety of a species bred through natural genetic selection, from the process of growing the plant out over time, and selecting progeny with desirable characteristics rather than gene mixing via intentional cross-pollination (resulting in a hybrid from two specific members of a species).

Variegation: Even or uneven color patterns found in leaves or flowers of plants that is mostly an inherited genetic trait. Probably adaptive but may also be induced by viral genetic meddling.

Plant Classifications

Binomial Nomenclature: The two-part naming system (genus-species) developed by a Swedish naturalist Carolus Linnaeus in the 18th century.

Cultivar: A specific, named variety of a certain species of plant, carefully cultivated to retain its desirable characteristics. The cultivar name is listed after the genus and species in a scientific name and is either preceded by the abbreviation cv., or surrounded by single quotation marks. Most cultivars are plants that produce showy flowers or unusual variegation, shape or size outside the norm for that genus/species. An example would be *Rosa multiflora cv. 'Lilliputian'*.

Taxonomist: These are the plant scientists that give plants their internationally recognized scientific names. They are also the ones that change the names about the time you have them memorized.

Family: This is a group of plants of various genera with broad similarities. According to the *International Code of Botanical Nomenclature*, all family names end in *-aceae*. For example, the rose family is *Rosaceae*.

Genus: A taxonomic subdivision of plant families which, in turn, contains a number of related species. The scientific name of all plants begins with the genus, which is usually Greek or Latin, and always capitalized. These names come from mythological figures, common (Greek or Latin) names for the plants, or are named in honor of someone involved in plant history. The genus for the rose family is *Rosa*.

Species: A sub-group (often large) of a genus with primary genetic characteristics similar enough to be identifiable, and whose individual members are able to interbreed freely. The second word in a scientific name is the species and is not capitalized. These words generally describe identifying characteristic of the plant. Sometimes the second word is *officinalis* or *officinale* (meaning "of the workshop") referring to its historical use as a traditional medicinal plant. A species for the rose family might be *multiflora* (many flowered),

Plant Nutrients

Chlorosis: A condition of a plant producing yellowing of the leaves, which decreases photosynthesis and therefore food production. Causes may be overwatering, environmental toxins, or deficiencies in magnesium, iron or nitrogen. The deficiencies may be caused from a lack of the nutrient in the soil, or from high or low pH causing the nutrients to be inaccessible to the plant.

Macronutrients: Mineral elements used in small amounts by plants for healthy growth and development. These are carbon (C), hydrogen (H), oxygen (O), nitrogen (N), phosphorus (P), potassium (K), sulfur (S) and calcium (Ca).

Micronutrients: Mineral elements used in small to tiny amounts by plants for healthy growth and development. These are magnesium (Mg), iron (Fe), copper (Cu), zinc (Zn), manganese (Mn), molybdenum (Mo) and boron (B).

NPK: Nitrogen, phosphorus and potassium and their relative amounts in a fertilizer or soil sample. All three are fundamentally important to normal, healthy plant growth.

pH: A scale from 1 to 14 assigning numbers to soil indicating relative acidity or alkalinity, 1 being extremely acidic, 14 extremely alkaline, and 7 being essentially neutral. Most plants will grow in a soil with a pH of 6.5 to 7, but some require a more acidic or alkaline soil for robust growth. A highly acidic or alkaline soil may also liberate excessive amounts of certain minerals that, although needed by plants in tiny proportions, would be toxic at higher levels. Even small increases or decreases in pH can profoundly affect nutrient uptake by the plant.

Trace Nutrients: Mineral elements used in tiny amounts by specific plants for healthy growth and development. These are chlorine (Cl), aluminum (Al), sodium (Na), silicon (Si) and cobalt (Co).

Obviously one could go into much greater depth regarding the anatomy and physiology of plants than I have in this chapter. Just the subject of plant cell function and structure could fill a book of its own. My hope is that this chapter has stimulated an interest in plants that goes beyond the day-to-day production of herbs, flowers, shrubs, vines and trees; that you will be stimulated to learn more, and use the information to give added meaning to an already enjoyable profession.

Chapter Four

Growing

Since growing plants is the crux of a horticultural business, I would like to spend some time in this chapter on basics. Learning how to grow without chemicals adds a dimension to the fundamentals that is challenging, but not really difficult. I consider it a thinking person's form of horticulture. Everything must be thought through carefully from seed to sale, with a dollop of vigilance and good sense thrown in. Your success depends not only on a good foundation of knowledge regarding propagation, soil, fertilizers and pest and disease management, but also on educating yourself about the specific plants you are growing. Much of your individual plant education will come from growing them in your nursery, but your understanding of the plants you sell should go beyond how they perform in a four-inch or six-inch pot. Later I will discuss the importance of growing these plants in your own garden to increase your understanding of how they behave in more mature stages. If you can tell your customer how the tomato tastes, describe the fragrance of a bloom, or illustrate the shape and habit of a shrub, they will more likely give the plant a try.

Given that people have varied levels of expertise going into a business of this kind, I have to make the assumption that there are those who don't have a clue how to get started. Some of this information applies to any plant business. Since we are small and have a chemical-free environment, much of what is written here will be related to my own experience. Pick and choose as you like.

Containers

In the industry, the pots you grow your plants in are referred to as *containers*. Materials used in making them are new and recycled plastic, clay, ceramic, metal and various kinds of natural fiber. Because they are the most economical, you will most likely be using the black, recycled plastic containers, easily obtained through most horticultural distributors.

Sizes will either be expressed in *inches* or in *volume*. For instance, many growers sell herbs, flowers and some vegetable plants in a round or square four-inch container. It is a good size for the customer who just wants one or two each of a small plant. However, many trees, shrubs and other perennials need to be sold in larger containers to accommodate a bigger, more developed root system. These plants are generally sold in containers that are measured in volume such as a quart or gallon. If you are growing bedding plants, such as flowers and vegetables, you might opt to use four-pack or six-pack containers.

It's helpful to know that there are *standard* sizes and *full* or *true* sizes of many containers. Standard sizes are generally just short of the stated size and full sizes are the exact size stated. For instance there are standard four-inch containers that range from 3-1/2 to 3-5/8 inches across, whereas the full four-inch is, well, four inches. Volume containers have the same kind of differences. The standard containers are used most often in horticulture. The plants are sold as the stated size, but money is saved in soil volume. Also, it's easier and cheaper to find carry trays for standard containers, and they take up less space on benches and in your delivery vehicle, allowing you to have more plants in a smaller space, again, saving you money.

Choosing which containers to use depends on what kinds of plants you intend to grow, how much money you are willing to shell out, how much space you have (such as bench width and length), and how much aggravation you are willing to put up with. There are a lot of choices including *blow-molded* or *injection-molded*, round versus square, black, white, green, terra cotta, smooth versus ridged, handle/no-handle, lip/no-lip, hanging baskets, bowls, window boxes, etc. Each has advantages and disadvantages. For instance, injection-molded containers are a rigid plastic and so stand up on benches better and are easier to carry, but roots tend to circle in these containers creating transplant problems for the customer if the plant has been in the container too long. On the other hand, blow-molded containers, which are made of a softer plastic, often have ridges that train roots to grow downward, but they are flimsy and fall over easily on benches, especially if the plant is overgrown. Ask your distributor to let you have some samples of containers you are considering so that you can check them out ahead of time.

There are also many choices in *carry trays* depending on what kind of containers you choose. Offered are multiple sizes and shapes of basic, inexpensive plastic "web" trays that carry different numbers of standard or full-sized, square containers. There are also molded plastic trays for round or special-sized containers. (A web or molded tray full of containerized plants is called a *flat*.)

Examine your options and get what suits your needs and budget. There are many retail nurseries that have piles of carry trays out back that they have no use for. Ask if you can look through them in order to see what other growers in your area are using. Take some home and play with them and the sample containers you got from your distributor. It might help you decide what is going to work best for you.

You will find that growers have some pretty strong opinions about pots. Don't always do what everyone else is doing. Use your instincts. Some years ago I decided that I really liked the quart size for many of the plants I grow. The nurseries kept telling me that it was not a good size to sell. I persisted because my plants looked great in that size container and I knew they would sell if the customers had more exposure to this size. Now quart-sized plants are in virtually every nursery. I obviously wasn't the only grower who thought it was a good idea.

The following are comments on containers that are strictly personal, but might help you make choices more wisely.

Standard Sizes. Generally we use the standard, square, black, four-inch pots; the standard, black plastic gallon; and the green standard six-inch. I have no use for round four-inch pots. You have to carry them in special, molded trays that are expensive and not especially sturdy. Standard six-inch pots fit nicely into most web trays.

Six-Packs. There are a number of different cells you can get from four-packs to 12-packs. Six is a good number for most bedding plants. We use the jumbo six-packs as opposed to the standard because the little bit of extra soil in the cell gives us a bigger, more vigorous transplant and, consequently, greater customer satisfaction.

Injection-Molded vs. Blow-Molded. Blow-molded containers are a softer plastic and therefore more flexible. They often have ridges running down the side, which really do train the roots to grow down. But these containers are just too flimsy for me. They tend to fall over on the bench, and forget anything that is top heavy. I prefer the more rigid injection-molded containers. They are a heavier plastic and are easier to

Rigid   Blow Molded

carry and settle on a bench. Plus, they can be re-used multiple times if necessary.

Hanging Baskets. These contain-
ers generally come in six-inch, eight-inch and ten-inch. They have differ-ent shapes and are often rigged to accommodate either a plastic or wire hanger. Colors vary from green (in different shades), to white and terra cotta. My personal preference is a green, round-shaped container with a wire hanger. I have had many cus-tomers tell me that plastic hangers make the basket look cheap. I'm not sure why they even make a six-inch hanging basket. There is not much you can grow for very long in a con-tainer of that size. Stick with the bigger sizes.

Molded Carry Trays. For the most part, I don't care for
these things. They're expensive, take up too much space, don't slide well on the benches, and they tear easily. People get them because containers fit more snugly in them so you have fewer "mishaps." They are handy for transporting the larger sized plants that tend to fall over in reg-ular web trays. We have used them for our quart aloes, which are often sold to floral departments of grocery stores. The trays make a nice retail presentation. But overall, they have limited practical use.

Sleeves. Sleeves are wrappers that contain your container-grown plant for easier transport. They come in paper or plastic and sizes ranging from small, four-inch to large sizes made to accommodate a wild and wool-ly ten-inch hanging basket. We also use these to transport any-thing that tends to fall over too easily with top growth. It not only preserves the integrity of your plants, but also allows you

to pack them in more tightly when loading. Paper holds its form a bit better than plastic and allows the plant to "breathe." They come off at the nursery and get recycled for the next batch of plants.

Soil

Most conventional growers consider the soil in which they grow their plants primarily a medium for allowing roots to form so that the plant doesn't fall over. In no way does it have anything to do with the overall health of the plant, except maybe in terms of its moisture-retaining properties. In fact, the medium is often referred to as a soil-*less* mix because it has very little resemblance to real soil. For most medium-to-large growers this is a control issue. These plants rely completely on the grower for food and growth commands because there is nothing in the "soil" to nourish the plant. Chemical fertilizers and growth regulators are formulated to make the plants perform to exact specifications. This gives the grower an edge on the mass market. By "forcing" growth, buds, and blooms they can get their product out faster to a consumer who expects and demands uniformity of size and shape. The problem is that once these plants leave the grower's greenhouse, they are removed from their source of chemical control. If they are not purchased quickly from the retailer and given a healthy home, they often go into a rapid decline.

I have known many self-proclaimed "organic" growers who used soil-less mixes, but most understand that to follow through with the concept one should build a potting soil that mimics some of the qualities of real soil; enough so that the plant will not wither and die during the interim between leaving your place and the time it gets into the retail customer's hands. If a nursery does not sell your plants in the first week they have them, you can bet they are going to be doing well to keep them watered, much less fertilized. The better the soil you have under that foliage, the better they will look in two or three weeks if they are not selling fast in their retail location. Retailers are much happier if your plants continue growing and looking perky until they are sold. With a good quality potting soil that provides ongoing nourishment, the plants will do well for a very long time.

What goes into a commercial soil mix? For plants six inches or smaller most growers use mixes containing largely peat moss with perlite, vermiculite or Styrofoam pellets. As the container and plant grow, you will probably see composted pine bark as an added ingredient. Some big growers which grow lots of shrubs and trees use mixes that are mostly bark and sand.

For the benefit of those who are not completely familiar with these components, I will define them individually to help you understand why they are used.

Peat Moss. What most people refer to as peat moss is the partially decomposed (carbonized) remains of any of various mosses of the genus sphagnum. These mosses have grown in massive bogs (very wet places) in various spots around the world, depositing layers and layers of plant debris over a few million years. These bogs have been mined to the point of depletion in Ireland and northern Europe. Now most quality peat comes from Canada. Louisiana has a few bogs being mined, but the peat moss is of an inferior quality that is excessively acidic. Peat moss is a finite resource for which we ought to find a replacement (see *Coir* below).

Peat moss is used as a primary ingredient in potting mixes because it is fluffy, inexpensive, easy to get, and holds moisture. That is, it holds moisture until it dries out. Then it will battle your best efforts to rehydrate it. Most bagged soil mixes have what's called a "wetting agent" mixed in to break the soil surface tension which allows the peat moss to re-wet more easily after drying out. In Texas, wetting agents are not allowed in the organic program. Peat moss is slightly acidic on the pH scale and even this will vary some from bale to bale. Speaking of bales, this is usually how the peat moss comes to your door if you are going to mix your own soil. The bales are generally compressed and have to be "fluffed" out to accurately measure volume.

Perlite. A natural, glass-like material heated to very high temperatures that pop it into a light, porous material that concurrently holds water and creates better drainage. Perlite "lightens" the soil. A word of caution. Perlite is very dusty when poured from the bag. You should wear a mask and goggles when handling the dry material. It really does feel like glass when you get it in your eye.

Vermiculite. A micaceous, hydrated, silicate mineral heated to very high temperatures, which expand it into a light, puffy material. In other words, it is puffed mica. It comes in various sizes from medium to extra coarse.

Pine Bark. This is a by-product of the lumber milling industry. The bark is removed from trees and sent through chopping blades and sieves which result in sizes from large chunks used in landscaping to very small pieces used in the container plant industry. When used in a potting soil mix it must be at least partially decomposed. Generally, composted pine bark is used when good drainage is vital. It adds a dimension to a soil mix that's difficult to duplicate. The decomposed pine bark used in soil mixes is often called *soil conditioner*.

Coir. This is a relatively new product to horticulture. Coir is the fibrous, outside hull of the coconut. The long strands have long been used to make things like rope and fiber mats, and the small, coarse by-product of this was for hundreds of years thrown into immense piles as waste. Some years back a few enlightened souls saw these mountains of discarded coir as a possible soil conditioner and maybe even a substitute for peat moss. It has been studied, tested, and analyzed with mixed reviews at this point. Its texture is gritty and it holds moisture quite well while providing good drainage. The one major drawback is that it has a rather salty chemistry. If you decide to try coir, be sure you are dealing with a reputable dealer that has a "washed" product. In other words, it has been through a process to rid it of excess salinity. I like the stuff. I just haven't taken the time to do any real trials with it, but I like the idea of a renewable resource.

Creating Your Potting Soil

There are a lot of companies providing bagged soil mixes that have various percentages of any of the above listed ingredients. There is something out there for every conventional grower's needs. My problem with the mixes was getting consistent quality and they *all* have chemical fertilizer charges along with the wetting agent. This is not allowed in the Texas organic program and I don't want the extras anyway. With a little inquiry, I gleaned the information needed to come up with the percentages of individual materials of some of the mixes I liked most. This gave me a basic soil mix that I could put together myself.

From this foundation, I was able to build a soil with a bit more nutritional "muscle" from natural, earth-given products. To a basic commercial mix one might add compost, earthworm castings, alfalfa meal, bat guano, bone meal, composted manure, fish meal, kelp meal, soft rock phosphate, green sand, granite sand, volcanic sand (basalt), sharp sand (silica), etc. There are many possibilities, and what you choose to use depends on personal preferences, what you are growing and where, and availability of materials. Remember, the point to adding the supplemental natural ingredients is to give your plants an extra edge. They will have a vitality and durability unmatched by conventional growers. Each supplemental material has unique properties which need to be taken into consideration when choosing what you will use.

I know there are people out there who insist that one can build a good organic potting soil without the use of the industry-standard peat moss, vermiculite, perlite and bark. I would have to say, of course you can, but there are three major problems I have encountered with *all* of the "organic" soil mixes that caring, intelligent, thoughtful people have put together.

1. A commercial grower would go out of business quickly using these mixes because they are very expensive to make and therefore inordinately expensive to buy.
2. If you wanted to put them together yourself, finding consistent sources and quality for the individual components would be a potential challenge that no doubt you will not have time to deal with.
3. I have dutifully tried every soil mix that I have been asked to try and, although the quality is excellent, I can't use them because they just don't drain well enough to use in a greenhouse environment, and they tend to be really heavy.

These soil mixes are wonderful for the backyard gardener who wants a natural alternative to the standard, peat-based mixes found in most garden centers, but they are just not practical for the commercial grower. This is not to say that if a good quality, natural potting soil came along that was inexpensive to make or buy and met my drainage standards I wouldn't use it. I would definitely give it a go. But for now, I am not going to change something that works well for me and gets a fine product to the customer.

A word on the importance of good drainage. No matter what soil you use, it is imperative that your plants do not sit in soggy soil. They will, very literally, be dead in the water. Soil needs moisture to move nutrients into the root hairs, but it also need oxygen. If the soil stays saturated it creates an anaerobic (no oxygen) situation, which eventually suffocates the roots. During the cooler months, in the rather humid environment of a greenhouse, water does not evaporate as quickly as it would outside. If the soil holds water too handily, it may take too long to rid itself of excess moisture. On the other hand, during the warmer months, evaporation may happen too quickly if your soil does not have some moisture *retaining* properties. It is a balance that each grower will have to discover in their own individual environment. Growing in the desert Southwest will be rather different than in muggy coastal areas.

Paramagnetism

While on the subject of soil, I would like to touch on the concept of *paramagnetism*. I am certain there are those who consider it voodoo, but it is something that actually makes a lot of sense to me. It is a scientific fact that all living beings are surrounded by electromagnetic fields, and that these fields continually interact with the environment. The earth itself is a rather incomprehensible magnet. While I don't fully understand the scientific basis of electromagnetism, I do understand that it is a part of our daily lives. Have you ever fuzzed up the radio or television by walking across the room? It is one of those things that happens all of the time, yet most people don't question how it happens. There are varying types and strengths of magnetism, from that which keeps us firmly grounded to earth, to the force which creates the rising and falling tide waters, to the horseshoe magnet that catches iron filings. Paramagnetism is the relatively weak magnetic force in the soil when certain elements are present. This weak (albeit important) force assists the movement of certain nutrients through the soil, making them more available to the plant roots. It can improve the uptake of nutrients that might already be present in the soil but that might otherwise be difficult for the plant to reach. Paramagnetism can be enhanced by the use of any of the crushed, volcanic (igneous type) rocks worked into the soil.

Misty Hill Farm Soil Mix
(Makes about 15 cubic feet)

6 cu ft (3 bags)	Composted pine bark ("soil conditioner")
3 cu ft	Peat moss (loose)
1 cu ft	Extra-coarse vermiculite
1 cu ft	Coarse vermiculite
1 cu ft	Perlite
1.5 cu ft (1 bag)	Back-to-Earth fine-screened soil conditioner (non-defoliated cotton burr compost)
5 gal bucket	Knippa basalt or decomposed granite sand (these come in bulk)
2 to 2-1/2 gal	Bat guano (about 6-7 lbs)
2 cans (28-30 oz)	Soft rock phosphate

The soil is easier to homogenize, (when mixing by hand), if spread out in even layers before mixing.

Any kind of igneous/volcanic rock may be used in the place of the basalt or granite.

To measure the bulk ingredients more easily, I found large plastic tubs at discount department stores and marked off cubic feet on them. I measured a cubic foot by taking a two-cubic-feet bag of something (like the pine bark), dividing it exactly in half, and dumping it into the tub to mark it. The ingredients can be broken down into percentages if you don't want to measure in cubic feet.

You can substitute some other kind of compost for the Back-to-Earth soil conditioner. I just really like that product.

Increase basalt and/or pine bark by 50 to 100 percent if working with large containers that need better drainage such as trees or shrubs.

Often you can locate hard-to-find stuff on the Internet. Most manufacturers now have websites with lists of distributors. If you can't find it that way, call your state department of agriculture or a state nursery association to see if they can refer suppliers to you.

Propagation

I am not going to pretend to be an expert on propagation because it has been the most challenging, and at times, frustrating aspect of growing for me. But the following observations and information come from hard-won experience and I would love for you to not make the same mistakes. Being a certified organic grower in Texas means that I either find organically grown plugs and rooted cuttings (which, if you *do* find them are unbelievably expensive) or do them myself. There have been times I have had to buy plants that were not grown by these standards, just to have stock, but I really grill the grower to find out exactly how the plant was treated and what chemicals have been used. However, the vast majority of plants grown in my "house" are grown from my own stock plants or from seeds that have been carefully selected from catalogs that offer organically grown and/or untreated stock. I'll share what I know and the rest you will have to get from a good book on propagation.

Plugs

The term *plug* is used to describe a plant grown from seed or cutting in a non-soil medium like perlite, vermiculite, peat moss, sand, or a mixture of any of these materials. The plants are germinated or rooted in a tray of multiple cells, each cell generally containing one plant (one seed or one cutting), which is called a *plug*. The number of cells per tray can vary from 18 to over 500, and the size of

the tray and number of cells will generally dictate what is grown in them. Cuttings are normally rooted in the larger cells (one-half inch and up) and seeds are sown and germinated in smaller cells (one inch or smaller). Plugs, when ready, are planted in soil-filled containers to continue growing out.

There are businesses that specialize in producing plug trays for commercial growers who do not want to spend time and energy germinating and rooting. It is convenient for the grower, but comes with a formidable price tag. Plus, for organic growers it is nearly impossible to find organic plugs. When you do find them, they are usually too expensive to be practical. If you do decide to try buying plug trays from these specialty growers, it is advisable to ask other growers who regularly buy plugs who has the best quality.

Seed Propagation

Seeds are the way to go if you need large numbers of plants in a relatively short period of time. Many herbs, flowers and vegetables are best started from seed because they sprout and grow quickly for the volume sales of spring and fall. Many perennials also may be grown from seed but generally tend to be slower to germinate and grow out. The biggest advantage of seeds is economy. Compared to the cost of buying plugs, seeds are cheap.

288 Plug Tray. Unless you are going into the plug growing business or you have ten acres of greenhouses, a simple vacuum seeder is all you need to do enough plugs to keep you in business. There are several companies  that make them, but they all operate on the same principle: A small vacuum motor is attached by a flexible hose to a metal box, which has a metal plate on top with small holes. Your seeds will adhere via suction to the metal plate until you turn the vacuum off, after inverting the box over your plug tray.

The plates come in hole patterns that match the plug tray you have decided to use so that when you invert the metal box, (with attached metal plate), over your plug tray, each seed will drop into one cell. They also come in different sized holes to match the seeds you are working with. Most growers use the

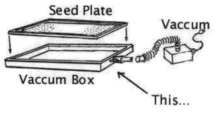

Seed Plate

Vaccum

Vaccum Box

This...

Plug Tray with Soil

turns over onto...

This.

plug tray with 288 cells, but they range in size from 72 to 512 cells. That is probably clear as mud, but you get the idea.

If you were the really handy type you could make one. But if you aren't, then the entire setup with several sizes of plates will cost you in the neighborhood of $1,000. That may seem like a lot of money, but I have used the dickens out of mine and it is still rolling along. It has paid for itself many times over considering the cost of purchasing plugs from someone else. You might as well put it in your budget.

There are also trays that have little rows built into them for doing those tiny little seeds the size of dust. I have tried just sprinkling the seeds over the 288-plug tray, which gives

Row Tray

you a small bunch of seedlings in each cell, but unless you have a remarkably steady hand you will end up with some cells stuffed with seedlings and some with only a few. I have also tried an open tray, just lightly broadcasting the seeds over the soil surface. Usually this is disastrous because no matter how lightly I think I am broadcasting, I still end up with this mass of seedlings that have to be laboriously teased apart, which is hard on them and on my patience. For really miniature seeds, lightly sprinkling in rows will give you something a little easier to work with.

The thing to remember is that some of those tiny seeds turn into rather large plants and so must be transplanted individually. If you plant something like thyme or Greek oregano in clusters you will have serious crowding in the pot.

The soil*less* mix I use for my seed trays (and also for some cuttings) is a mixture of 50 percent peat moss, 25 percent medium vermiculite, and 25 percent perlite. I also throw in a little soft rock phosphate and bat guano but that is not absolutely necessary. I think it just makes me feel better as I imagine I am giving those baby plants a little something to munch on when they put on a show of leaves. The mixture should be slightly moist when you are ready to use it. If it is dry, add water until you get a moist cake consistency.

Fill the plug tray by heaping the soil over the cells and tapping the sides to make sure there are no air pockets in the cells. Do not pack it in. You can lightly firm the soil in, but pressing too hard will remove the small air spaces between soil particles which are necessary for good drainage and healthy root development. Smooth the topsoil off and you are ready to seed your tray. After seeding I use some of the loose plug mixture to lightly cover the seeds that need darkness or soil depth for better germination. The tiny seeds and the ones that specifically need light for germination I just leave on top of the soil. They will nestle in when you water.

Water your tray immediately with a mister or fogger. Droplets any bigger than this might displace the seeds and/or pack them in too forcefully. *Do not ever let your plug trays dry out.* They must be watched vigilantly. Misting

Mister/Fogger

benches with timers are great if your weather conditions are exactly the same every day. Around here, a very humid, sunny day might follow a humid, cloudy day, which might follow a dry, sunny day. Each of those days will require different watering strategies. If you let the plug trays dry out when germination first occurs, you will most likely lose the whole tray. If they dry out severely after the cotyledon stage, the plants that do survive will likely be weak, stunted and generally perform poorly. You might as well start over.

It is a good idea to have a written record of what seeds you sow, when they germinated, and when they were planted. I have developed several different kinds of logs over the years, trying to come up with something that made it so easy that I would have no excuses for not recording my work. The one I am currently using is by far the easiest, but I still procrastinate about logging. The thing is, it is really nice to look back over a season or two to see the patterns of germination. It can be very useful when you are trying to work out your growing plan. It is also an excellent way to track which varieties of plants have performed well for you.

Varmints 'n' Such

Depending on where you live, you will likely have varmint problems. I have come into the greenhouse early in the morning to find the plug trays literally mined for seeds by mice; they go through the trays and pluck them out. What they don't eat on the spot they gather in their mouths and deposit somewhere else in the greenhouse. I then find my crops of seeds coming up in pots everywhere, even outside in the garden. If it weren't so frustrating it would be funny. I have to admit, I

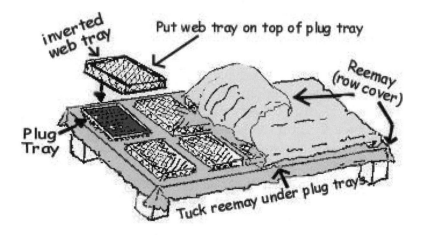

have gotten a chuckle or two when we find the caches of seeds sprouting in various places.

I have tried many different tactics to keep the mice out of my trays, but the only thing I have found that really works consistently is *reemay* (row cover). For those who don't know, reemay is a very light, spun polyester generally used to cover rows of crops to protect them from inclement weather or bugs. I have used it for a variety of things, and it worked very well to keep the mice out. I lay a piece on top of the bench (because they can get up through the mesh on the bench), and set the plug trays on top of this. At night, (which is when they are so busy), I invert a web tray over each of my plug trays and lay another sheet of reemay over the entire bench and tuck it in under the trays.

I know it sounds like I have gone around the bend, but those little dickens had foiled every other attempt I made to keep them out, including traps. A grower friend of mine has gotten so

AHAH !!!

frustrated with the mice that he has been dreaming up a way to actually suspend the plug benches from the ceiling so they can't climb up the bench supports. It sounded like a good idea to me, but then one day one of my house cats decided he wanted to go live in my greenhouse and that was the end of the mice. Why didn't I think of that?

Another problem I have experienced with plug trays is certain insects. The ones I have battled the hardest are thrips and leaf miners. They establish themselves early and cause poor growth habit, stunting and mottling. Since we do not use standard greenhouse poisons, it is a challenge to come up with strategies for keeping these pests off my infant plants. The best plan, of course, is to keep the overall "load" of insects down in your houses. This will be discussed in the chapter on disease and pest control. But even with best intentions and vigilance they occasionally get out of hand. Putting up sticky traps all around the plug bench gets a surprising number of the adult forms of these insects. *Bacillus thuringiensis* and beneficial nematodes will get many of the soil-dwelling larvae. If you are really frustrated, you could spray with a mixture of insecticidal soap and maybe pyrethrum or neem. Just be aware that these can be kind of hard on those tiny seedlings, so I would only recommend this as a last resort. You will have to figure it out as you go.

Rooted Cuttings

If you plan to do rooted cuttings from stock plants, bear in mind that all plants do not root well year round. Some do best during winter dormancy, some in mid- to late spring, and some in early to late fall. Some don't care when you cut on them. Again, for basic methodology you will have to refer to a good book on propagation, but mostly you will have to work with the plants you want to grow and see what they want.

There are two mediums we use most often to root cuttings. For mint and other plants that root readily in water, we simply place them in a tub of perlite and water. The perlite keeps the upper foliage out of the water and upright while the lower portion of the stem dangles in the water. Rooting will take place in five to seven days on average. The biggest drawback to rooting in water is that the roots are relatively fragile and there is often an adjustment period for the plant. There is a big difference between swimming in water and the relatively low moisture level of moist soil. You can reduce the amount of shock experienced by the plant by not letting the roots get too big (not more than one-half inch) before removing the plant from the water. The other medium we use is the previously mentioned plug mixture. This is used on the tougher perennials (woody, herbaceous plants) or plants that would rot in water (succulent-type plants). Sometimes I use open trays and sometimes the 72- or 120-cell plug trays. I know people who have very good success with simply rooting everything in plain vermiculite. Other mediums used are cedar flakes, sand and coir. You will find your own preferences along the way.

The foliage of your cuttings must stay humid or moist until they are rooted. If they dry out then rooting might not occur. (Note: The exception to this would be dormant, hardwood cuttings done in winter.) Setting up a misting bench on a timer or with a soil moisture sensor is the ultimate way to do this, but I have rooted plants fairly successfully by just misting with a fogger (attached to the hose) several times during the day. Cuttings also need to be protected from really bright light. Give them their own shade area or set them under a tree outside. I have not tried the outside method, but I have heard that setting cutting trays down on the earth makes plants root earlier. I guess they figure that's where the soil is and that's where they need to send the roots, pronto.

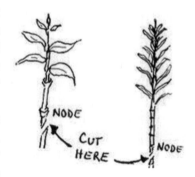

I have found that cuttings no more than three inches do best. Just strip or trim off the lower one-half to two-thirds of the leaves. In most cases with foliar plants all you need is two sets of leaves. There is a delicate balance between leaving too many leaves (for the rootless plant to support) and keeping enough on to support it with stored nutrients while it forms roots. I have even cut very large leaves in half with a pair of scissors to reduce the total leaf surface area. It is a good idea to soak stems in a weak seaweed solution while waiting to place them into the rooting material. Misting every so often helps if you have a large number of cuttings waiting for processing. If the cuttings are going into a soil mixture of some kind, be sure it is moist (not wet) *before* putting the cuttings in. Make a hole with something like a chopstick (called a *dibble stick*), slip the cutting in, and gently firm the soil in around the stem.

The stem *must* have contact with the soil to realize that it now needs to change gears and make roots. Try to position the cutting so that the lower leaves are not touch-

ing the soil. The moist soil will rot the leaves touching it.

The following are some additional observations. Again, none of this is meant to be comprehensive. My intention is only to give you guidelines.

> Do not take cuttings in the heat of the day. Early morning is best.
>
> Be sure the stock plant is well hydrated before cutting pieces from it.
>
> Late spring and fall are good times to do perennial cuttings. At these two times of the year the plant will have the right type of growth for excellent results. Late spring will have new growth from breaking winter dormancy and mid to late fall will have new growth from breaking summer dormancy. The latter is more evident here in the South where even the most drought-tolerant plants struggle to survive the brutal heat of summer. When the temperatures cool down in the fall, perennials will put on several months of vigorous growth.

The best, most plum cutting will have a slight darkening at the base (the new growth has matured some) and a tip bursting with new growth.

Be patient. Some cuttings will root right away and some might take as long as several months. If the top and stem are still green, then the plant is still viable. I check them by giving a very light tug. If they give resistance, they are probably ready. If you pull out one of your green stems that has been there a while, but still has no roots, check the base of the stem. If it has some weird little knobby things attached to the bottom then put it back in the soil. Those little nubs are the beginnings of a root system.

Remember to dry out the cut ends of "wet," succulent-type plants before rooting. I give it at least 24 hours. Fleshy plants store more than enough water in their leaves to get through a day or two without being attached to anything. This scabbing process will prevent bacteria or fungus from entering the newly cut stem, which can make a big, mushy mess in your soil if put straight in.

Potting

You might not think there is much to planting in containers, but my dedicated worker bees will tell you there are aspects of it I am rather picky about. This is where, to me, growing becomes as much an art as it is a skill. I realize I stand a bit alone in the world of mechanized horticulture and even among many of the smaller growers who depend, as I do, on human labor to produce our products. I suppose my attentiveness to certain aspects of growing is attributable to the same part of my personality that made me a good nurse. I really care about

the process and the ultimate health of the plant. Here are a few of the things I have learned along the way.

Planting Plugs

You will know your plugs are ready to get planted when they have grown past their first "milk" leaves (cotyledons) by several sets of "true" leaves. The roots should be white and full, but not so thick that you cannot tease them apart. I have planted plugs purchased from other growers that had roots so tight that they never grew out. They stayed in that tight little ball in the soil with a few straggling roots breaking free, but mostly intact, just as it came out of the cell. Plugs are perfect when they are full enough to begin molding to the cell but are loose enough to carry on healthy growth in the new soil without manipulation or teasing. At this stage, the less you mess with those delicate roots, the less lag time you will have before the plant begins active growth.

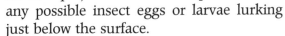

There are fancy "plug poppers" of various designs that will get those babies out of their cells at light speed, but we just do it one cell at a time. I have found the thick end of the larger diameter chopsticks works well to push or "pop" the plug out of the cell from the bottom drain hole. It is really not too bad when you get into an assembly line mode. One person pops and sorts, setting the plugs out onto trays, and the other person plants. We always remove the topsoil on the plug because it often is a little mossy (which will spread quickly to the new pot) and this also helps to remove any possible insect eggs or larvae lurking just below the surface.

True Leaves

I have grown so many different types of plants fairly successfully that the abysmal failures do not daunt me for long. However, something has come out of this experience that is pretty important. You must know your plants. You need to know how tall, wide, bushy or thick they will get. You need to ask yourself how they most likely will be handled by the end consumer. Is it a plant that doesn't mind a bit of crowding or does it need three-foot spacing? Would you know how to grow it in your own garden? Do you know what it looks like fully grown? Could you honestly tell someone where to put it in their garden if they asked?

This is important because you have to decide the most prudent method of growing out tiny plugs. I get aggravated when I see containers absolutely stuffed with plants that should be grown as singles, or at least in smaller, looser clumps. Many growers will put clumps of plants into four-inch containers to get faster "cover" (it looks fuller), ergo, quicker turnover (faster sales). The result, in most cases, is weaker individual plants with hopelessly overgrown and tangled root systems. If you peek under the bottom leaves, there is a mat of brown and yellow foliar die-off from lack of airflow. Water and nutrition needs go up, which is bad news when it gets to the nursery. This is a grave disservice to your wholesale customers and to the end consumer.

When you are ready to put the plug into a container, think about these things and make the choice that will give everyone a better, healthier plant. Some things need to grow out alone and some things do well in clumps. An example of something that can grow in a clump is German chamomile, but I beseech you; do not think you must start with a large clump. It grows very quickly and will give you wonderful cover in a short time. Conversely, cilantro is often grown in thick clumps, which goes against its nature. Individual plants get quite large and full, given adequate space. Would you rather have a clump of weak, spindly plants or several that are gloriously tall and full?

Pre-fill your pots and flats. Find a tool (we use old rubber spatula handles) to push the soil aside while concurrently slid-

Example: I went through several phases with basil. I started out putting three plugs in each four-inch container. They were beautiful, but ultimately not very practical for the consumer. It is simply not a good idea to grow three basil plants that close together in a garden. Besides, it was costly. I looked at the single basil out in the nurseries and was not impressed with how that looked. Finally, after several years of vacillating, I settled on two plants, spaced well in the container. It gives pretty good cover and they are not so crowded that they can't be pulled apart and planted separately if wanted, or planted as is, together. My point is that deciding how many basil plugs to put in a four-inch container was a process. I had to experience the plant in many ways (including growing it in my garden), to make the final decision about how to present it to the consumer.

ing the plug into the hole. The soil will cooperate more if it is slightly moist. If it is dry it will just fall back into the hole before you can get the plant in. Please don't cram the little plant into the soil. The microscopic root hairs on these plants are very delicate and pushing down too hard will damage them. As I said earlier, this will delay their adjustment to their new environment. We also do a cursory inspection of the leaves before planting as aphids and spider mites will show up even at this stage. When you have a flat of infant plants snuggled neatly into their new pots, water thoroughly. Then I log it in. (Remember the log?)

Stepping Up

There are times when you will have plants that have (intentionally or not) outgrown the container they are in. This will be evidenced by roots that have over-filled the container, or top growth that is choking itself out. Either way, it's time to re-pot the plant into a larger container. This process is called _stepping up._

Sometimes it is necessary to do this because a few flats of four-inch pots have not sold and growing them out in larger containers is the logical next step (assuming there is a market for the larger version of what you had in the smaller size). Sometimes stepping up is a process necessary to get a tree, shrub or other perennial to the size most likely to be marketable. Nurseries will not buy some plants, such as trees, in small containers.

Transplanting should be handled mindfully. Inspect the foliage for bugs or disease and examine the roots for color and texture. If stepping up is part of a growing-out process, then the plant should be transplanted before it becomes overgrown. The roots should fill the pot but should "tease out" easily. The top growth should be full but not crowded. Be sure the plant is well hydrated to reduce the stress and potential shock. As with

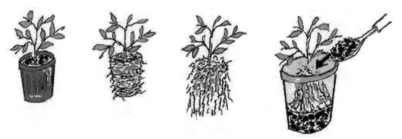

plugs, we always remove the top layer of soil and debris before placing into the new container. If roots are well formed to the shape of the pot but not circling tightly, gently pull down on bottom roots to loosen before placing into the new container. Place enough soil in the new container to allow the plant to sit upright at the appropriate level. Pour soil around the perimeter of the root ball, firming gently as you go. Fill until the soil surface matches the place on the stem where the soil surface was in the old container.

Be sure to leave about one-half inch of "head" space between the soil and the container rim so water does not overflow and wash the soil out. And do not be too stingy with soil either. The level will automatically drop some when you water, as water displaces the air that was in your nice, fluffy soil. Over time, it compacts even more. If you start out with too little soil, you could end up with a container half full of roots struggling to anchor themselves in a piddling amount of soil. It is a good idea to log what you planted, what size container you used, and how many you potted.

When you are stepping up because the roots are "bound" up or overgrown, there are several approaches I have used successfully. If the root ball comes out of the pot in a solid mass, there are a couple of approaches. Assuming the bottom of the ball does not tease out easily with your fingers, then take a sharp, clean knife and slice about one-half inch off the bottom of the root. Then, from the top, rake your fingers down the sides of the ball to untangle the bound-up roots. If the roots are so thick and tight that this is impossible, then you might have to slice more of the root ball off. I have sliced a root ball in half at times to get to a place where I can begin loosening the roots.

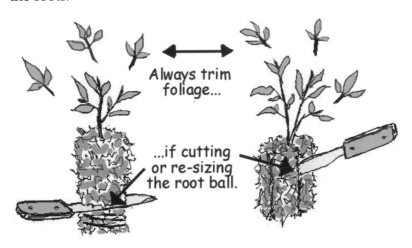

Always trim foliage...

...if cutting or re-sizing the root ball.

This is rather drastic, but the plant is probably pretty stressed anyway, so ultimately you are doing it a *big* favor. The whole point is to re-train the roots into thinking there is more to the world than the inside of that container. If you do have to trim off a bunch of the root system, be sure to trim off a comparable amount of the top growth. The new, traumatized— yet invigorated—root system cannot support the same amount of leafy stuff that it did before. Don't forget to give it a good drink and some fertilizer after replanting. It will no doubt need a little extra TLC and you singing the "Hallelujah" chorus a few times to really get its juices flowing.

One more thing about replanting: during the active growing season when plants are bent on taking over the world, replanting is tolerated quite well. But remember that some plants despise being roughed up and need to be handled with care. This is something you will have to figure out on your own as you work with your chosen varieties. They will let you know in short order.

Fertilizing

If you are growing commercially, no matter what you are growing in containers or what soil mixture you use, you will need to fertilize. This is especially important during active growth when nutrient needs rise sharply. In addition, during the warm/hot months, increased watering washes nutrients out of the soil and these nutrients need to be replaced in the form of a soil drench or foliar application. Feeding your newly planted plugs regularly is important, at least until they have an established and healthy root system. Plants whose root systems have been even slightly disturbed in transplanting will need extra nourishment until the new roots have formed.

Commercial growers most often use chemical fertilizers because it is the easy way to get nutrients to the plant. These fertilizers come in many formulations of NPK (nitrogen/phosphorus/potassium) and are easy to apply as a liquid soil drench, in time-released pellets ("prills"), or granular forms that are mixed into the soil. Some are formulated to "force" specific types of growth such as foliage or flowers. They are also designed to move growth along at a quick pace to get plants out to the nurseries in a timely manner. Fertilizer is especially important when the grower is using a soil-less mix.

Call me an organic purist, but I tend to equate chemical fertilizers with heroin. The plants will be fine as long as they are getting the steady supply of calculated N-P-K. In fact, they will respond quite well. Several things bother me about this process. One, the fertilizer was made in some chemical-manufacturing lab and it is totally artificial. Two, I have a problem force-feeding any living thing. Three, a plant grown this way is like building a house with cardboard rather than bricks; the plants just don't hold up in the long term if exposed to any stress.

When a plant is allowed to grow at a genetic rate (rather than a chemically calculated rate) it will have a stronger overall constitution. When you give your plants a natural, earth-made fertilizer it is like sitting down to dinner for the plant. If it is hungry, it will use what is available. If not, it won't. Simple, gentle and sensible. Folks, I could pay my July electric bill if I had a dollar for every time someone has said to me, "Your plants look so *healthy.*" That's because they are. Anyone can grow plants, but to grow sturdy, vigorous, vital plants takes a different frame of reference and mind—it becomes a thing of beauty.

The following is a basic list of fertilizers and soil amendments that can be used in organic horticulture. It is not intended to be comprehensive; it is meant only to acquaint you with some of the most common products and how they are used. I will not even mention N-P-K numbers as people depend too heavily on these when trying to decide on a product. Natural products such as these generally do not have high N-P-K numbers, but offer a wealth of readily available nutrients to plants in a living soil.

Alfalfa Meal: Alfalfa is a perennial legume that is used as fodder for animals, green manure for crops and, when cut, dried and ground into a meal, it makes a great soil amendment. Some of the many nutritional benefits alfalfa meal offers are nitrogen, phosphorus, potassium, calcium, magnesium, trace minerals, triacontanol (a growth stimulant), sugars, starches and a bank of amino acids. It can be mixed directly into your soil or made into a "tea" and used as a soil drench or foliar spray. If you make the tea in warm weather, don't let it sit more than a couple of days. The smell will knock your socks off.

Blood Meal: This is dried, slaughterhouse blood. Very malodorous and rather expensive. High in nitrogen. Probably better off in your garden than in your soil mix.

Bone Meal: A by-product of the meat industry, bone meal is animal bones that have been pasteurized, dried and ground into a powder. Used as a calcium and phosphorus amendment, but also contains some nitrogen. Can mix directly into your soil or dip your plug roots that need extra calcium into the meal before planting. Note: In an organic setup, both bone meal and blood meal should be used only if there is nothing else available that will provide the same benefits. There also should be a full disclosure of where the bone or blood meal is from and how it was processed to avoid contamination of organic plants with products that are not organic.

Calcium Sulfate: Gypsum, as it is commonly called, is a mined or industrial by-product material used to correct calcium deficiency (especially in alkaline soils) and to loosen up tight clay soils allowing better drainage, which can release excess sodium if present. Would be used in garden soil for the most part, but is good to know about.

Colloidal Phosphate: Often referred to as soft rock phosphate, this is mined, crushed phosphate that has been suspended in clay. Good, long-term source of calcium and phosphorus. We dip our flowering-fruiting plug roots in the powder before planting.

Compost: Although many different organic substances are used to make compost, the fundamental nature of it is the same. The end product is the result of digestion of these substances by microorganisms (bacteria, fungi, etc.) and some macro-organisms such as earthworms. The process releases nutrients from the original material and creates a soil conditioner rich in humus, humic acid, vitamins, minerals and nitrogen. Final analysis of any compost depends on what original materials were used. Some commonly used are manure, cotton burr, vegetable and other plant waste (hay, grass, leaves, tree twigs/bark, etc.), mushrooms, rice hulls, paunch manure (cow stomach contents), and even the hulls of certain nuts. Compost can be worked into the soil, used as a mulch/top-dressing, or made into a "tea" and used as a soil drench or foliar spray. (For more information on compost see Chapter Six.)

Cotton Burr Compost: Another by-product of the cotton industry, this is the wickedly sharp calyx of the cotton flower in which the boll rests. There is only one company I know of who uses only organic cotton burrs and aerobically composts them into a wonderful, earthy soil amendment. As with the seed meal, it is a good, slow release source of nitrogen, phosphorus and potassium. I'm in love with the smell. I use the fine-screened product in my soil mix.

Cottonseed Meal: A by-product of cotton ginning, the seed is ground into a meal and used as a soil amendment. It is a slow-release nitrogen, phosphorus and potassium source. This is a good product, but due to the large number of chemicals used to grow cotton (pesticides, herbicides), one should be certain that the source of the meal is only from organically grown cotton. Good luck.

Earthworm Castings: Earthworm poop is finely digested organic matter. It has all the same basic benefits of compost, but in a more compact, easy-to-use form. This is a great addition to potting soil and even can be used safely in plug mixtures. Commercially available from small earthworm farms.

Fish Emulsion: As the name implies, it is an emulsified fish by-product in a concentrated form. When mixed with water it can be used as a soil drench or a foliar spray. It is valued for its nitrogen, phosphorus and trace minerals. When I first started using fish emulsion, I was not sure I was going to be able to get past the smell. I found that not only did I get used to the smell, it was virtually gone by the next day. Most importantly, my plants love it.

Granite: This coarse-grained, light-colored, hard igneous rock is often used by landscapers in crushed (gravel-like) form as mulch and in garden pathways. In organic horticulture the sand or meal is mixed with soil as a source of potassium and other trace minerals. It also has paramagnetic properties, which as you recall, helps other nutrients become more available to the roots. If possible, try to find the partially decomposed granite.

Green Sand: Mined from ancient ocean beds, this silica-based material—officially called *glauconite*—is greenish colored sand that is loaded with potassium. It also contains iron and other elemental nutrients. Best if used in a soil that has good microbial activity.

Guano: This is aged, dried poop from bats and sea birds. Most of what you see commercially is bat guano, but some garden supply catalogs have droppings from birds that live on sea cliffs. They are all high in nitrogen, humus (a good soil builder), microorganisms, vitamins and minerals. It is good stuff, but has a very strong urine-like odor. I would avoid top dressing the soil of pots with it because it has an odd, almost greasy consistency when wet and just doesn't seem to work its way down like compost. It is better worked into the soil ahead of time. It is a fine powder so you should wear a mask when mixing it.

Lava Sand: Generally a combination of crushed volcanic rock often including basalt. Can be used as a soil amendment for drainage, minerals and paramagnetic properties.

Lime: This is a general term referring to the various white, powdery materials containing a substantial amount of calcium carbonate. Some also have a generous amount of magnesium, so before using as a garden soil amendment do a soil test and see what you really need. Often used to adjust an acid soil pH higher. *Caution:* do not buy lime intended for industrial use as it may have toxic heavy metals.

Manure: Any animal manure can be used as a nitrogen source in soil mixes as long as it has been well aged, pasteurized and/or composted. Some might be considered mild enough to use directly, but why take the chance? Different manures have varying levels of nitrogen. I would check out what the animals are being fed. If the manure is full of hormones, antibiotics or other chemicals, you will not want to grow plants in it. Always wash your hands thoroughly after handling manure of any kind—better yet, wear gloves.

Molasses: This sweet, thick, black syrup is a by-product of the cane sugar industry. It comes in various grades, but the blackstrap grade retains the most nutritional components and is good for people as well as plants. Molasses can be added to foliar sprays or to soil drenches and adds iron, sulfur, potassium and other trace elements as well as sugar to feed the beneficial micro-organisms in the soil and on plant leaf surfaces. Can be used as a "sticker" instead of soap or oil when spraying botanicals for insect control.

Seaweed: This product is kelp that is ecologically harvested, dried and ground into a powder. It comes to you in either powder or liquid concentrate. Mixed with water, it can be used alone or with fish emulsion as a foliar spray or soil drench. This is the "black gold" of organic fertilizers. Packed with trace minerals and natural hormones, this product not only fortifies overall health but assists in the uptake of other nutrients.

Sulfur: This yellow powder is a natural mineral that binds with calcium in garden soil to bring an alkaline pH down. Often called elemental sulfur or flower (flour) of sulfur.

At one time I was so bad about fertilizing my plants that it only happened when "I got around to it." Now I fertilize every seven days (on average) during the spring, summer and early fall and about every 10 days to two weeks (depending on what I'm growing) during the winter when growth is slow or dormant. Sometimes, if I am overwintering completely dormant plants, I don't fertilize at all.

The mixture I use is fish emulsion and seaweed with a little molasses thrown in. When I first started growing I used compost tea, which the plants loved, but it was a lot of trouble. I felt like I was constantly making new batches, which I guess I was. I have to admit, it's nice now to just open a bottle and mix with water.

A lot of people have asked me about how I fertilize and I always have to laugh because, in the beginning, my system was quite archaic and laborious. You might as well forget about fancy mixer/sprayers if you plan to use fish emulsion. It is just too thick and has too much residue, which clogs up those tiny emitters, even if you strain it. My "system" was a 15-gallon sprayer sitting on a four-wheel handtruck, with a diaphragm pump hooked up to a 12-volt battery.

I would have used a bigger tank, but the fish and seaweed needs to get sloshed around periodically to keep it from settling and as strong as I am, sloshing 15 or so gallons of fluid on wheels is challenge enough. Plus, rolling that thing down the middle of the greenhouse with 120 pounds of fertilizer five or six times over kept me as fit as I wanted to be.

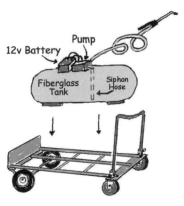

A while back we were at a farm and tractor store and we were trying to come up with ideas for a larger system that would fertilize four or five times the number of plants. I needed something *big*. Finding the big tank was easy enough. The

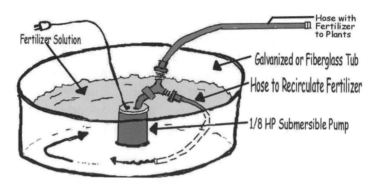

Fertilizer Solution

Hose with Fertilizer to Plants

Galvanized or Fiberglass Tub

Hose to Recirculate Fertilizer

1/8 HP Submersible Pump

challenge was figuring out a way to keep all that fish and sea-weed agitated in a 150- to 300-gallon tank. Obviously sloshing was not going to work. The man who was helping us was one of those amazing people that comes up with ideas faster than you can breathe. His suggestion was to place an immersible sump pump into the tank with a Y or T connector on the pump outlet. Then connect a short hose to one side that recirculates the fluid and a long hose on the other side for fertilizing the plants. I was astounded at how simple yet rational the plan was. I tested the theory using a 150-gallon tank and some old garden hose. *Voila!* It worked so well that it cut hours off my fertilizing time.

Watering

I will probably never have any kind of automated watering system because we grow too many different things in too many different sized containers. The only way you will be successful with a controlled watering system is if you are monocropping and if your plants are evenly spaced on the benches with good airflow to all containers. It is a fact that containers on the out-side of benches and flats dry out faster than the rest of the con-tainers. If all containers are being watered equally all the time, some will be over watered. I think it is much easier to *over*wa-ter than *under*water and hand watering can be tricky. Soil may appear dry on top but be very moist underneath. If you are heavy-handed with the hose, things might get a bit soggy.

Perfect soil is slightly moist, not wet. If soil stays wet, the plant will suffer. As I mentioned before, water fills the natural soil air spaces when you water. If it is never allowed to dry out, either from over watering or from soil that does not drain well enough, the plant will ultimately die from oxygen deprivation. Wet soil also breeds fungus gnats, mold, and moss. A little moss is not harmful, but if it covers the top of the pot, it can affect soil drainage and oxygen exchange. Don't ignore moss. It is a *signature* of either overwatering or poor drainage.

Conversely, do not let your plants stay dry too long either. Most will recover with a deep watering, but if they are allowed to stay dry too long the roots will sustain damage that may not be reparable. Occasionally, if a plant has been exposed to dry conditions often enough, it will become stunted and weak.

By examining the root system of an established plant, one can pretty well tell how evenly the plant has been watered. If the roots are well distributed, fat and white, then you have done a good job. If the roots are shallow (primarily in the top half of the soil), then moisture is not penetrating to the bottom of the container. The plant keeps putting out superficial, shallow, dense roots to be sure it gets enough moisture to support the top growth. As the roots become more dense on top, less water can get through to the bottom thus creating a cycle of moisture deprivation. If the roots are all on the bottom, then chances are you have a container drainage problem. If the drainage holes are clogged or there are not enough holes to suit the drainage needs of the plant, then the water will sit at the bottom of the container and roots will congregate there. I have pulled plants out of containers that had a mass of thick white roots on the bottom and precious few in the middle or top. Often the soil (and sometimes the decayed roots) will just fall away. There are cases, of course, where the plant is trying to send a taproot down and it ends up curling around the bottom of the container. Not the same thing. That is just a big root looking for China in the bottom of your pot.

Obviously, watering is something one must do with a great deal of conscious thought. Use the finger test to check soil moisture before you soak those plants. I have found that some of the inexpensive soil moisture meters are really pretty accurate. You can watch the meter reading change as the probe goes deeper into the soil where moisture is generally higher. If you are training someone to do the watering (and if you haven't figured it out yet, I don't consider this a flunky job), have them use the moisture meter and then feel the soil to get a correlation. It will help them to evaluate how much water, if any, is needed.

Air temperature as well as humidity affects soil moisture quite a bit. In general, plants do not dry out in the cool temperatures of winter as quickly as they do in the heat of summer. If you factor in dry, cold air or humid, hot air, it changes the evaporation levels noticeably. All these things must be considered when deciding whether or not to add moisture to soil.

This piggy got none...

Sometimes water temperature can make a difference. In winter, if the water you are using is too cold for the comfort of your own body, then it may actually slow growth temporarily. The shock can impact plant growth for up to 24 hours. Warm it up a bit and the plants will be able to use it without missing a beat. Even room temperature is better than that ice-cold stuff that comes out of the faucet in the dead of winter. And in the heat of summer, when you notice that the plants are drooping despite good soil moisture, just mist them with some cool water. It is amazing how fast they perk up. I even stand under that mist sometimes when I'm about laid out from the heat and, by golly, it makes me feel better too.

Primping, Pruning (and Makin' Pretty)

The reason we grow plants professionally is because we are what my husband affectionately calls "plant people." Plant people care about plants. We care about how they look and how they grow. It is a passion that can be happily shared with other plant people. Furthermore, the grower has an opportunity to provide the plant consumer with the focus of their obsession—beautiful, healthy, interesting, useful, tasty, fragrant, wonderful plants.

When we work on various projects around our place we compulsively pick dead, discolored or distorted-looking leaves; pinch growing tips; pitch dead or dying plants; and pop plants out of containers to check root health and growth status. It becomes so second nature to growers that I've noticed that we even do it to other people's plants, especially the leaf-picking thing. We just can't stand to see an otherwise nice looking plant with this yellow/brown leaf hanging off a branch or stem—so off it comes, just like that. The plant feels better, we feel better.

We primp plants. Because we are not a Mega-Mart horticultural business with 25 acres of greenhouses, we are able to take the time to look over the plants before they go out. We usually begin the process a couple of days before delivery, selecting the best flats, consolidating and grading plants for size, checking for empty containers or cells in the middle of a flat or six-pack, looking under leaves for bugs, cleaning debris off the soil surface (and adding soil if needed), picking off yellow, brown or mottled leaves, and trimming away any unruly growth. Granted this is time consuming, but believe me, I feel better knowing that the plants leaving my place have been thoroughly inspected and look the best they possibly can. If they do not meet my approval, they do not go. I admit there have been times when I have had to send out plants that did not meet my highest standards, but if you expect the highest quality, then coming down a notch or two at times is not so bad. The plants I turn back to the bench are often perfectly acceptable by some growers' standards, but if another week on the bench will bring those plants up to my high standards, then that's what we do. It is not worth it to me to sell a plant

this week that looks "unready" when one more week will make it look spectacular. Sometimes it amazes me what a difference a week makes.

The point is that attention to detail can make a big difference when you go to market your plants. Scrutinize thoughtfully. One or two off-color or broken leaves can make the whole plant look unattractive so take them off. Even if it makes the plant look less full, it will appear healthier. Debris on the soil surface looks unkempt—clean it off. Hydrate the plants well before they leave. Deadhead old blooms. Snip, trim, primp, and make pretty.

Interlude

A Photo Tour
of Misty Hill Farm

*Post holes were the first step in
constructing our greenhouse.*

Laying out the side posts.

Connecting rafters (ribs) to side posts.

Attaching eave runners and purlins.

Finishing the end wall.

Pulling plastic over rafters.

Securing plastic to the side.

Plastic in place and fully inflated.

Finished screen on end wall and sides.

Laying down the weed cloth.

Shade cloth in place.

Germination bench.

Empty 288 and seedlings.

Plugs laid out on soil-filled six-packs.

The perfect plug.

Graded plugs in a dish.

Plug planter.

A bench of newly planted six-packs.

A "salad" bowl.

Finished six-packs.

The author checking sticky traps.

Papa's peppers.

Louise, standing, with Marilyn and helper Cleo.

Four different types of Aloes.

Indoor show.

Outdoor show.

Someone eyeing the cart.

Talking about organics and soil.

Corner display.

Preparing plants for customers.

The gardens around our greenhouse grew to reflect our organic philosophy.

Chapter Five

Making Compost

Anyone who has gardening in their genes gets an endorphin rush when they slide their hands into a pile of well-made compost. It is such a primal pleasure to feel the fluffy, soft texture; to sniff the earthy fragrance; and to admire the perfect, granular consistency and dark brown color of finished compost. The appreciation for me also extends to the knowledge that it will do wonderful things for my soil, whether it is an addition to my commercial potting soil, or being mixed into a garden bed, under a shrub or tomato plant. It can be worked into the soil, used as a mulch/top-dressing, or made into a "tea" and used as a fertilizer in the form of a soil drench or foliar spray. No matter how you use it, the end result is extraordinarily healthy plants.

Compost is an integral ingredient in any organic growing business. If you grow in containers, then it *must* be in your soil mix. If you grow plants in a garden or crops in fields, it must be incorporated into your soil. Without the addition of compost, there is no life in your soil. It is the soul of good earth.

As stated in the chapter on *Growing*, no matter what organic materials you use to make your compost, the principle nature of it is the same. Compost is the result of the digestion of organic materials by microorganisms (bacteria, fungi, etc.) and some macro-organisms such as earthworms. The process releases nutrients from the original material and creates a soil conditioner rich in humus, humic acid, vitamins, minerals and nitrogen. Final analysis of any compost depends on the original material utilized. Some commonly used materials are animal manure, paunch manure (cow stomach contents), cotton burr and cotton seed meal, vegetable scraps, hay, grass, leaves, tree twigs/bark, mushroom waste (from mushroom growers), rice hulls, peanut hulls and even the hulls of certain nuts like pecan and walnut.

Compost is a vital addition to any soil depleted of humus, microorganisms and other macro- and micronutrients. Making good compost can be as easy as piling miscellaneous garden trimmings and kitchen scraps into a corner of your yard or as technical as layering different complementary materials in specific ratios with carefully planned days for turning the pile and with vigilant observance of ideal moisture levels. Both methods will give you good quality compost, although the first method will take up to two years and the second method as little as three weeks.

If you are planning to use your own compost in your commercial organic potting soil, it should be prepared using consistent methodology and materials. In other words, use the same bins, the same carbonaceous and nitrogenous material, the same formula, and the same cyclic timing. This is the only way to ensure consistent quality without having to buy commercially prepared compost. You also want to use materials that have not been tainted with herbicides, pesticides (or any other -*cide*), hormones, antibiotics or other man-made chemicals or substances. As a rule this means using materials from your own farm or ranch or from one that you know to be free of the aforementioned substances. If you are *certified organic* then it is imperative to make sure all materials come from chemical-free sources.

If the compost is going into your garden, you still need to be sure there are no chemicals or other synthetics, but you can relax a bit regarding the variety of organic materials used. However, the following should *not* go into the pile if you are concerned about contamination:

Hay or straw that has been treated with herbicides, pesticides or chemical fertilizers. Most commercially produced hay is loaded with this stuff.

Grass or vegetative material that grows along roads and highways. There is an accumulation of dust, dirt and road grime, and many counties–and often the department of transportation–use herbicides to control grasses and weeds in areas where they cannot get the mowers very easily.

Grass or vegetative material from fencerows of ranches and farms that use herbicides and pesticides.

Manure, urine, paunch manure, bloodmeal or any other byproducts from animals that have been treated prophylactically with antibiotics, hormones or pesticides.

Diseased animal waste or byproducts.

Human waste.

Sewage sludge. This may contain any manner of chemicals and heavy metals that have been poured down drains in one vile concoction or another.

Although a very hot compost pile will kill most pathogenic organisms found on plants, if you are not sure what the pathogen is or whether your piles get hot enough to destroy them, then burn, bury or throw away the diseased plant material.

Necessary Elements for Compost

Microorganisms

Aerobic: Needing oxygen to survive; *i.e.,* environment with lots of air space.

Anaerobic: Needing little or no oxygen to survive such as soggy or tightly packed soil.

Psychrophile: Organisms preferring a cold or cool environment (Greek *psychro-* cold and *phile-* love or strong affinity).

Mesophile: Organisms preferring a moderate range in temperature (Greek *meso-* middle, center, intermediate).

Thermophile: Organisms preferring a very warm or hot environment (Greek *thermo-* pertaining to or caused by heat).

Interesting Facts About Microorganisms

Without these microscopic organisms, nothing would decompose. That means our world would be filled to the heavens with organic waste.

Many species of microorganisms have individual preferences regarding pH, nitrogen and carbon levels and moisture levels. Some aren't picky at all.

There are approximately 70 pounds of microorganisms in 1,000 square feet of root zone (that includes about 12 inches of healthy topsoil).

There are over 900 billion microorganisms in each pound of healthy soil.

One hundred pounds of dead microorganisms puts approximately this amount of nutrients back into the soil: ten pounds of nitrogen; two pounds of potassium; one-half pound of magnesium oxide; five pounds of phosphorus; one-half pound of calcium oxide; and one-third pound of sulfate.

Moisture

All organisms need water to survive. Aerobic microorganisms need some (but not too much) water to break down organic matter. Ideal environment is "moist," not wet. If it is too dry, then decomposition will slow or stop. Excessive water attracts anaerobic organisms and, overall, slows decomposition. Be sure compost piles are covered in rainy weather to avoid leaching nutrients and to avoid water saturation, which decreases oxygen supply to aerobic microorganisms.

Air (oxygen)

Organic material to be decomposed should have some air space between particles to allow aerobic microorganisms to have oxygen available to them. If airspace is removed by compression of material or soggy, wet conditions, then anaerobic organisms will take over and/or decomposition will slow down or stop.

Carbon

Carbon is the "calories" for microorganisms. It primarily comes in the form of dried vegetative material such as straw, hay, leaves, twigs, vines, (dried) grass, seed or nut hulls, bark, wood chips, etc.

Nitrogen

Nitrogen is the "protein" for microorganisms. It will be provided by any fresh-cut (green) vegetation, manure, vegetable kitchen scraps, animal by-products such as bloodmeal and fish scraps or meal, feather meal, human hair or animal fur, etc. (Do not put meat or fat in compost piles as they slow down decomposition and may cause the pile to smell.) Plants in the legume family make excellent "green manure" because they are high in nitrogen and can be tilled directly into the soil from which they grew, or harvested (with roots) and used to make compost.

Principles of Composting

Carbon to Nitrogen (C/N) Ratio. This ratio should be around 25:1 to 30:1. This is not a measure of volume but rather percentage of carbonaceous to nitrogenous materials. To accurately figure the ratio in your pile you have to know the ratio of carbon to nitrogen in the carbonaceous material you are choosing to use. All plants have carbon and nitrogen, but the amount and ratio of one to the other varies widely by the individual plant, what kind of soil the plant was grown in, and if it was fertilized before harvesting. For instance, coastal Bermuda hay is lower in nitrogen than alfalfa, but both of those grasses have much more nitrogen than cornhusks, pine needles, newspaper or sawdust. The higher the carbon content, the more need for nitrogenous materials to balance the ratio. Remember, the beneficial organisms need both, but in appropriate quantities. Too much of either and they won't thrive.

So how do you know how much of what material to use? There is no good way for the average gardener to measure this very accurately, so to get a good ratio it will take trial and error. It depends a lot on what materials you are using. For instance, if you are using rotted manure for your nitrogen, then you would need only a small layer between larger layers of carbon material. But if you are using freshly cut, green plant material (which is high in nitrogen), then you would use a larger volume of this between layers of dried material because it is not as "dense" in nature. It also depends on the particle size of the fresh material. Fresh-cut lawn grass is a much smaller particle size than fresh-cut vetch or alfalfa, so you would use a smaller layer of the grass than the other. The main thing to remember is that the microorganisms cannot break down the carbonaceous material without adequate nitrogen. If the pile is decomposing too slowly, then it might need more nitrogenous material. If it is smelling strongly of ammonia, then you have too much nitrogen.

If this is confusing and you don't have a clue what C/N ratio you have in your materials, then simply start out by using a general volume percentage of two-thirds or three-fourths (dried) carbonaceous material to one-third or one-fourth nitrogenous material, evenly layered. If it is slow to cook, then you need more nitrogen. If it begins to smell, then you need to add more carbon. If it stops completely, then you need more moisture. This is a place to start. Eventually you will find the right ratio.

If you plan to make your own compost for commercial use, you will see how important it is to use consistent resource materials. Otherwise, you will be reinventing your formula constantly.

The smaller the particles of organic material, the faster decomposition will occur. If possible, chop the large material into smaller pieces. This does not mean that everything has to be the same size. As a matter of fact, differently sized particles help keep the pile mixed and aerated. But if you want fast compost, keeping the overall individual particle size small helps the process.

The more a pile is turned, the faster it will decompose. If you have limited space and want to make compost quickly (in a few weeks), then turning every three to seven days will speed up the process. If you have large, out-of-the-way areas where you can pile organic matter as you acquire it, then turning "when you get around to it" will be fine. In the latter situation it might take as long as a year or two to have useable compost not only because it is not being turned as often, but also the C/N ratio is not necessarily being observed. Nature will take care of it eventually.

Decomposition happens faster in warm temperatures. What this means is, you will probably have to adjust your turning times. The warmer the ambient temperature is, the sooner you can turn the pile.

Finishing the pile. A properly layered compost pile will heat up to around 150-160°F within 24 hours and will slowly decrease in temperature by about five to ten degrees each day until it is turned again. When turned, it will heat up again to its maximum potential (between 120° and 160°F) and will do so each time until the organic matter has been sufficiently broken down. How much it heats up between turnings depends on how much material is left to be decomposed. If you want compost fast, then turn it every three to seven days. If you can't get to it but every 10 to 14 days, that is perfectly fine. It just won't be ready as soon.

When the compost pile is "cooked," turning will no longer activate it. It can then be sifted and stored for use with potting soil or used as-is for mulch or as a garden soil conditioner. Some compost pundits believe that storing it for a few weeks before using it is preferable to using it right away, perhaps to make sure it is truly "done cooking." If it is stored, it is preferable to put it somewhere out of the rain so valuable nutrients are not leached away and perhaps covered to prevent moisture loss and insect or weed seed infestation.

Additional Techniques for Successful Compost

If you are interested in going the extra mile in making perfect compost, then consider the following:

To ensure adequate air (oxygen) is getting to the middle of the pile, a plastic PVC or metal cylinder with holes drilled around and down the length of it placed in the center of the pile will guarantee that air gets to the middle of the entire pile from top to bottom. It must be placed so that the material is layered evenly around it on all sides all the way to the top. The top of the cylinder, however, must not be covered by the composting material to make sure air is able to enter and work its way down to the bottom of the pile. The diameter of the cylinder depends on the size of the pile. The wider and deeper the pile, the wider the diameter of the cylinder needs to be to be useful for bringing oxygen to the center of the mass.

To make sure your pile is heating up properly, check the internal temperature with a meat or candy thermometer inserted into a place near the center. If the pile was set up correctly, with appropriate carbon to nitrogen ratios and moisture levels, in 24 to 48 hours the core temperature will be between 140-160°F. It will cycle up and down each day, with peak temperatures coming down by about 5-10 degrees each day until it reaches around 120°F. This will be anywhere from five to seven days, depending on outside temperatures and the types and quality of raw materials you used. It is then that you turn the pile to reactivate the microorganisms and get the pile hot again.

Build the pile around the cylinder

Cylinder with holes

Check temperature near the center of the pile.

If you are checking temperatures regularly and the pile is not getting hot enough, then you might need to adjust the nitrogen ratio up. Also, if the material is not moist enough, the microorganisms will not thrive. A dry pile is a dormant pile. You might need to reassemble and adjust your pile a few times until you find what works for you. Take good notes so you can duplicate the process from then on. It is not an exact science, but if you want consistent quality in your compost, you need to have a method that works predictably well.

If your composting materials are in a closed container like a metal or plastic barrel or trash container, you must drill holes in the sides and top to make sure the busy microorganisms have access to oxygen.

Compost Containers

Composting can be as simple or as technical as you want it to be. If you have lots of space and time, then slowly built piles in out-of-the-way places might suit you just fine. It will likely be a year or two before you have usable compost, but nature takes care of everything eventually. The advantages are that you don't have to worry about layering and turning, and you can just add to it whenever you get a fresh bunch of trimmings, weeds or leaves. This is my kind of compost pile.

Composting in open piles can also be a method of getting hot, fast compost. If all your materials (nitrogenous and carbonaceous) are assembled, you can layer them into a neat pile and simply turn the pile every three to seven days onto another spot near-

Open Pile

by. It takes a little more space than containers and is not very attractive, but it gets the job done if finished compost is what you are after.

There are many creative and efficient container ideas that are easy to assemble and simple to use. Thirty-six-inch welded wire can be cut into six- or eight-foot pieces and formed into a cylinder to contain the compost material. Snow fencing can be constructed in the same way. Many excellent portable bins are made from wood pallets, lashed together in a square shape. When it is time to turn the pile, unhook or untie the end pieces

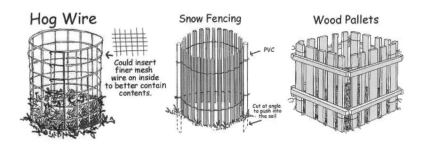

Hog Wire

Could insert finer mesh wire on inside to better contain contents.

Snow Fencing

← PVC

Cut at angle to push into the soil

Wood Pallets

that are holding it together, remove it from the pile, reassemble it next to the original spot, and fork the contents into the reassembled container.

More permanent containers can be built from hay bales, cinder blocks, lumber or any durable material. They can be single, double or triple containers. Having multiple bins allows you to move the material from one container bin to another with much less mess and effort. Having *three* bins allows you to store the finished compost in a separate area from the two that are being used for turning. Some wood bin designs allow you to remove slats in the front and/or in-between for greater accessibility. The cinder block designs should have the holes facing out to allow air to get to the composting material. Chicken wire can be attached to the inside of the blocks to keep material from spilling out of the holes.

Hay Bales

With either transportable or permanent bins another consideration is a cover of some kind to keep excessive rain from getting into your pile and leeching nutrients. A simple plastic tarp works well enough in most cases. But more sophisticated hinged lids made of fiberglass or metal may be preferable on the permanent structures. They should be made so that the lid can be opened fully on dry days.

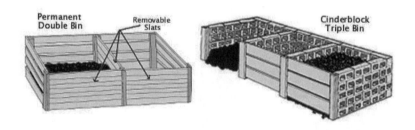

Permanent Double Bin   Removable Slats   Cinderblock Triple Bin

Chapter Six

Disease & Pest Management

 This chapter is not designed to help you identify specific pests or diseases. There are multitudes of very good books available with practical, photographic guides to help you in this area. If you cannot find your bug or disease in a book, take it to your county agricultural extension agent. In Texas, if the agent can't find the insect or disease in their books, they will likely send it to Texas A & M. You could send a sample yourself directly to an agricultural university that can do this sort of work in your state. If all else fails, you could ask growers in your area since it is likely that whatever you are facing, they have dealt with before. You may have an alternate solution to the problem, but getting a fix on what is eating or killing your plants is something about which all growers share a concern.

As I have mentioned before, we do a lot of "scouting" inside and out. Daily walk-throughs can give you a lot of early information about what might be invading your space. If you know your plants thoroughly, aberrations will be more apparent. Look at the new growth for stunting, chlorosis (yellowing), curling or anything that looks unusual. Spot check the undersides of leaves, especially on plants that are generally more susceptible to certain types of diseases or insects. What is flying up and out of the foliage when you water? What is crawling on the soil surface? And look down into leaf/flower buds and leaf axils for those munching, sucking, rasping mini-monsters. They may be small, but they are murderers. Pull off and inspect any leaves with odd coloring, spots, flecks, bumps or anything else that is not supposed to be there. Check it out now. Tomorrow may be too late.

Disease Prevention and Treatment

Most preventive techniques are plain common sense. Here is where my nursing background came in handy. Many of the techniques we have implemented in disease prevention in humans apply to the home in which plants live. The following are a few things to think about:

Keep your house clean. Have a regular cleaning day to sweep, straighten, wash, dust, etc. It amazes me how fast things get cluttered and dirty in the growing area. We have weed cloth down on the floor of the greenhouse and we just take a broom to it. If moss begins to collect in low areas, we occasionally mop with a weak bleach solution. Mop any areas that tend to "puddle." These areas breed fungus and annoying insects like mosquitoes. Pick up as much debris off of the benches and floor as possible. This has been hard for me because I tend to pick and drop. We try to carry debris buck-

ets with us when we are working on the plants so refuse does not end up on the bench or floor. It does no good to remove a leaf suspected of harboring pests and then leave it on the floor of your greenhouse.

As previously suggested, clean the soil surface of debris. Old, dropped leaves get moldy and rotten creating great conditions for fungal problems, not to mention fungus gnats. If you spot-clean on a regular basis, overall fungus load goes down.

Good air circulation is imperative. You must have fans that circulate air at all times in the greenhouse. When humidity is high for days (or weeks) at a time, you might need to set up extra fans in "problem" areas to get you through. We had a rainy/cloudy period once that lasted about eight days (with humidity in the 80 to100 percent range). I started seeing fungal problems I had never seen before. It was rather scary, but cleared up as soon as the sun came out again.

Remember that pests that come into the house from outside can transmit disease to your plants inside. Keeping pest populations down helps, but you can't control where the bugs have been before they come to your place. Just be vigilant.

Wash your hands often and well. Plain soap and water gets rid of most transmittable diseases. We keep a "final wash" bucket filled with soapy water and some bleach to help control viral transmission.

Keep your cutting utensils clean. Wash scissors, pruners, knives, etc. frequently with a soapy bleach solution. I keep one of those green scrubbers available for removing the resin build-up on the blades.

Examine plants brought in from other growers or nurseries. It is best to quarantine new plants from your other plants until you are sure there are no disease problems.

Consider using one of the beneficial fungal (mycorrhizal) drenches on your plug trays to prevent pathological fungus for the life of the plant. This attaches itself to the root system of the plant and not only competes with the destructive fungi such as Rhizoctinia, Fusarium and Pythium, but also develops a symbiotic relationship with the root, allowing better flow of nutrients into the plant tissue while making use of certain nutrients for itself. The result is stronger, healthier root and top growth, which is more resistant to disease.

Good microbial activity in your soil mix also helps battle the bad guys. The good microbes will compete with the pathogenic ones if the balance is right. The result, again, is healthier root and top growth.

When you find plants ravaged by disease, throw them away or burn them. Some diseases will be destroyed in a good, hot compost pile, but why take the chance of re-introducing problems through your compost?

Remove suspicious spots or markings. If you find only one or two leaves on a plant that look suspicious, try just removing the affected leaves from the plant and soil surface. Sometimes that is all you need to do. These are often random bacterial or fungal spores that land on the leaves of plants in a localized area. They may only bloom if conditions such as humidity, temperature, light levels, etc., are exactly right. If you act quickly, you can often nip the problem in the bud (no pun intended).

Try baking soda. I have had good results combating fungal problems of all sorts with good old baking soda (sodium bicarbonate). I have even gotten rid of gray mold and black spot with it. One tablespoon of baking soda in a gallon of water with a teaspoon of soap or molasses to make it stick is the recipe I use. You might have to be persistent and spray every day for a few days, but it works. (I have been told that you can also use potassium bicarbonate, and that it might be a little easier on the plants.)

Pest Prevention and Treatment

If you live in the South, you are going to have insect pests. They are out there and no stop sign is going to halt their journey to your greenhouse. The best you can do is be ready when they show their ugly faces. I have read for years that if your plants are healthy, the pests will leave them alone. This is generally true in nature where the sickly and weak plants will go first. But if pests get into your greenhouse, they figure they have died and gone to that big, all-you-can-eat plant buffet in the sky. This is an artificial environment and once they are in, you are stuck with them.

There is however a definite benefit to having healthy plants. If they are suddenly hit hard by something ravenous, they will have a better chance of bouncing back and resisting disease. You cannot keep pests away. Weather conditions and climatic changes dramatically affect insect populations. Your best defense is to know what you are dealing with and be prepared ahead of time because pests can rock your greenhouse world while you are sleeping.

Here are a few pest-fighting suggestions:

Screening in your greenhouse is probably a good idea if you live in an area that has all the seasonal pests (aphids, leaf miners, whiteflies, mealy bugs, grasshoppers, etc.). This is especially true in the warmer season when most people open houses up. If you do have closed-in screening, make everyone shut the door behind them. I swear I have seen unwanted guests near the door just waiting for someone to open it so they can fly (or hop) in.

Become knowledgeable about the insects you may encounter. Ask your neighbors and other local nursery folks what bugs they have had problems with in the past and in what part of the year they occur. I know a lot of growers don't want to admit that they have problems, as if it is a reflection of their overall competence, but trust me, all growers have to face insect challenges occasionally.

Inspect new plant material carefully before mingling it with your established stock. Some of the larval forms of these bugs can hide themselves really well from probing eyes.

Get to know a good source for beneficial insects and have that order number handy when you see any of the pests showing up. Better yet, if you know when the pests are most likely to show up, order ahead of time so they can ship them ASAP and you can get the good guys established before the invasion takes over the battlefield. The biggest problem with this is that the beneficials need to eat, and if there is not enough food (that is, insect pests) for them to sustain themselves, then you have to provide sustenance for them until they can munch on their

favorite foods like aphids, spider mites, mealy bugs, etc. Most insectaries have a manufactured food source you can put out for your beneficials until the populations of pests are high enough to sustain them.

Obtain a good magnifying glass to enable you to properly identify insects on your plants. Most of the malicious creatures will be on the undersides of the leaves but, as I have said before, they could also be on top of the leaf and in the flower buds and leaf axils. Some larvae wriggle around (stuffing themselves) inside the leaf and then drop into the soil to pupate. Many have larval and pupal stages that happen in the soil. They will get you coming and going.

Learn the difference between good bugs and bad bugs. Some, to the untrained eye, are hard to tell apart. For instance, there

is a spider mite predator that you might mistake for a spider mite if you were not aware of the differences. People who have bug phobia are likely to kill anything that moves. If you inadvertent- ly kill some of the helpers, you might be get- ting rid of several potential generations of help. I tell new employees that they are not allowed to kill any bugs until they have prop- erly named it and found out what it does. It is fun to watch their astonishment as they learn that those weird little orange and black alligators are lady beetle larvae or that the mealy bug destroyer larvae looks almost identical to the mealy bug. Finally, spiders live happily in my greenhouse. Although they occasionally grab and eat the good bugs along with the bad, they are good predators of things that eat plants.

Educate yourself about the different stages of insect development. If you can identify the eggs, larvae/pupae or nymph, and adult stages of your friends and your foes, you will be a long way toward preventing problems early. It also keeps you from smooshing the eggs of something that would have hatched a brood of hungry pest predators. It is interesting to know that some insects are pests during one stage of their development and neutral or beneficial in another.

Greenhouse infestations can literally hap-pen overnight, especially with things like aphids who give (live) birth to large populations of little plant suckers in a very short period of time. If the population is new  and localized (only on a few plants), then your thumb and fore-finger could be the organic solution. If the population is a bit more than you can mash with your fingers, then take it to the sink and wash the plant. We lay it on its side and using a strong, fine spray thoroughly wash the undersides and tops of all leaf surfaces. Do not bring the pesticide spray bottle out  unless the problem is really out of hand. Even then, check the plant for any ben-eficials that may be happily munching and remove them before you spray.

If you have to spray, then at least know what you are using. There are many different approaches that can help you knock down the large populations if you are feeling a bit over-whelmed.

Low-Toxicity Pest Control

Bacillus Thuringiensis (Bt)

Bt is a rod-shaped bacterium that is harmless to humans but deadly to larval forms of butterflies and moths. The bacil-lus must be ingested by the larvae, so the environment and/or food source must be saturated. There are several varieties available that target specific pests, but they all work on the insect the same way. The bacillus releases a toxin into the digestive tract; the bugs get a severe tummy ache and stop eat-ing, and then they sort of implode. The next day you will see shriveled-up little carcasses all over the place. Kind of sad real-ly, but better them than my plants. There are several different varieties of Bt, each working best on specific pests, so be sure you get the Bt that you need for the problem you have (it should say on the product label). I did discover quite accidentally that the Bt I was using for fungus gnat larvae also worked on leaf miner larvae.

Citrus Oil (d-limonene)

This is the powerful oil from the skins of citrus fruit (oranges, grapefruit, lemons, etc.). Alone, or in combination with other products, it can repel and even kill some insects. It is produced commercially in concentrated form, but you can also make your own solution by soaking or boiling chopped citrus peel in water.

Compost Tea, Seaweed and Molasses

All three of these things mixed together or used separately in foliar application, have insect-repelling qualities. Much of the benefit comes from giving plants a nutritional boost, which in turn makes it less desirable to insects looking for stressed plants.

Diatomaceous Earth (D.E.)

This soft, powdery substance is the crushed skeletal remains of one-celled diatoms from ancient oceans. It feels softer than baby powder, but has microscopic, needle-sharp edges that essentially impale the cuticle of insects, causing them to desiccate. It can be mixed with water and sprayed onto plants, but will leave a white film that I have had a dickens of a time getting off. I don't know this for a fact, but my guess is that the film, if left on too long, might interfere with photosynthesis. It is probably better used on the ground or around the bottom of containers for ants and other crawling things. It is great for fleas and ants.

Horticultural Oils

There are various grades of petroleum-based oils on the market for insecticidal use. Read the directions carefully to be certain you have the right oil for the correct situation. Basically oils smother the insect or eggs. *Dormant oil* is used in the winter or early spring on trees and shrubs that have over wintering eggs or insects on them. It must be used before the plants break dormancy, as it can be toxic to the new growth. The other lighter oils are called *summer* or *horticultural oils* and can be used in the warmer months. These break down faster and are not as phytotoxic. Vegetable oils can be used to the same end as the petroleum oils and might be preferable for someone trying to stay completely organic. I am not much on using oils. Scale is said to be one of the pesky insects that oil is effective against. When I find soft-bodied scale, I reach for a wet rag and just wipe them off the leaves and stems. I have tried oil on hard-bodied scale and did not find it to be particularly useful. I usually end up pitching the plants.

Insecticidal Soap

This product is made from potassium salts from natural plant oils and animal fats. This soap penetrates the protective membrane of soft-bodied insects and kills them. It generally has no effect on insects with tough exoskeletons such as beetles or grasshoppers. It can also be used as a "sticker" for other products being applied to make sure they stay in place. There is some concern by organic pundits now about soap killing beneficial microbes on the leaf surface. It should never be applied on a sunny, hot day as it sometimes can damage the leaves.

Neem Oil

Neem is a tall, native East Indian tree (*Azadirachta indica*) cultivated in tropical Asia for timber, bark, resin and neem oil. It is said that its seeds are placed in granaries to repel insects. Oil extracted from the neem seed (azadirachtin) is a very effective insect repellent and appetite suppressant. It also interferes with growth, development and reproduction of certain insects. Strange smelling stuff, but it really works well.

Pyrethrum

This is a powder made from the crushed, white, daisy-like flowers of certain chrysanthemum family members. The two most commonly used are *C. cinerariifolium* and *C. coccineum*. It is a powerful contact poison that immediately affects the nervous system of the insect. Pyre*thrin* is a viscous liquid ester extracted from the aforementioned chrysanthemum flowers. Pyre*throids* are laboratory produced, synthetic compounds that have similar effects of the natural substance. In an organic program, only *pyrethrum* and *pyrethrin* should be used. Know the difference.

Rotenone

This is a white, crystalline compound derived from the roots of either derris (a woody vine of tropical Asia) or cubé (a woody plant in the pea family found in tropical America). This toxic stuff leaves a residue on the leaves of plants for up to a week. My understanding is that it is a stomach poison that interferes with insect feeding and causes starvation. It is powerful enough that it is used to kill fish when stock ponds are being cleared of "trash" fish in order to stock them with the desired fish. Use with care around animals and ground water.

Sabadilla

This is the powdered seed of *Schoenocaulon officinale* (a member of the lily family) found in Central America and Mexico. It has been used as an insecticide for centuries, but also has some historical, medicinal uses. It is hard to find but can be useful on some of the hard-to-kill bugs.

Sticky Traps

These are yellow or blue cards about the size of index cards that have a very tacky, sticky substance on them. They attract adult flying insects with the color and trap them in the goo when they land. Generally these are used for monitoring insect populations in your greenhouse. The yellow traps attract most small insects and the blue are designed to attract specific insects like white fly and thrip. I have found them handy in trapping amazingly large numbers of adult thrip, fungus gnats and leaf miners to begin the process of population reduction.

You can make your own by buying the sticky goop in a can and painting it onto your own yellow or blue cards. The advantage is that if you use plastic cards you can wipe them clean (when they are full of pests) with plain cooking oil, and start over. The disadvantage is that it is a mess to deal with.

Don't forget the importance of maintaining the grounds around your operation. Mowing vacant lots or open fields can keep pest populations down. Grow gardens around your greenhouses that have plants that attract beneficial insects and/or trap

crops for the pests. It is awesome to me to see the millions of tiny beneficial insects busying themselves in the foliage and blossoms of my plants outside. Most of the insects you see outside are good bugs and the less you spray the more of them you will see. Sometimes I think I have every honeybee in the county in my garden and on my container plants outside.

It may take time, experience and a little frustration, but eventually equilibrium takes place. The gardens can provide a  sort of screen that takes care of most of the pests before they have a chance to enter the greenhouse. After a few years of trial and bafflement, I can honestly say that insect pests do not conduct the reign of terror they had over me initially. I just had to learn about the balance of nature.

Chapter Seven

The Demonstration Garden

 For several years after I started my business, I dreamed of having a display garden where people could come and see, first-hand, how the plants we sell grow in our climate. My father and I hauled some huge native sandstone rocks from near the house down to the area next to the greenhouse where I envisioned my garden-to-be. We placed them in arrangements that made them look as though they had always been there. Some rocks were used to gently and subtly define garden beds and others just accented a path or plant. It was a beginning. Little did I know then how long it would take to actually create the garden I wanted.

The first several years I put a few plants in, but the area was still a bit wild and needed more taming before anything was going to survive. Besides, the grasshoppers skeletonized almost everything I planted, except the rosemary, and I just was not dedicated enough to the project to keep things watered and mulched. I was too absorbed in learning how to grow things *inside* the greenhouse to put the kind of energy and thought into the garden that it needed. I would visit nurseries that had beautiful gardens and wonder how they had the time, energy and resources to develop and maintain something like that.

Somewhere around the second year, I put in a beautiful ornamental pepper plant. It was incredibly vibrant and healthy when I planted it and it set its roots down right away. Then the  grasshoppers came and ate it down to a green nub. I was shocked and outraged. The plant kept trying to put out new growth and as soon as it had a few beautiful leaves, the prehistoric insects would return to nibble it back down to a nub. (Everything else I planted suffered the same insult and injury.) The pepper plant struggled the whole year, and in late fall, I put the poor baby to bed with five inches of mulch. The next spring the plant came back. That year the grasshoppers ate big holes in the leaves and stems, but left the plant basically intact. It never got very big (and it was still pretty awful looking), but it survived. In the late fall, I put it to bed again with five inches of mulch. The next spring it came back and grew into a big, beautiful shrub with virtually no grasshopper damage. I had heard about plants adapting to environmental stresses, but had never witnessed it first hand. Since that year, I have seen other plants develop the same kind of adaptation to the grasshoppers. Even so, I have decided that it is easier to just stick with the plants that they do not particularly care for, which is hard when you want to plant *everything.*

With the adaptive revelation and a renewed determination, that year became a turning point for me and for my garden. I have relaxed a bit and the plants, insects and I are getting along in relative equilibrium. I have learned to allow plants to go through their adaptive phases whether it is insects or other environmental challenges. By leaving some of the garden wild and taming the rest with plants of my own choosing, I have created a place that is vibrant with color, texture and interest. I have a trust now in the spirit and innate vitality of the garden.

And How Does Your Garden Grow?

A visitor came out one day and was inspired to do something similar on her own homestead. She asked me where you start when you have acres of "wildness." It is pretty over-whelming, especially in this day of instant gratification. I told her that I had to live with it for a few years, watching the native plants and their growth habits to figure out what I wanted to get rid of (or move to another place) and what I felt I could leave. I studied it all carefully, making mental notes on the lay of the land and how the plants looked and acted at different times of the year. Then, one foot at a time, on my hands and knees, or bent over a grubbing hoe or shovel, I worked to create the gar-den, clearing out stuff I didn't want and leaving or moving stuff I did. I did not have a plan. It just sort of hap-pened.

One thing I have tried to do is develop "zones" for plants with similar needs. Much of this was inspired by the natural growth in the area. I watched sun patterns (which change throughout the year), subtle differences in native soil from one side of the garden to the other, drainage trends, slopes, etc. All these things have helped me make decisions about where to put the plants I *want* in my garden. Placing plants with com-parable requirements for things like moisture, sun, drainage, etc., in general proximity to each other prevents disasters down the road; *i.e.*, my water-loving malvas do not drown out my xeric rosemary.

One reason I like to grow the plants we sell in containers in my garden is to be able to take pictures of them at maturity or in bloom. These pictures graphically demonstrate the charac-teristics of the plant. There is nothing like a good photograph to convince someone to try a plant in their own garden, espe-cially if it is in a small size when you are selling it. It might otherwise take some powerful imagination or trust to convince them that this little four-inch baby plant will someday grow up to be a big, beautiful shrub.

It is also a good idea to have experience with the plants you sell. How tall or wide will it get? What color and size are the blooms? How long does it bloom? Does it need to be cut back before fall? Does it overwinter well? How soon does it come up in the spring from the root or from scattered, dropped seed from last year's plant? Does it tolerate some frost? And, more importantly in Texas, does it tolerate the heat of summer? Do the "bad boy" bugs really like it? Do the butterflies, bees or beneficial insects use it for pollen or nectar? All of this experience with plants gives you an edge. This goes for vegetable transplants too. If you grow them out and actually harvest and eat them, you will be more convincing when it comes time to sell those varieties to your retail or wholesale customers.

Garden Magic

One of the most important reasons to have a garden in front of or surrounding your greenhouse, especially if you are involved in organic container plant production, is the diminished load of pest insects. Some beneficial insects need nectar for a specific phase of their developmental cycle, and so must have flowers available to sustain them. If you are growing a variety of blooming native or well-adapted annuals and perennials, you will provide them with a steady supply of food. And since pests will likely go to your garden if they are around, your army of beneficials will take care of them before they have a chance to enter your greenhouse. This provides something like a screen. If pests do enter your greenhouse, the load will be light and easy to deal with. Besides, if you have beneficials outside, they will often work their way into the greenhouse thereby taking care of the majority of any pests that enter. It is positively miraculous how well this system works.

If you are not sure what plants to use, contact your local native plant society, your county extension agent, a local garden club, a university in your state with a horticultural department, or just get in the car and drive around, looking at some of the really nice gardens in your area. Talk to your neighbors. Find out what they have had success with and what has failed.

Retail nurseries that sell native and naturalized plants can give you lots of ideas, not only for your own garden, but they can give you a glimpse of what plants people desire. Subscribe to publications that share information on what grows well in your area. Join associations that focus on horticulture or on the types of plants that you want to grow commercially.

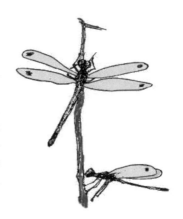

Your Garden Soil

It goes without saying that I recommend the use of organic techniques for sustaining and maintaining your garden. If your soil needs help, find out what it needs (basic soil test kits are available through most agricultural extension offices), but bear in mind that good quality compost will salvage most soils (see *Chapter 6, Making Compost*). It provides bulk and moisture retention for sandy soils and tilth and friability to clay soils. (If you want to find out what kind of soil you have, do a soil texture analysis. See *Appendix* for instructions.) Compost also provides the nutrients, growth factors, microorganisms and humus needed to create a healthy, living soil. If, after a year or so of amending your soil with compost, you are still having problems with pH or specific mineral deficiencies, you can judiciously add the supplements needed to balance the soil. Just remember that compost by nature is a soil balancer because the microbial activity contributes a continuous supply of nutrients by breaking down carbonaceous material. Many pH or deficiency problems disappear after the soil has been sufficiently amended with compost. Nutrients that were "locked up" will become available to your plants as the pH works itself to a more neutral level. Besides, if you are growing native or well adapted plants, there is no need for extra rich, heavily amended soil. Only if you are trying to grow finicky, fussy plants will you need to monitor levels of specific nutrients. If you have to make your soil more acidic or alkaline on a regular basis to grow the plants that you want to grow, then you are creating a tremendous amount of work for yourself. Ultimately, the plants will not thrive as their roots get farther into an incompatible, native soil.

Mulching

Adequately mulching your plants throughout the year is a simple, sustainable technique that will save you time in garden maintenance and money in water usage. The following advantages of mulching should make a convert out of anyone:

1. Moderates soil temperature during extreme heat and cold. Light-colored mulch reflects heat away from soil in summer and dark-colored mulch absorbs heat in winter when soil (and roots) needs warming.
2. Conserves moisture by preventing evaporation.
3. Prevents erosion of soil.
4. Controls weed growth. Those that do make it through the mulch are easy to pull out.
5. Prevents crusting of soil, improving water absorption.
6. Keeps rain or irrigation water from splashing onto lower part of the plant. Splashing water droplets often infect lower leaves with soil-borne pathogens.
7. Reduces compaction of soil as you walk through and work in the garden.
8. Organic mulch placed over a healthy, living soil will decompose, thereby further adding nutrients and tilth.

Use whatever you have available. *Partially composted* grass, leaves, twigs, straw, hay (make sure it has not been sprayed with chemicals), shredded hardwood, grain hulls, pine bark, peanut hulls and garden waste all make excellent mulch. If you live near forests of conifers, then gather and use the fallen leaves ("needles") and pinecones, although the cones will probably need to be chopped or shredded to be useful. Avoid using raw materials like sawdust as mulch. The excessive carbon will trigger increased activity by microorganisms, which uses up available nitrogen in the soil, causing temporary deficiency in the plants. Using material that has been at least partially composted prevents this problem.

And in the End

Your garden can be anything you imagine. If you prefer straight lines, geometrical forms, and/or circles, then formal gardens may give you more pleasure. You will just need to do a bit more planning and ultimately need to gather a few more materials to line the beds and define the walkways. It does not matter how you do it, just as long as it pleases you and suits your needs and resources. This is a garden you should be delighted to share with others.

My garden is as organic in structure as it is in soil composition and maintenance. There are no straight lines, and the areas of plantings (there are no real "beds") rise and fall with the natural lay of the ground in which they grow. Some might find this too wild for their tastes, but in reality it is a reflection of my intense desire to "sit among the briars," so to speak, to experience the full gift of nature's lessons in balance and force. I delight in spring surprises and accept the occasional defeat from summer's tortuous heat or winter's icy grip. It is all part of learning to live and grow with patience, adaptability and tolerance.

Your display or demonstration garden should be a reflection of you, not what you think people want to see. All over the country there are formal gardens and botanical centers that offer folks a glimpse of what one can achieve with grants and old money. Your garden can be a place to show visitors what they might do creatively on their own little piece of earth, with plants that are proven to do well in your part of the world.

Besides, planting a garden is just plain good for the soul.

Chapter Eight
Marketing & Merchandising

You have a good product. Now you have to sell it to your customers. Does your product stand out from the other growers that are producing similar plants? Do you give your customers a reason to choose plants from your list rather than from your competitor's? Can you sell them something that they don't know they want? What makes you so special?

Marketing Your Product

We talked about finding your market in *Chapter One (Market Research)*. Now we will focus on how to let these potential markets know that you have something to sell. Although merchandising is a weighty factor in whether they will want your product when they see it, I want to cover marketing first because there are some important things to know about plant buyers that will influence how you approach them in the beginning.

First of all, plant buyers are busy people. They sift through lists of plants every week and have to make choices of what to buy based on the season, what is left on their shelves or benches, what they can afford, and often how the last weekend went in terms of sales. If they do not know you or your product, it will be hard to get an order from them by phone or fax. It is not that they don't like having new and interesting choices from growers, it is just that many of them do not have the risk tolerance to buy new products sight unseen or they are already getting it from someone else and do not see the necessity to change vendors.

You have to go and show them. Load the van, truck or trailer up with a good variety of what you have to offer and go to the places where you would like to do business. It might also be a good idea to call ahead to make sure there will be someone there who can buy your plants off the truck. Even if there is not someone there who can buy your plants that day, there will almost always be someone there who can at least look at the plants and make an assessment of whether they would be interested in what you have to offer. When my husband Chris did deliveries for the business, he was much more organized than I would have thought to be. He always took a three-ring notebook with alphabetized tabs and created a page for each new place he went to visit. On the page he noted the name of the business, address, phone number, fax number, e-mail (if available), the names of the decision-makers for the business, and any other important contacts and their titles. If the person you need to see is not there, find out what days and times they are available so you can either give them a call or come by next time you are coming through the area. Make a note of time and date you dropped by and anything useful you learn. For instance, if they tell you, "Oh, we already buy vegetable transplants from Evil Giant Nurseries," then go take a look at EGN's plants to see how your plants stack up to theirs.

People who work in nurseries are just like you. They love plants. If you have good looking stuff, you will get someone to take a peek. If your plants are smashing (as I know they will be), don't be surprised if you draw a crowd. If the right people are there, they might buy—if they like what they see. A good thing to remember is that most growers deliver between Wednesday and Friday each week. If you go over on a Thursday, you will catch them getting their product for the weekend and they might just want to add yours to the weekend stock. I have made supplemental sales on delivery days because nurseries did not get as much of a certain kind of plant as they thought they were going to get or they have sold down on something and did not get a replenishment order in for the week. You just never know.

You might have to do this for a while until the retail buyers get to know you and the quality of your plants. It does not hurt to start sending out your weekly availability list (by fax or e-mail) during this time so the retailers start seeing your name every week in print. It doesn't mean they will start ordering right away, but eventually they will notice. When they do start ordering, unless you are selling out of your availability right away, you might need to make followup calls. For instance, if you sent your list to 20 retailers on Sunday, and receive four orders on Monday, then call the businesses that did not order, on Tuesday. Ask them if they received the availability list. If they did, then ask them if there is anything they can use. I have found that sometimes retailers will want a few items but opt not to call in the order because they did not think it would be worth your time to bring by an order that small. When you are still a minor player in the plant supply trade, small orders are fine. Reassure the retailer that you would be in their neighborhood anyway (even if you really have to go a little out of your way), so small orders are no trouble. You need their business. The more you sell them, the more they see your plants and remember how good they look.

If you still have plants available on delivery day, take them with you on your delivery run. Point them out to the customers whose orders you are delivering. In the peak of the season, they will often pick out a few more things to add to their order. As you are making your deliveries, stop by other places that did not place orders or visit a garden center you have never been to before. As time goes by you will learn who will buy off the truck and who will not. We even have a few customers who notoriously will not place an order but will buy lots of plants off the truck if we swing by on delivery day.

If you want to expand your market beyond garden centers, try selling to grocery stores that have floral departments. Floral buyers are often looking for new and interesting plants to put on display. Although most grocery chains buy quantities of cheap, seasonal plants from large commercial growers for all their stores, you might be able to talk individual floral buyers into giving your plants a try, especially if you are offering something like good quality, organic herbs. Your plants stand out among the average looking "color" hanging baskets and benches of Pothos Ivy. Grocery stores can be a very lucrative market if you have enough plants to supply them on a regular basis, but they can also be fickle. What was in yesterday may be out tomorrow, literally in a blink of the eye. Additionally, they are very season oriented. Through Christmas, Valentine's Day, Easter, Mother's Day, etc., they focus on what is going to grab attention and sell quickly and cheaply. Unless you have a lot of plants you need to unload for seasonal promotions, it might be better to focus your energy elsewhere during those times. If you want to check out this market, just stop by a store on a delivery day with some extra plants and see what you can develop. I had the best luck with individual stores, such as the local Whole Foods Market, rather than the large conventional grocery chain operations.

As your business gets bigger, you might want to construct minimum quantity orders for retailers that are in out-of-the-way locations. This is standard practice and most retailers understand and comply if they know you have to travel extra miles and/or hours to get to their business. I have one very loyal customer about 60 miles away who always orders enough to make it worth my time to come to his place. It is a courtesy that he offered to us on his own from the beginning. He was never asked to do that.

If you are a small grower with seasonal sales, they may forget who you are from the end of one growing season to the beginning of the next. There is also a lot of buyer/manager turnover in this business. You may have to reintroduce yourself every spring for a few years until you become established.

The Availability List

You will need to design a plant availability list to let your customers know what you have for them to buy and I suppose it is no surprise that I have some suggestions regarding this subject. I have redesigned my availability list many times to make it user friendly for the buyers. Not everyone has good quality fax reception, so if you send by fax, my first advice is that the page you send out must be very easy to read. Here are a few things that must be on it:

1. The date.
2. The name of your business.
3. Your telephone *and* your fax number.
4. A place beside each item where buyers can mark desired quantity.
5. With each item listed you *must* tell them how it comes (gallon-each; four-inch, 18-count flat; quart nine-count flat, etc.), how many you have of each or how many flats, and how much the individual item or flat costs.
6. If you have room for a brief description of each item, it could help the buyer decide if they want to try it, especially if they are not familiar with the plant. Do not assume they know everything about all plants.
7. The form must have a place for the name of the company or buyer so that you know who made the order when they fax it back to you.

Retailers might want to phone in their order rather than return the fax to you, but I always encourage them to send back the written order so there is no miscommunication. I don't know about you, but when I am busy, I make mental errors. Even if you read the order back to them (which you should always do), you may still have a number in the incorrect column or have inadvertently marked the wrong item. Does it sound like I have experience here? You bet.

The last thing I have to say about marketing is that if you have good quality plants with a difference that makes them desirable, you probably will not need to advertise unless you plan to sell plants retail out of your place of business. Of course, it never hurts to have a nice business card that you can hand out at appropriate times or to join a small business association or professional (growers) association where you can network with other like-minded business associates. You can always get on the speaking list of garden clubs or botanical garden centers. In the end, an excellent product is the best marketing strategy for getting the attention of your target customers.

Merchandising Your Product

Labeling Options

When the end consumer sees your plants, it is likely that the first thing they will notice is quality. Then they will look for the pot label to tell them something about the plant. If the label does not tell them what they need or want to know, then it is possible they will not buy the plant. It is that simple. Granted, some folks know exactly what they want when they come to a nursery, but most gardeners and plant people are browsers and if something catches their attention, they want to know what it is.

The following is a brief course on the pros and cons of different labels.

Hand-Printed Tags/Labels

You can obtain blank labels from label printing companies or horticultural distributors. These are generally made from wood, plastic or metal. The advantage for small growers just starting out is that you can label your plants as needed. The disadvantage is that it is seriously time consuming and, unless you have a very legible hand, it can be hard for anyone to decipher what is written on the tag. At the least, the information should be printed, but even with the steadiest hand these labels look rather unprofessional and do not provide enough information.

Pre-Printed Tags/Labels

It is relatively easy to get labels with pre-printed information on standard flowers, trees, shrubs and herbs. These can range from simple, straight-to-the-point text or text with a picture of the plant fully grown or blooming. Some of these are quite nice. Many of the larger seed companies and plug producers now supply pot labels for the seeds and plants they offer, but most growers get them from label supply companies.

The advantage of these tags is that someone else has done the work. The disadvantage is that you often have to order minimums, often in the hundreds, which can be costly if it is not a plant you grow regularly or in large quantities. Also, you are stuck with the information on the tag and it may not be appropriate for your part of the country. For instance, a plant may be a perennial in zone 10-7, but must be grown as an annual in the more northern climates. If your tag says that the plant is a perennial and you live in zone five, you are giving erroneous information to the customer.

Other growers we have talked to who use pre-printed tags say that one of the biggest problems is storing them. If you are like most growers, you will have hundreds of different plants in your inventory. Multiply those hundreds with the hundreds of each tag you will need to have on hand and you have tens of thousands of labels to keep track of. One place we know in East Texas ended up having to build a storage shed just for labels.

Custom Tags and Labels

Label companies offer custom labeling in a lot of different styles. Like the pre-printed labels, they can be simple text or fancy with pictures you supply yourself or from the label company archives. You can design a logo, have your name printed on top or on the back and create whatever format you want for the text.

The advantage is that these sorts of tags and labels are distinctive and really set your business apart. They tell the customer that you care about quality beyond producing a good plant. The disadvantage is that they are costly, especially if you grow a wide variety of plants, because you still have to order minimums.

Label/Tag Printers

Another option is to purchase your own label printer. Again, there are many options here from simple black-and-white dot-matrix and heat-transfer printers to high-tech computers that print out superior quality, multicolor, very professional-looking tags or labels. The simpler text printers are like any other printer and work off your home/office computer with software that allows you to create the format and information for the tags or pressure-sensitive labels you need.

There are several advantages to buying your own software and printer. First of all, it is a very flexible system. In just a few minutes you can change the content, format or color of a tag or label if you feel a change is necessary. Second, you can print only one or print 200, whatever you need at a given time.

MALVA, Windsor Castle (M. Sylvestris) Biennial
"Magic Hollyhock". Sun. Ht. 48", Sp. 2'. Rich soil kept moist
Stately plants w/regal, purple-veined blooms w/wavy-edged petals.

Example of our pot tags. Plant information on the front, our name and ph # on the back

Certified Organically Grown
MISTY HILL FARM
(512) 376-2817

Third, you can add new labels and tags to your repertoire at any time. Fourth, it gives you a distinction. People will learn to recognize your tags or labels and, hopefully, will look for them in their favorite garden center.

The disadvantage is the initial cost and the time it takes to set up your label information. The latter can take some time indeed if you have a lot of different plants. Then there is changing the rolls of tags/labels and ink ribbons, etc. Frankly, it is worth it to me (I have a heat-transfer printer) to have tags at my fingertips whenever I want them. Recently I learned that there is software and labels that you can use with an ordinary office printer that runs off any computer. It is getting simpler and more accessible to make your own labels. It is definitely worth considering.

Customer Information

Early in my business, when I did farmers markets and plant shows, I found that if I wanted to save my voice, I needed to provide my customers with information they could read. I also found nursery buyers responded well to information. Besides, it is just fascinating learning all you can about the plants you are selling. Where did they originate? What are their characteristics? Do they have specific growing requirements? How should they be used in the landscape or garden? And in the case of herbs and vegetables, how do you use them? Is there any interesting history or lore associated with them? This research is especially important if you do not have up close and personal experience with these plants in your own garden, landscape or kitchen.

I research the plants I sell and put the information into a format. These are printed out ahead—usually three or four to a page—and handed to both retail and wholesale customers when they purchase the plants. It takes a tremendous amount of time and effort to create these information sheets (see example below), but once they are done the information is at your fingertips, stored on your computer, waiting for a print command. Unless you have tried this, you have no idea how positive the response is to these little sheets of information. To retail customers it is an added value to the beautiful plants they are buying. Often it encourages them to purchase some-

---

MALVA, Windsor Castle ("Magic Hollyhock")
(Malva sylvestris)
Malvaceae

Origin: *M. sylvestris* ("Common Mallow" or "Wild Mallow") is native to Europe and introduced to North America where it can be found growing wild along roadsides and in waste areas.

Characteristics: A **biennial** to **perennial** herb, the Windsor Castle Malva are stately plants with regal, purple-veined blooms with very pronounced wavy-edged petals. Blooms from May to October. **Height to 4'. Space 2'.**

Culture: Prefers **rich soil kept moist**, and **full sun**.

Uses: Ideal for herbaceous borders, landscaping and natural planting. Use individual blooms for unique table decorations. Common Mallow was an old, favorite country remedy, and was also cooked and eaten as a vegetable.

Certified Organically Grown • Misty Hill Farm
2280 Sand Hill Rd., Dale, Texas 78616 • (512) 376-2817

---

thing they might not otherwise try since they have the information they need to give them a shot at success. I also put our phone number on the sheets and on our pot tags so if people have questions they can just give me a call.

Plant people are sponges for information. They want to be successful with the plants they are buying and they really appreciate help with their endeavor. Nursery buyers like being able to talk intelligently about the plants they are putting on their shelves. They do not know everything about all plants and definitely value the added guidance.

Nomenclature

Please get the plant name right. If you are going to sell a plant to the public, do everyone a favor and be sure you have the correct botanical name. Believe me, I know for a fact that this is not always easy. First of all, those crazy botanists that do all the naming are forever changing the classifications of plants. What you thought was in one family or genus is now in another. Even the species "signature" can change when the scientists decide that "Yes it does have the *multiflora* characteristic, but I think *grandiflora* describes it more succinctly." And so it changes.

Never call a plant solely by its "common name." There are often several different plants that have the same common name. It is best if you also have a botanical name beside it so folks can differentiate this plant from the others. At least give people the genus. For instance, if you have a passionflower vine and you do not know which species or variety it is, then call it *Passiflora spp.* Then you can tell them whether it is red or purple or yellow, etc.

We have a more educated retail plant customer now. They watch garden shows on television, listen to the garden radio shows, belong to garden clubs, and read plant books. There are even gardening chat rooms on the Internet, some of which are pretty sophisticated. Do not assume that no one is going to notice if you do not have the correct name on a plant—least of all the retail nursery plant buyer. I sold a plant for two years with an erroneous species identification without realizing it. I thought I had done a thorough search for the correct classification. Although the plants were in the same genus, there was a big difference between the plant I thought I had identified and the one I really had. It can happen. It is a painful lesson, but it is necessary to make it right.

How do you make sure you have the right name? One place to get information is in bookstores. You can use them kind of like a library and browse through the many botanical tomes to locate and identify your plant in question. This also gets you acquainted with the latest references on all manner of plants, and you might find something you need for your own personal library. I have accumulated quite a library of reference books myself. My favorite way to identify plants is via the Internet. Information, pictures, lists are all available with searches through plant/seed sellers, universities and other botanical websites. With a little patience and persistence you should be able to find your plant. There is an incredible wealth of information out there in that magical web of wires and energy. Of course, there is the real library. However, unless you live near a large city with a good municipal library, your search might be frustrating. If you are lucky or know a student or educator, you might get into a university library with a good botany section, but I have spent too much time in libraries with too little benefit. I have found it too hard to do it that way.

There is always the tactic of taking your plant with you and stopping at every nursery along the way to ask if anyone knows the name of your plant. If you stop at enough places someone is bound to know. I would consider that only a starting place. If someone tells you it is a *Wabish plutoria* you really need to do further research. You might find that there are a lot of members of the *Wabish* genus and they all look very similar. You need to know *for certain* if it is a *W. plutoria* or if, in fact, it is a *W. congoria*.

Knowing your plants is a good way to show nursery buyers that you are a professional. They have a lot of respect for those growers who put effort into accurate plant identification.

Delivering Your Product

Here are a few points that might make the whole experience of delivering plants to customers a bit nicer for both you and the customer.

Be organized. Put plants on the shelves in reverse order of delivery or at least systematized so that it is easy to locate the customer's order. No one has time to stand and wait for you to find the plants. It makes delivery day very long indeed if you have to rummage through the shelves at each stop to pull the customer's order.

Before you load them on the truck, van or trailer, make sure that all plants have tags and that the tags are placed in the containers in a neat fashion. Consider how every flat or plant looks before loading, so you are not straightening everything later as you unload. You do not want your plants to look messy.

Try a smile. It does not matter how harried or rushed you are, this is your chance to work on public relations. You really can take five minutes to chat with the customer. This is where they get to know who you are and what you are all about. On the other hand, do not overstay your welcome. They have work to do too.

Do not expect your customers to help you unload. Some places will and some won't. Find out early in your relationship where it is customary to unload your inventory, and just go to it when you get there. Even the ones that usually help you might be too busy to rush over and assist when you arrive.

Check invoices and order forms. Most places will check off what you have brought, not only to scrutinize the quality of your plants, but also in some cases, to compare it to an order sheet (P.O. or purchase order). When they OK the delivery, get them to sign the invoice in case there are disputes later about the order. Give them a copy and keep one for yourself.

Retail Sales

Although my primary focus is wholesale, I have done quite a few plant shows, farmers markets and festivals. Selling plants retail in a very small space is challenging. It takes a great deal of creativity to make it attractive enough to get people in to take a look at what you are offering.

If you are going to sell retail, then first visit some plant shows, farmers markets, shops, nurseries, stores, malls, flea markets, etc. and take notes. What is your first impression regarding attractiveness, neatness, accessibility, signage, courtesy, help, information, cleanliness, product variety and product quality? If the first thing you notice when you walk in a shop or store is chaos, then that image will likely taint your perception of the product. If you notice bright colors and organized shelves with signs that are easy to read, then consciously or unconsciously you will probably want to explore this place of business a little further.

First impressions are very powerful. Whether you have a permanent retail location or you are just planning to sell from vendor stalls at shows and markets, you must look at your place of business through the eyes of a new customer. What is going to make them stop here and what is going to make them want to come in once they have paused? What would make you stop and look? Is there anything that sets you apart?

Storefront Signage

One of the first things people should notice is your sign announcing who you are. Is it in a place that is easy to find with the eyes? Is it big enough to be read from a reasonable distance? Does it stand out through color or design? This is your first opportunity to catch the customer's attention. If it is bold and assertive, then folks will see it. Use large lettering. Work with colors. The design should be simple and to the point, but reflective of who you are. This is not the time to be timid. If you are proud of your product, then let people know.

> **Howdy!**
> **We're Sho Nuf**
> **Open Fer**
> **Business!**
> **Y'all C'mon**
> **In!!**

For our business we actually have two banner-type signs. One is made from green striped awning fabric that is about six-feet long and 18-inches wide that announces in large, red letters, "Certified Organic Plants." Then we have another rectangular, plain white sign with large black and red letters that says

Misty Hill Farm, etc. Placed strategically, they tell customers at a distance who we are and what we have for sale.

Organization

When a customer stops to take a look at what you are selling, is it clear to them how to proceed through the shop or market stall? Are you forcing them to walk through a chaotic maze of shelves and displays that have no apparent reason to be there except to give you a place to set your product? Have you ever been in a store that does not seem to have any logic relating to where the products are placed? If you have, then you understand how frustrating (and downright annoying) it is to walk past shelves of seemingly unrelated products. Many grocery chains actually move products to new locations periodically just to make you have to walk through the whole store to find them. To me, this is a negative rather than a positive experience.

You want to invite rather than repel your customers. Here are a few things to think about:

Have clear pathways. Ask yourself if two people can pass each other in the aisle if both are carrying a basket, pushing or pulling a cart, or carrying plants.

Do not overcrowd the shelves. It is very hard to find what you are looking for if you have to rummage through tightly packed shelves.

Organize your products into meaningful *categories.* Try to get inside the head of a customer. Would basil be lumped into an annual herbs category or a culinary herbs category? Whatever system you decide to use, apply it to everything consistently.

Label plant categories. When you decide on your categories, label them with signs large enough to catch the attention of shoppers. There really is no point in making customers look over the entire inventory of plants or product if they have something specific they are trying to find. Make it easier, not harder.

If you do not want to do categories, then at least label the plants or products clearly. Don't make customers hunt for information. People do not want to have to ask for help. At the very least, put an identification tag in the pot or on the product.

Price your products clearly. How many times have you been interested in something for sale and found there is no price on it? As often as not, I will just set it back down and walk away. It is irresponsible for a retailer to not have things properly priced and it frustrates your customers.

Be courteous, available and friendly, but do not hover. Avoid *watching* your customers. Let them shop without interference. It doesn't hurt to be aware of obvious questions they have and volunteer to help them get the answers they need, but then leave them alone to do the rest of their shopping.

Provide information. Information sheets or labels can save you a lot of time (and your vocal chords) if placed alongside your products or plants. I have observed customers reading every one of them as they work their way through an area. If they find out that they get a copy of the information sheet when they buy the plant, they are thrilled.

Make it flow. Is it easy to flow through the display area or is it "herky jerky"? If the customer is spending more time trying to figure out how to get through the maze than looking at your products on the shelves, then there is something amiss.

Make your product accessible. Don't make your customers reach over things to secure the item of their interest. Shelving should have the product within easy reach. Building tiers is OK, but they should not extend out so far that a person has to stretch beyond balance to get to the top shelf.

Presentation

Stand back and take a good look at your product. If it is plants, do they have a few yellow or brown leaves or broken stems? Are the pot tags or labels all facing different directions? Is there old leaf debris on the surface of the pots? Do you see plants lying on their side? Has

Don't Leave Pot Tags Untidy

soil spilled out? Are they dry and parched or soggy and mossy?

Are there aphids under the leaves, spider mite webs, or fungus gnats swarming on the soil? Is there inconsistent quality in a flat of the same plants? Do your foliar plants have a yellowish color instead of a solid, healthy green? Are there spent blooms among the new flower buds?

If you get some perspective on your display, you might figure out ways to make it look clean and more inviting. It might not seem important in the big picture, but to a customer looking at your plants, it makes a difference. Pick off those bad leaves, discard ugly debris, straighten the tags, remove diseased or bug-ridden plants, water the plants if needed, dead-head the blooms, etc. Always, always, always try to look at what you are selling through the eyes of a buyer.

If a flat only has three or four plants left in it, either put a new, full flat in its place or pull the plants together and place them to the front of the flat. Oddly, customers have a reluctance to buy the last one or two in a flat. Unless it is something they really want, they may have the perception that those last few plants are the culls. When we do shows, we are constantly replacing flats or consolidating. If we run out of something, the sign comes down and something else is put in that space. It takes vigilance and persistence to keep a retail area looking attractive.

Do you have something really unusual or showy? Put it near the entrance. Why do you think nurseries often put their blooming

Consolidate

annuals and perennials near the front? It is eye catching. It draws you in. Do you have a lot of something that you need to move? Put them together in a tidy display near the entrance with a description of their use (or value) and a reasonable price tag. If it is one of the first things people see and it looks like a good deal, they will often buy one. People just cannot resist a bargain. (Just make sure it really *is* a good buy.)

Decisions, Decisions, Decisions

In the beginning, when we traveled around Texas visiting different growers looking for a business model that might suit us, we began to notice a pattern. In many cases the business owners had set out to do one thing, and in a year or two ended up doing something altogether different—for instance, a container grower who ended up in the cut flower business; another in the herbal product business; another in the bulk compost business, etc. I also observed container plant growers who started out growing one type of plant and ended up either growing something entirely different or adding other types of plants to the original growing plan. Some were completely retail, some completely wholesale, and some were both. We learned how labor intensive cut herbs are, how hard it is to maintain a wholesale/retail business, and how complicated some businesses had become, diversifying beyond reason, trying to figure out how to make a profit.

After careful consideration, we decided to make wholesale container plants the core of our business. My passion at the time was herbs, so that was my focus. As time went by, I became interested in heirloom vegetable plants and the fascinating history behind each seed line. I developed a desire to offer these plants to customers for their home gardens to help them appreciate how tasty they are, to understand how important it is to save our seed heritage, and to relearn the art of plant selection and seed saving. At first, I got a lukewarm reception from the garden centers about the fact that they were heirlooms, but after a couple of years consumer interest began to increase, and soon there was an outright demand for the plants.

Another area that began to interest me along the way was native plants and water conservation. As my awareness increased, so did my concern about offering only herbs that do well in our region. I began to appreciate the beauty of native, regional plants and learned more about them in my own garden. Consequently, as I developed more familiarity with these plants, I added them to my inventory.

After a few years I realized that I had done exactly what I had observed many other growers doing when we first went out looking at established businesses. I have learned over time that it is a part of any successful business. Start with a firm plan, but be flexible enough to evolve and custom fit the business to your interests. Find out what the market will support. Use your instincts. Using organic techniques, your plants will be beautiful, no matter what you decide to grow; so grow what makes the most sense to you and market your plants with confidence. You will learn soon enough what works and what does not. One thing I noticed when I began selling the heirloom vegetable plants was that people bought them not because they were heirlooms, but because they were robust, beautiful plants. Their recognition of the importance of heirloom plants came later.

With a couple of years of wholesale business under our belt, we decided to dabble in retail and spent a few years doing seasonal plant shows and farmers markets. Our location was not suitable for retail traffic, so this was the only way we would be able to experience this side of business for ourselves. It was incredibly hard work for often little financial reward, but the perspective you get selling retail is invaluable. You see how consumers react to your plants, you hear the questions they have, and you find out what they are looking for. All this helps you sell plants to your wholesale customers, who are selling retail to those same customers.

After a few years of plant shows and markets we decided that, in the end, they took too much time and energy away from our wholesale business. We ditched the retail aspect and went back to being entirely wholesale. If we had not experienced retail, we would not have known that it was something we would rather not pursue. By doing it the way we did, we did not invest more time, energy and money than we were able to support, but we still gained the experience we needed to get the retail perspective.

Some people start out wholesale and evolve completely to retail, and some do the reverse. Some people get into the plant growing business and find after a couple of years that it is not what they thought it would be, so they move on to something else. The important thing for a budding entrepreneur to remember is that the time you spend researching and planning before you jump into a business will support you well in the first few years. You get the benefit of seeing how other people have succeeded or failed, which gives you a firmer foundation on which to build the business you want. Do not be afraid to restructure your vision as you gain experience and knowledge. If your business is solid, then as you go along you can test the market with a few new ideas, work in new marketing tools, develop new production techniques and try new aspects or venues of the business without risking the basic integrity of your plan.

The goal of any small business is to create enough financial return to support the owner and to allow for growth of the business. On the way to that profit, it is very satisfying and rewarding to provide consumers with a real value for their money. The customer's perception of that merit has a lot to do with your attention to detail and your real desire to have them come back and shop again. Thorough, thoughtful marketing and conscientious merchandising can be pivotal in determining whether your business survives or thrives.

Chapter Nine

Employees

If and when your business needs the support of outside employees, there are many things to consider and understand before you get mired in the muck. If you have owned businesses in the past that supported employees, then most of this will not be new to you. If you have never done this before, sit up and listen. It is not hard, but there are lots of ducks to get in that row.

Before getting into the details, lets have a word about contract help. There is almost no way you can hire a person in horticulture who wants to work by contract. I know how tempting it is to hire someone who will take full responsibility for their Medicare and Social Security taxes, but there are very specific laws regarding who may hire themselves out for contract and who may hire them. First of all, there has to be a very carefully constructed contract for a very specific job that has a beginning and an end. Second, the person hired must have all his or her own tools for the job to be done—they cannot use your tools. You cannot supervise them or tell them what to do. None of this fits into horticulture. You need someone who can do multiple tasks and can go from one task to another under your supervision. You might as well just prepare yourself for hiring employees, be they full-time, part-time or temporary.

Ads and Interviews

Getting good, reliable help is a challenge. If you are like most horticulture businesses, you cannot pay much and the available work force is limited. Rural areas especially can be a challenge. If you are not near a good-sized town, you might have some trouble finding anyone, much less the right one. You might have to piece it together with a lot of part-timers.

That's the bad news. The good news is that there are an amazing number of people out there who love working with plants. Trainable people. There are housewives, retired folks, students and out-of-work people who just want a little income to get by. I have hired several college students who did fine work and have lucked into some good people with various college degrees who just want to work in the plant business. I have been very blessed in this area.

Where do you find people who want to work? Word of mouth works pretty well, but you get into some sticky situations when you decide not to hire someone who is a friend of a friend. Another way is to list your position on job boards at high schools, colleges, employment offices, etc. You may have to fill out some forms, but it can help you clarify, in your own mind, what and who you are looking for. Laundromats frequently have bulletin boards and you will often see people perusing the board while their clothes are drying. Then, of course, there are the classifieds in the local newspapers or any publication that is distributed free of charge.

When you begin wording your ad, I suggest you keep it simple. You do not have to go into lengthy job descriptions. Just state who you are, where you are (especially if you are rural), general job title, how much you pay, and your phone number. If qualifications are important, then describe briefly. I have found that I attract the right kind of people with just the statement, "Must love plants." Plant people come scrambling out of the woodpile. You will likely get calls from an amazing assortment of folks.

When you start interviewing, give yourself a cut-off date. Let everyone know that you will make a decision by such-and-such a date. This way they will know ahead of time that if they have not heard from you by the date you have given them, they are not hired. This saves you a lot of time and anxiety about having to call people back. If you find the perfect person the first day, keep your word and continue the interviews until the cut-off date. If they want the job badly enough, they will wait.

Make your interview as informal as possible without losing professionalism. Have something for them to fill out that gives you basic information about them, (name, address, phone number, horticulture-related work, back or other medical problems that might interfere with this type of work, etc.). I

The Interview

Peat Moss

also state our employee health insurance status, refer to the seasonal nature of the business, quote a starting salary and make them sign the bottom. I think a lot of the information on standard application forms is useless, so I made my own form. It works well for me. Get only the information you must have. This is not an IBM executive we're talking about.

I also ask them why they want this job. If their immediate response is, "I love working with plants," then you probably have a winner. If they say something like, "I just need a job," or, "It's all I could find," then ask a few other questions to see if there is a light on in the plant tower. Some people think that there is nothing to working with plants—"Well how hard can it be?" Remember, this is *your* livelihood and small mistakes can create whole batches of unmarketable plants. People who enjoy working with plants are less likely to do stupid things. Your plants become their plants. When they come in to work they will go see how *their* basil is doing.

How much you pay will not be a primary issue with the right people. Everyone here starts at minimum wage and I can honestly say that it has never been a deciding factor for the people I wanted to hire. Truly, if they have their own garden or grow lots of plants in containers, then they are good candidates, whether they have formal horticulture experience or not.

During the interview I will also give them a thumbnail overview of our business (including our philosophy regarding the environment), and, if they want, a quick tour. Then they get to ask me questions. It is amazing what you can learn about a person by the questions they ask you. This is not a test to see how intelligent they are. It is strictly an opportunity to open communication. The questions will vary from clarification of working hours to elucidation about how one becomes certified to carry the "organic" label. If you conduct lots of interviews, you might want to make notes to yourself (after they leave) to remind you of what impressed (or did not impress) you about the person. When you decide to hire, listen to your instincts. If it is between someone who has commercial horticulture experience but is kind of distant and odd and someone who just has lots of experience with their own gardens and is very enthusiastic about plants, you have to go with your gut feeling. Guess which one I would choose?

Hiring

Once you have decided on the employee(s) you want to work in your business, call them right away. I don't know about you, but I have been on the "waiting to hear" end of a job hunt and it can be excruciating. Especially if you have interviewed in several places and are holding out to hear from the one you really want. That is why the cut-off date is helpful for those who are out of the picture, especially if you do not feel comfortable calling people to let them know they have not been hired. Call the ones you want as soon as you know and set up a starting date and time. If you have hired more than one employee, even if they are working different hours and days, schedule them to come in at the same day and time for orientation. It is not good management of your time to go over the material several times in the course of a few days or a week. Besides, it gives them time to get to know each other a bit before getting to work.

When your new help arrives, introduce them to anyone already employed if they had not already met them in the interview. Show them around; here is the bathroom, there is the work area, here is the supply shed, there is the drinking water and break area, etc. Then take them to a quiet, comfortable area to fill out tax forms, settle on schedules, read the orientation manual, and go over basic *dos* and *don'ts* of working in horticulture. If you do not have an orientation manual, then consider writing one. You want to cover all your bases right up front and have something they can refer to later to refresh their memories. A manual can consist of simple guidelines for many of the routine tasks or step-by-step instructions for things you do every day. I also suggest you have guidelines on disease prevention, acceptable and non-acceptable behavior between employees, tardiness and absenteeism, work habits, back care, safety, lunches and breaks, and any other expectations you have concerning employment with your business.

Be sure they understand that time sheets are their responsibility and have them start one right away to be sure they know how to fill it out. The method you choose should be simple for the

Break Area

employee to use and easy for the person doing payroll to interpret. I played with a lot of different time sheets until I finally developed one that works well for everyone. When you decide on one, I suggest that it have places for the employee to sign in and out at least a couple of times in a day. This allows them to take long lunches or to do split shifts if necessary. I have been in situations where we had to go out of town for shows or conventions and I just needed someone to come and water and check on things several times a day while we were gone. The employee just signed in and out each time he or she came. We also use the quarter hour method for simplicity. In other words, they record the hour with a quarter decimal; *i.e.*, 8.00, 8.25, 8.50, 8.75. They record the time they are closest to when they arrive or leave. When I first started using this method I was afraid there would be discrepancies. What I discovered was that the numbers always evened out. And it makes bookkeeping a breeze.

Keeping Employees

Alright, you have hired some people, you have a work schedule, and production is rolling along. What do you offer that would prevent your employees from quitting suddenly at an inopportune time like, say, the middle of spring? Yikes! It is a tough dilemma if you are only paying minimum wage and have no health insurance benefits. What can you give them to make them stick around? If you hired "plant people," then the ability to buy plants at wholesale prices is a big plus. My folks walk out of here with an armload of plants and love it. But even that is not enough if they are not happy in their work. Here are some thoughts.

You should be approachable. Work alongside employees until they feel comfortable in the routine tasks. This way you can correct mistakes right away and offer encouragement when employees feel frustrated. This teaches them that they can always come to you with a question about how to attempt a task without risk of embarrassment.

Give kudos for good work. People love being thanked for their hard work and complemented on exceptional production. It is heartwarming to see their proud smiles. I know it sounds silly, but a round of applause after finishing a particularly big job can lift everyone's spirits.

Be patient. Everyone does not learn at the same pace or in the same way. You might need to work with some people more than others and repeat instructions more than a few times. This is why routine tasks should be in writing, in a step-by-step format, and in a notebook or tacked onto a bulletin board for reference. Oftentimes the problem is not a matter of intelligence, but perhaps a learning challenge such as dyslexia. If you ask people how they learn best, they will answer with a clue as to how you can approach teaching them. For instance, they might say, "I have to do things myself in order to learn how to do it," or, "Just show me first, then I can do it." Whatever they tell you, use that information to help them learn the tasks they need to know. At the same time, do not assume that your quick learners are doing things right. Follow up on their work or check in at intervals. They may need some fine-tuning along the way.

Take a few minutes now and then to relate to employees as individuals. Everyone has a life that is important to them. If they have children, ask about them. If they have an ailing family member, ask how they are doing. Assuming this does not make them uncomfortable, it might actually give them a sense that you care about them in ways other than how many flats of basil they can plant in a workday. It can also give you a read on any problems brewing that might cause stress or lack of concentration at work. I have sent people home that were showing serious lack of focus due to personal issues. As sympathetic as I am about personal difficulties, I am better off working short-staffed than with someone who might mess up a whole bench of plants. You have to draw a line somewhere. Be gentle but firm.

Correct mistakes immediately, but do it in a positive way. In other words, tell them what they are doing right first, then show them what you want them to change. I have found that people will respond much more readily to correction (or in some circumstances change) if there is a valid, logical reason for why you want things done in a certain way. More often than not, the reasons I do things in a particular way are from experience doing it the hard way or in an unproductive, inefficient manner. Telling employees my blundering stories sometimes helps them understand the means and the end.

You will have grueling days. Your employees will have days of blunder. There are times when it really does seem like there is some cosmic conspiracy keeping you from completing the work. I honestly believe that days and times like this are often created by our own misguided expectations of ourselves and our employees. Try to step out of this stress vortex and get perspective. Think about your situation as though it is a sitcom on television. Find the humor in what is going on and give it a chuckle. Share this amusement with your employees—lighten it up. You will be amazed at how much better everyone feels when it becomes clear that this week-from-hell is only a microsecond of your entire life. You have always heard the expression, "You will laugh about this later." Well, laugh now, it pays huge dividends.

Give raises when you can. Even if it is 50 cents an hour. It is not the amount, it is the sentiment behind it. We have never had enough money coming in to pay people well, but I try to give my good employees some kind of raise at intervals. They will not consider a small raise an insult if they truly understand your situation.

Give employees responsibility. There was a time, early in my nursing management experience, that I mistakenly thought that most people would feel their worth in a position by how much money they made. I am sure there are still some who feel this way, but I have found over the years that most people achieve self-validation through responsibility and doing a job well. Give each of your employees an area of the routine tasks to oversee, with specific guidelines and expectations. They are responsible for checking the area daily, reporting problems, and making suggestions for improvement. Even part-timers can have specific areas of responsibility if it is something that only needs to be checked a few times a week, such as grading/sorting the salable plants in flats. Some things, however, need doing every day, like scouting for insects and disease.

An example from my business is the Aloe area. It is ongoing. There are always pups to be planted into four-inch pots, grown-out four-inch plants to be planted into quarts, and overgrown quarts to be stepped up into gallons. We need this area to flow because we sell Aloes almost every week of the year. If one step of the process is not heeded, we sell out of a particular size and have to wait for production to catch up. If one person is responsible for overseeing Aloe production, then there are fewer interruptions in the process and that employee feels good about being an integral part of the fiber of the business. Now this does not mean they necessarily do all the work. It simply means they must make sure someone is doing the work or call it to my attention.

Deal with tension. If you are noticing tension or unease between employees, deal with it. Often it is a simple misunderstanding. If it is personality differences, then you may need to mediate a compromise that is suitable to both parties. One way to prevent disputes from the start is to have short, informal, Monday morning meetings to plan out the tasks for the coming week. If everyone has specific tasks and the anticipation of working as a team, then there is less room for disputes to occur. (By the way, having lists of tasks to cross off when done gives everyone a sense of accomplishment at the end of the week.) Sometimes, if the conflict is serious, there may be nothing you can do to remedy the situation. One time I arranged a meeting with two employees to try to work out a brewing problem. It ended with rather explosive anger bordering on violence from one of the employees toward the other. He was let go immediately. He was a good worker, but there is no room for that in the workplace.

Be as flexible as you can with schedules. There are always times when an employee needs a few hours off to go to a doctor's appointment or run an important errand. I allow them to do whatever they need to do as long as the work is getting done. They can always stay late, come in on a day off, or trade days with someone else if this works for them. Most employees are very willing to make up the hours another time if it is necessary. Flexibility goes a long way to building loyalty.

If people come in sick, they need to go home and get well. I am rather adamant about this. You will not get productive work out of someone who is running to the bathroom every 15 minutes or has a nose, lungs and/or mouth oozing fluids. I have never thought it fair to expose other

employees to whatever vile virus a sick employee is harboring. People still do not understand that rest and fluids really will get them better faster than working through it. In the end they will thank you. If you are the flexible employer we are talking about, then you might be able to work out an adjustment in the schedule to allow them the time to recuperate. It is really a loving, caring thing to do. Have them check in with you by phone every day to give you a health progress report. This helps you plan your days in their absence and supports their understanding that you care.

Most of what I have said is common sense, but I also know that dealing sensibly with employees is easier for some than others. When I was involved in management positions in the past, I tried simply to treat my employees with the same respect that I would desire of an employer. Strive always to put yourself in their shoes and to truly understand their position. Only then is it a real team.

Payroll Liabilities and Taxes

This is one of those duties that can be hard or easy depending on how you want to proceed. The thing is, it has to be done no matter how you decide to do it, even if you have only one part-time employee.

The first thing you will have to do is file with IRS for a business Employer Identification Number (EIN, see *Chapter One*). You will need this before you pay one cent to any employee. This is how the IRS keeps track of you and your employees as long as your business exists. It will be on any and all forms you file whether you owe taxes or not.

It is the law that you take Social Security and Medicare taxes out of every check that goes to an employee. This is calculated by multiplying the total earnings by a percentage currently assigned to each tax. When your employee gets the check, it will be minus whatever amount you have calculated.

If you only have a small number of employees, chances are you will only have to file your taxes on a quarterly tax report, but it *must* be accompanied by a check that has the amount of Social Security and Medicare taxes you have withheld from the paychecks, plus a matching amount contributed by your business. At the end of the year you file a summary report (W-3), which states how much you owed, how much you paid, and to whom this amount was attributed (which employee). You file a W-2 report, which is in quadruplicate so everyone gets a copy.

There is also the Federal Unemployment Tax. This you pay if you have a certain number of employees to whom you are paying a certain amount of wages in a certain period of time. The government has it all figured out and will take you for quite a ride trying to figure out if you are obligated to pay this outrageous tax, but it is the law.

Then there is Workers Compensation. As with the unemployment tax, the state workforce commission has a formula for figuring out if you are responsible for paying into this plan to ensure that injured workers are properly cared for. Of course, your business can take on the expense of injured workers in lieu of Workers Compensation, but it could get mighty expensive if it involves physical rehabilitation. It's a gamble.

There are many other payroll considerations such as overtime, health insurance, retirement and pension plans, sick pay, vacations, bonuses, etc. All have specific requirements attached to them regarding U.S. Treasury Law. All are covered in the Circular E (Employer's Tax Guide) put out by IRS. This and any other publication, guide or form is available to you by contacting IRS.

Here are the most current methods for contacting the IRS:
1. Internet: (www.irs.ustreas.gov). This will give you access to forms, instructions, lists of publications, answers to questions via email, and help calculating your withholding. This is by far the easiest way to get the information you need.
2. Fax machine: Dial (703) 368-9694 from your fax machine to get the most requested forms and instructions.
3. Telephone: Call IRS at 1-800-829-3676 to order current forms, instructions and publications. They will arrive by mail in a week to 10 days.
4. Post offices, libraries, and IRS offices carry many of the forms, information and publications you will need.

5. There are also CD-ROMS you can buy and forms you can fill out to order information by mail. It might all seem a bit intimidating at first, but you'll get the hang of it pretty quickly.

Since it is generally assumed that you will have a computer associated with your business, I recommend that you get a good business bookkeeping program that includes payroll. These programs will calculate payroll taxes for you if you fill in the tax rates, and will print out all manner of reports for you. Some will even print out the checks if you have the right printer and check blanks. When I started out, I was calculating everything by hand and it was pretty time consuming. With the payroll program (we use QuickBooks) we just type in the number of hours worked and the computer calculates everything else. Easy.

You could do all your own day-to-day bookkeeping, quarterly taxes and such, but many business owners choose to work with a CPA (certified public accountant) at the end of the year to file the IRS paperwork. If you are not familiar with the different forms to fill out and how to apply the financial statements you have generated, then it would probably save you a lot of stress (and probably some money) if you have someone do it that knows the ropes. A good CPA will be able to guide you through the process and help you understand how to make the numbers work for you.

If you do not feel comfortable doing the daily bookkeeping tasks then, if you can afford it, you might consider hiring a CPA your first year or two to assist you in setting up your books. If you do not know by now, your time is extremely valuable and it might be worth the extra money in the beginning to get the help, rather than spend hours and hours hammering it out by trial, error and blunder. In business bookkeeping, ignorance can cost you a bundle.

Chapter Ten

Safety

Back Care

Most people don't give enough thought to back health. We bend and twist the whole day long and don't consider our backs until the end of the day when the throbbing starts. We slouch, curl, lock our knees, and bend our necks until our backs and necks are screaming. How in the world can we possibly justify doing such thoughtless things to the part of our body that holds us upright our whole lives? If you do not already have back problems, then I guarantee you will hear some spinal squawking after a few years in this business. There is a lot of lifting, carrying, bending, stooping, walking and reaching, and if you are doing all these things without thought to body mechanics, you will be taking a lot of analgesics.

Let's review some basics. I'm sure you've heard them before, but they are very important. Do not ever assume that youth or good health will protect you from back injury.

When carrying large or heavy objects (especially if they are unwieldy), hold them as close to your body as possible. Carrying heavy objects transfers your center of gravity to an unnatural place and your small back muscles try to pick up the slack. At least don't bend forward. Use your arm muscles and stand or walk as straight as possible. If the object is too heavy, use a cart or dolly.

When picking up objects from a low area, let your large leg muscles do the work, not your small back muscles. If the object is on the floor or a very low place, do not reach for it until you have squatted down. Placing one foot slightly in front of the other, with shoulder width between

them, squat, pick up the object, pull it into your body and stand using your leg muscles to lift you. If the object is in an awkward place for you to comfortably grab it, then push or pull it into a spot that allows you to pick it up without reaching or twisting. If it is too heavy to move, get help. If someone is helping you pick up a heavy object, coordinate your movements so that the weight is evenly distributed and it comes up in a smooth, balanced motion.

Never pick up an object if your body is not square with it. In other words, don't twist and lift. No matter how many objects you are moving, square yourself off before picking something up and before setting it back down. It just takes a few extra seconds. As much as possible, use both arms to carry something balancing the weight.

Move your body with thought. Sometimes we get in such a hurry our movements get fast and jerky. This is when you are more likely to

No Twisting!

injure yourself. Think about what you are doing. Move deliberately. When you walk, visualize your body being held up by a string that runs up the middle of your spinal cord and out the top of your head. Look forward, head up, and keep shoulders straight.

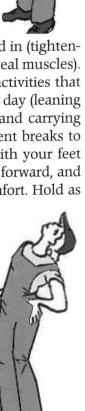

If you are engaged in an activity where you are standing for a long time at a work table, either get a tall stool to lean on to relieve the spinal pressure or have a step stool to rest a foot on. At the very least, do not stand with knees

locked or shifting weight back and forth from hip to hip. If you have to stand in place for long periods of time, your knees should be slightly bent and your pelvis tucked in (tightening the abdominal and gluteal muscles).

If you are engaged in activities that make you bend forward all day (leaning over benches, picking up and carrying flats, etc.), then take frequent breaks to relieve the strain on your back muscles. Stand with your feet shoulder-width apart, hands flat on hips, thumbs forward, and slowly bend backward as far as you can with comfort. Hold as long as you are able to get the most benefit. This realigns your spine and relaxes the back muscles. It makes a huge difference in how your back feels at the end of the day.

It is just as important to be aware of body mechanics when you are sitting. Stools (with no backs) are actually best for sitting long periods at a work table. This allows you to move more and use good sitting mechanics. The important thing to remember is to keep the slight curve in your low back. If you are bending over enough to round that curve out, then you are putting too much stress on your back muscles. If you are sitting with your knees too high or too low, you are likely cutting off circulation to your legs and causing undue stretching of hip tendons and ligaments. If you are engaged in an activity that is making you look down constantly, every five minutes or so bend your neck back to relieve the muscle pressure in your neck.

Back First Aid

Backs will often "go out" even in relatively benign activities because the muscles are tired and stressed. Maintaining good body mechanics, and resting when you are too tired to go on, can prevent many injuries. Here are some suggestions for acute back pain.

1. At the first sign of back pain, immediately lie down on the floor or ground; face down, with arms extended along the side of the body. Stay in this position for at least five minutes to let the back muscles relax.
2. After five minutes bend your arms and place elbows to either side of your chest, with hands flat on the ground (palms down) pointing forward. Slowly lift your torso up with your arms, leaving the pelvis flat on the ground and relaxed. This movement realigns your spine by recreating the natural curve (lordosis), which will allow your back muscles to work properly. It may be somewhat painful (if not downright), but maintain this position for at least a couple of minutes; preferably about five.
3. Slowly let your torso back down, and yes, it probably hurts. Relax again, face down for a few more minutes.
4. After relaxing, bend your elbows again, this time placing hands flat on the ground to either side of your chest (push-up style).
5. Slowly push your torso up with your arms as high as you can, again leaving the pelvis flat on the ground. Hold for a couple of seconds, then let yourself back down slowly. Repeat this ten times and then relax.

Note: If pain is more on one side than the other, then slide your hips slightly away from the painful side to do the stretches.

When you are ready to get up, roll onto your side, bend your knees and, if necessary, have someone assist you onto

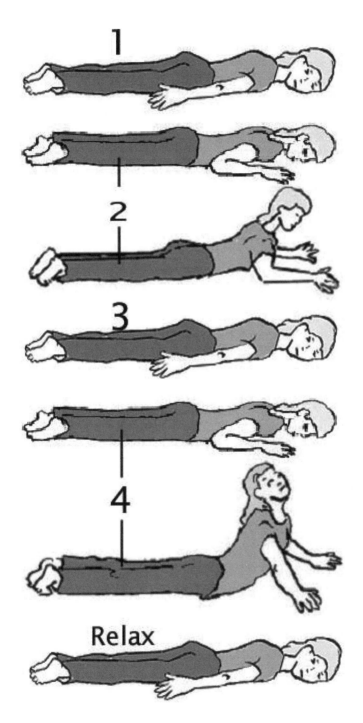

Relax

your hands and knees. From this position, rock back onto your feet and slowly lift yourself with your leg muscles, back into a standing position. Walk around slowly (using good body mechanics), to evaluate your back. Generally, unless there are torn or strained muscles, the spasms will slowly go away. This does not mean that you can go back to lifting. The muscles are obviously in need of some rest and relaxation. This does not necessarily mean go to bed. It simply means you should not do anything that would re-aggravate those muscles until they feel better. Some cold packs could also help ease the spasms.

If the pain does not lessen after the stretches, then go to bed and place a rolled up towel in the small of your back and curve of your waist. It really does make a difference in comfort when you are sleeping at night. After a day of rest, begin the stretches as described above, and repeat every two hours throughout the day. These exercises can be done indefinitely, and in fact, are good maintenance for your back. As the pain lessens you can reduce the number of times per day you do them until you get to a comfortable level for your needs.

This back first aid is from a wonderful book recommended to me by an orthopedic physician I saw a few years back. I had been having progressively severe back pain that ultimately interfered with daily activities as simple as dressing in the morning and brushing my teeth. I was petrified that I would be crippled in a year's time. Although the doctor suspected a couple of disc herniations, he knew that I could not afford the expensive tests and was not going to do surgery. I explained to him that I would do whatever I needed to do, on my own, to get better. I just needed some guidance. The guidance came in the form of a little book called, *Treat your Own Back,* by Robin McKenzie (Spinal Publications Ltd.). I immediately sent Chris out to get a copy of the book and I began doing the exercises the same day. I was 30 percent better in three days and 50 percent within a month. I was so thrilled with the results that I told everyone I knew who had back problems to get this book and try the exercises. At this writing, I am as functional as I was before the crisis began. I am also much more aware of my body movements now and take much more care when I am working. I have to say that, in a way, it was life changing. I recommend it for anyone doing physical work, whether they have back pain now or not. The exercises and spinal education should be a part of employee orientation.

First Aid

I worked for the Red Cross for a couple of years and taught lots of first aid and CPR. If it is possible, I suggest taking the Red Cross standard first aid course. It has both CPR and First Aid and could keep things in hand when emergencies occur. Everyone needs the information, not just for work, but also for life. At least one person in the work area should know what to do in an emergency. You really just never know when something is going to happen.

My intent here is to describe a few of the things you are most likely to deal with in this business. It's not supposed to be a first aid course. It's only to increase your awareness and give you a few guidelines.

Heat Exhaustion

Here in Texas it gets mighty hot in the summer. When the ambient temperatures rise into the 90s, then plastic-covered greenhouse temperatures will be in the 100s. I try to start the day early in the morning and work until about two. From two until five or six I rest and get things done around the homestead. Then I go back to work when the sun is a bit lower in the sky and put in a few more hours. Unless it is a cool day, employees go home at 2:00 or 2:30.

Despite these precautions, many of us have suffered a bit of heat exhaustion. The most common symptoms are red face, profuse sweating, light-headedness, nausea or abdominal cramping, rapid (and often pounding) heartbeat, weakness, sometimes confusion and often extreme thirst. These symptoms are very dangerous because the next step is shock and potentially death in extreme cases. It often occurs when humidity is high because the skin is not able to cool itself as effectively through evaporation of perspiration. Consequently the body core temperature rises rapidly—often before you even notice.

If the symptoms are mild, sit the person down and wrap a wet towel around their head, neck and perhaps the torso. Offer tepid (not cold) water to drink in small, frequent sips. If they are weak, lay them down with their feet elevated slightly above the level of the heart. Someone should stay with them until they feel better.

If the symptoms are moderate to severe, lay them down, with feet elevated above the level of the heart, and sprinkle them with cool water from a hose or a watering can. If there is a fan available, place it where it can cool (but not chill) the person more quickly. Offer sips of tepid water only if they are fully conscious. Stay with them. If they have lost consciousness or continue to stay confused, with pale skin, and shallow respirations, call 911. If you know how, monitor respirations and heart rate until EMS shows up. Folks, this is no joke. People die from heat stroke.

Cuts/Scratches/Abrasions

Basically we are talking about breaks in the skin. All of these, if relatively superficial, can be treated the same way. Just wash the area thoroughly with plain soap and water, dry with a clean paper or cloth towel, and cover with some kind of adhesive wound dressing. If you want to put something on the wound like triple antibiotic ointment, that's fine. Personally, I prefer a little fresh Aloe Vera gel from the many plants we grow here. With Aloe, it will no doubt be healed in a couple of days.

If the cut is deep and bleeding rather profusely, first put a towel over the wound and then apply direct pressure. If it is a really severe wound, raise the body part to a place above the level of the heart. Here is where you have to make a judgment call. If the wound is small but deep, you may be able to wash it after slowing the bleeding with pressure. The sooner you can wash a wound, the less chance there will be of infection. Your first aid kit should have "butterfly" adhesive strips that can be used to pull two sides of a small wound together to help stop the bleeding and lessen tissue damage. This is generally only temporary to give the person time to get to the doctor for stitches if needed. If the wound is large and you are having trouble stopping the bleeding, maintain it above the level of the heart and simply place a thick, sterile dressing over the wound and wrap snugly with gauze or clean cloth strips. Then get them to an emergency room.

Note: Any time you are dealing with someone else's wound, you must have protective gloves on to avoid contact with their blood. These vinyl, plastic, or latex gloves should be a part of your first aid kit and readily available to the person giving assistance.

Sprains/Strains/Contusions

The injuries in this section are internal damage to blood vessels and/or ligaments generally caused by a forceful blow or wrenching of a body part, often a joint. The tissue surrounding the wound will swell and become discolored from internal bleeding. Fortunately, they are not life threatening but can be unbearably painful.

Contusions (bruises) should simply be treated with an ice pack if severe. Do not rub the area. This only increases the internal bleeding if there is significant blood vessel damage. Place a dry, cloth towel over the wound and then an ice pack. If possible, wrap it with gauze or anything that will keep it in place for 20 minutes or so. Bruised comfrey leaf, used as a poultice externally, helps heal the wound if you are willing to give it a try.

Sprains and strains can be more serious and in severe situations, where ligaments and/or tendons have been torn, might need surgery. For the most part though, first aid is all that is needed. First sit the person down and elevate the joint. Elevating an injury of this kind will help reduce the amount of swelling. As with bruises, place a dry towel over the affected area and then an ice pack. This also helps reduce the swelling and internal bleeding. The person must not use the injured joint for a couple of days, or longer, depending on the severity of the injury. Ice packs should be used continuously for at least 24 hours. (If the cold is too uncomfortable, apply 20 minutes on, then 20 minutes off). Never put heat on an injury of this kind for at least 24 hours. Whenever there is a question about the severity of a wound of this type, have a doctor look at it. Again, I recommend a bruised comfrey poultice perhaps mixed with fresh Aloe Vera. You will see astounding healing in a short time.

Snakebite

I am including this because we are in a rural area and the snakes have been having a few good years. Get a good field book to help you identify the snakes in your area. Venomous snakes are in the minority of those you will see, and the others may help quite a  bit with the rat and mouse populations. It is really a good idea not to kill your helpers.

If someone has been bitten, try to get a person to identify the offending reptile while you help the wounded. Keep the person as calm as possible and the bitten area below the level of the heart. A cold pack might help relieve some of the pain but should not be used long term. *Do not slice the wound open and try to suck out the venom by mouth or with a suction cup.* This action wastes valuable time and only makes the person more vulnerable to infection from the wound. Getting the person to a hospital is your priority. Knowing what kind of snake bit them is important. There are different toxins that affect the body in vastly different ways. If the snake has been killed, bring it with you. Snake bites do not often kill, but they can make you very ill. The sooner you get help, the better one's chance of a speedy recovery.

Foreign Objects in the Eye

No matter how careful you are, you will get stuff in your eyes. If it is something like perlite it can be very painful. Some simple guidelines will help you deal with this rather annoying occurrence.

First, the second you feel something hit your eye, close your lids and look up. With your lids closed keep your eyes rolled up and move them slowly back and forth from left-up to right-up. If your eyes are watering, this may flush the object down to the bottom lid or to the corner of the eye where it will be easier to extract.

If you are unable to move it out this way, get a cup of water (preferably non-chlorinated because chlorine really burns), and with your head down over the cup, hold your affected eye in the water and blink, blink, blink. You can get what is called an eye cup that is specifically for washing out eyes. It fits perfectly around the eye. I also recommend using real eyewash if you can. This is generally just saline solution (mildly salty water), but is so much more comfortable to the delicate tissue of the eye. There are also bottles of saline wash that have a squirt top to irrigate the foreign particle out. Just lay the person down, pick up the eyelashes, and squirt under the lid.

I do not recommend probing around with sticks or cotton swabs. Leave this to an eye care professional. If the cornea has been scratched, medication may be needed to ease the pain. When in doubt, go to an eye doctor. Taping an eye patch over the (closed) affected eye will help immobilize it until you can get help.

Insect Stings

For the most part, I do not get too excited about insect stings, but it is a good idea to find out if your workers have allergies, and, if they do, how severe their allergy is. If they have had severe reactions to insect stings they need to bring an adrenaline kit with them to work (as ordered by their doctor) and know how to use it. Anaphylactic reactions can happen in a matter of minutes and it might not be enough time to get the EMS team there. It is pretty scary. If the reaction is slow coming on, sometimes all that is needed is a strong antihistamine. Whatever the case, be as prepared as you can be.

Most of the time people will have the standard reaction of pain and localized swelling. This reaction may be enhanced if you are hot and sweaty. Sometimes people think they are allergic when it may just be the state of their body at the time they were stung. There might even be a slight systemic (whole body) response if your blood is really pumping. It depends on a lot of factors including your own immune system, the type of insect, and the state of your body at the time you are stung.

If it is a good-sized hornet or bee, look for the remains of the stinger. If it is visible, try scraping it off/out with something stiff like a credit card or driver's license. Then, put a cold pack on the sting if you are concerned about swelling. It is normal to have some tingling and perhaps soreness the next day in the area of the sting, especially if it was a hornet or something like a bumblebee. I have found Calendula flowers, rubbed onto the affected area right away, take a lot of the sting and swelling out. This even works for fire ants and stinging or bull nettle.

Supplies for a Simple First Aid Kit

Ace Bandages. Have a couple of different sizes (two to three inches) with clips or safety pins to secure in place when applied. These bandages are good for holding bulky dressings in place and for supporting an ankle or wrist that has been injured. The bandage should be snug but not tight and you must check circulation in the area below the bandage to make sure it is not too constricted.

Adhesive Dressings. Prepackaged and in different sizes from small to large.

Antibiotic Ointment. If not used up within a year, replace with a new tube.

Butterfly Adhesive Strips. These are used to close open wounds long enough to get the person to a doctor for sutures if necessary.

Eye Cup. Made of ceramic or glass and used for cleaning debris out of eyes.

Eye Patches. Gauze patches made especially for eye injuries. Can be secured in place with an eye patch sling or tape.

Eye Wash. Saline solution in squirt bottles to help rinse debris out of eyes.

Fabric Strips. Clean, one- and two-inch strips, torn (or cut) from an old sheet and rolled up. Can be used for holding dressings in place, or in the case of serious injuries like a broken limb, to secure a splint in place.

Gauze. Prepackaged gauze squares in various sizes and rolls of sterile gauze to dress and wrap wounds.

Notepad and Pen/Pencil. For taking down vital signs or observations in times of emergencies.

Plastic/Latex Gloves. Can be purchased in boxes and are used any time you are exposed to a person's body fluids like blood or mucous membranes.

Safety Pins. All sizes for securing ace bandages or fabric strips on dressings.

Scissors and Tape. Clean bandage scissors (not the ones used to snip your plants) for cutting gauze and fabric and first aid tape for securing dressings in place.

Splints. For broken fingers or for immobilizing a wounded area of the hand. Popsicle sticks can be used. These sticks are readily available at craft stores.

Square Fabric for Arm Sling. Should be about 24-36" square to be folded in half and tied at the shoulder to immobilize an arm or shoulder.

Tweezers. Get good-quality, fine-point tweezers for picking out thorns or splinters. The ones with an attached magnifying glass are great for finding those invisible little stickers that you know are there because you can feel them, but you can't see them without help.

Remember, this was not designed to be a first aid course. It's just a brief glimpse of things you are most likely to see in the day-to-day running of a business of this sort. I still recommend a real course in first aid. It can help everyone be more calm and effective in an emergency situation and may save a life.

Hydration

On any given day, every adult should consume up to two quarts of water. You can easily double that amount if you work in a hot, humid greenhouse environment. Do *not* wait until you are thirsty. If you wait that long, your body is already in a deficit. Now I mean *water* (H_2O), not tea, soft drinks, beer or other carbonated beverages. Leave the caffeine at home. Caffeine actually dehydrates you more by encouraging diuresis (makes you pee more). Your body needs water to keep joints and mucous membranes lubricated, flush out toxins and metabolic by-products, keep your blood flowing, maintain brain function and muscle health, etc. If you want nutrients, eat some fruit, raw nuts or an energy bar. You do not need calories in your water. If you do not care for water, squeeze a lemon or lime into your jug in the morning before you head out to work. It adds virtually no calories but enough flavor to make it more palatable to finicky water drinkers.

I have always encouraged my workers to bring their own thermos or cooler if they want cold water to drink. Of course we have water at the greenhouse, which is available to anyone, but people have very specific preferences in the area of water. Some want cold water, some want bottled water, and some just bring a cup. I don't care as long as they drink water. It is kind of amusing how we sort of check up on each other to see if everybody is drinking their water.

Eye, Lung and Skin Care

This is just to remind you of some simple things you can do to protect yourself from the ravages of the horticulture business. If you are working with dry materials like perlite, vermiculite and peat moss, wearing a simple dust mask and clear, protective goggles may save your delicate eye and lung tissues from damage. If you have ever mixed your own soil with these products without protection, you were probably picking the stuff out of your eyes and nose the next morning. Remember, perlite is a glass-like substance and the fine dust you breathe into your lungs may irritate at the least, and possibly even embed itself into the lung lining—not worth the risk in my opinion.

My hands look ten to 15 years older than my chronological age because I have a hard time using gloves for simple activities like potting plants and mixing soil. The grit and dirt really does dry out the skin and I have small- to medium-sized scratches, nicks and cuts on my hands all the time. If you are concerned about your hands, there are some really good quality garden gloves available that are flexible enough to work in comfortably and sturdy enough to protect your skin. I am a very tactile person so gloves make me crazy, but I do wear them when doing heavy lifting, weeding, clearing and whenever I am putting my hands into a space I can't see (where unknown creepy crawlers might be lurking).

Regarding sunscreen, if you are fair-to-medium skinned it is probably a good idea to wear sunscreen. Most likely, hats and shade are the only things that are really going to protect you. I sweat so much in the summer that sunscreen would be a waste of time. Even long sleeves don't protect much in Texas summers. The current wisdom is to avoid burning. If you expose your skin very gradually (as you would if you worked from winter into spring), you minimize some of the damage and give your skin time to adapt to sunny conditions. I use comfrey oil on my skin in the morning before I go out and at night before bed for skin lubrication and to help heal any potential damage. Regularly using something on your skin that aids in healing UV damage is a good idea.

Work Area

Try to get most of your outside work done in the early morning or cool evening hours to avoid exposure to the high, intensely hot summer sun. If possible, set up a well-shaded work area inside or outside the greenhouse for tasks during the day. By setting up your day this way, you can dodge the most dangerous conditions and still get your work done. And if you are really smart, you can set up your day so that most of your work is done between 6:30 or 7:00 a.m. and 1:30 or 2:00 p.m. Then rest for a few hours and come back when the sun is lower in the sky and temperatures are cooler. I do this in the late spring and summer and average seven to nine hours per day of productive greenhouse and garden work.

Keeping your work area uncluttered is probably going to be one of your greatest challenges. We often mimic my father when we trip over something blocking our path as he often releases several verbal expletives, mumbling something about how there is always something in the way. As hard as we try, the work area just gets cluttered. Every few days we signal "time out" and clean it up a bit, but when there is a lot of activity going on in the area it is hard to keep it neat. Marilyn, my loyal help, is always picking up after me and putting things away. If it were not for her, we would never be able to find anything. Keeping your work area organized can relieve a lot of stress and perhaps prevent a few mishaps as well. Following are some ideas that I use in my business.

Keep a tool bucket, drawer or container of some kind to hold things you use every day such as scissors, pocket knives, pruners and any miscellaneous stuff you find handy for working with plants. We keep our plug poppers and plug planting utensils in our container too.

We have lots of hand-written labels for our newly planted flats to make sure we know what we planted. It is also for the benefit of those who come through who are not so familiar with the plants. When the permanent pot labels go in, the flat labels come out, and often go into a rather unorganized pile. It was really a pain to have to go through the pile every time I wanted to label a plug tray or flat and I often would make new labels (waste, waste, waste). Now we have an alphabetized system using old six-pack plant containers and the labels to be recycled go into the appropriate slot.

Keep a real tool box with wrenches, pliers, screw drivers, files (for keeping tools sharp), spare hose washers, hose cutoff valves, WD-40, Teflon pipe tape, electrical tape, duct tape (indispensable), and anything else you can think of that you might use as maintenance supplies and equipment.

Think long and hard about how to put your work area together. Consider the various activities you will be engaged in and arrange work stations that flow. For instance, if you are popping plugs and planting, you have four distinct activities going on:

1. Someone is getting the plugs ready for planting.
2. Someone is pre-filling containers and trays for planting.
3. Someone is planting the plugs.
4. Someone is taking the planted flats, putting them on the bench, then watering and fertilizing them.

There may only be one or two of you doing this work, but you can make it flow. If your soil bin is near the planting station, then there is no time wasted in carrying the soil-filled flats over to the planting area. If your plug prep station is near the planting area then the readied plugs can just be handed off to the planter. I realize this is ideal, but it really is something to think about. I have rearranged our work area many times trying to get the right organization, and things flow pretty well right now.

Last, but not least, have comfortable heights for work tables and chairs or stools. Working at an uncomfortable height is very stressful on the neck and back. I recommend stools because they are much easier to get on and off quickly, and to get out of with a flat in hand. It is also easier to sit with good posture on a stool.

Benches

Have your greenhouse benches at a good height. If you are not sure what this height is for you then try taking a ground to hip measurement and start with that. You should be able to comfortably reach the center of your bench without bending too much. If you have to bend way over to pick up a flat, you are setting yourself up for low back pain. Height is also important to consider when you are hand watering. If the bench is too high, you will put a lot of stress on your upper back and shoulders while wielding the watering wand.

If your benches are made with wire mesh, be sure all stray wires are tucked in around the edges. If wood is used, sand down rough places and break or saw off splintered pieces. If there is something to get you, it will.

Carts and Hand Trucks (Dollies)

We have two carts with big, air-inflated, spoke-type wheels and we use them constant-ly. We use them for hauling bags of soil supplies to the bin, for 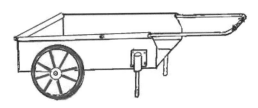 carrying plants from inside to outside benches (and vice versa), for carrying garden weeds to the compost pile, etc. The big wheels make the difference in terms of ease in use. I don't know how we ever got along without these beauties. They are a must for anyone carting a lot of things back and forth.

 Hand trucks (dollies) are good for moving items that have a solid shape like boxes, shrink-wrapped containers or large, heavy bags. I have a hand truck that converts to a cart for carrying things on four wheels. I used to keep my 15-gallon sprayer on it, but since I rarely use that anymore, it is now used for carrying multiple flats from one place to anoth-er. It is really quite handy. Either carts or hand trucks are bet-

ter than trying to carry heavy or unwieldy supplies, plants or trash unaided.

Keeping your workplace safe and dealing with emergencies means thinking ahead and using good sense. If you have the plans in place you will save yourself and others a lot of trouble.

Epilogue

Since I began writing this book several years ago, I have witnessed a subtle change in the horticulture industry. In mainstream horticulture journals there are more articles on alternative pest management, mandatory water reclamation, and low-impact fertilizing, with more emphasis on cultural practices to manage pest problems and plant growth and development. Although the changes are slow and there are many in the business that still can't think beyond the deep groove of habit in which they are entrenched, there is no doubt that many are deciding to reduce the environmental impact they are creating in the day-to-day production of container plants.

I am sure now that in my lifetime the management of container plants described in this book (or certainly something similar) will be the normal and customary method used. Not only is the consumer demanding a safer world, but the industry is losing its fear that the change will have a negative impact on profitability. Organic methods are simply a different way of dealing with the challenges of commercial plant production. As distributors of horticultural products see the shift, there will be more organic, low-impact supplies available to those who want to move in that direction. As it is right now, many distributors won't carry these products because there is not enough demand. That is where you come in. Demand it. Exert your right to have these products as readily available as the chemicals and old (tired) standard products.

You are the future of horticulture. Make it count. Show the industry how it is done. Give your customers an alternative. Demonstrate to other growers why this is the better, saner method. Be the poster person for organic horticulture.

I wouldn't do it any other way.

Dear Mother

So often I have pondered why my
   spirit's drawn to you.
What is this energy you have, to do
   the things you do?
To work these forces 'round us with
   the flicker of your hand.
(I hardly fathom how you turn a
   mountain into sand.)

And cycles, oh my goodness, how they never seem deterred.
Seeds with awesome powers, and migration of the birds.
A brown and dormant twig bursts into life with coming spring.
In fall your children put to bed awaiting winter's sting.

I admit I'm still amazed at the tenacity
   you yield.
The constant tests we put you through
   you manage yet to heal.
Your patience with our blunders now we
   rarely do deserve.
You barely have recovered when we throw
   another curve.

So many of your children really want to make you proud.
I stand before you now as one who wants to show you how.
Your Earth is safe in this small patch, the place I call my own.
My garden is a haven, safe from horrors you have known.

Your flowers grow and fliers fly
  and buzzers buzz away.
Your birds sing songs contentedly
  in trees allowed to stay.
Your spiders, lizards, snakes and frogs
  are welcome living here.
Even mice and other furry creatures
  have no fear.

I just want to be a part of all that makes you what you are.
To let you work your magic while I watch you, not too far.
To know your breath in wind and feel your cooling gentle rain.
Reflecting on the facets of your exquisite domain.

I'll sit among the briars and I'll tolerate the heat.
Your precious weeds grow vigorously underneath my feet.
I've endured the bites and stings of creeping, crawling things.
I've felt the nip of icy winds and all that winter brings.

These things I know are all a part of this place you've given us.
We are the shepherds of this stead and care for it we must.
So Mother dear, please don't despair, I promise we will try.
We know the wonder of your Earth, your trust we won't belie.

—*Louise Placek*

Appendices

Appendix A
Activity Logs & Miscellaneous Forms

I created the following logs to assist in record keeping. Each was developed for specific tasks to keep track of all the activity relating to germination, plug planting, stepping up, cuttings, etc. These records are useful when you sit down to do your growing plan for the season as they help you determine time frames for plant development and sale cycles. All the logs were kept in a three-ring notebook at the greenhouse for easy access. I have found managers to have very personal preferences regarding flow charts, logs and other paperwork, so use these templates as they are, or let them be an inspiration for something that works for you. *(Note: The forms on pages 216-220 and the employee handbook on pages 221-229 have been reduced for space considerations. They can be enlarged on a photocopier. These pages are also available as downloadable files at www.acresusa.com/extras/madefromscratch.htm.)*

Plant Activity Log. Use this form when you are stepping up a large number of established plants. If you have eight flats of four-inch rosemary that need to be repotted, you can record the date, root condition, old and new pot size, number planted, and any notes on the plant condition.

2/20/99 Plant: Rosemary - Upright   Root Condition: ___Weak ✓Strong ✓Thick ___Thin

From: ___PT ___2" ___4" ___Qt ___6" ___Gal ___Other Rooted Cuttings   Plants/pot: 1

To: ___6 Pk ___2" ✓4" ___Qt ___6" ___Gal ___2 G ___3 G ___HB 8" ___HB 10" ___Planter (___)

Planted: 333 Note: Approx 95% rooted - Good Batch (about 16½ flats - 20ct)

Germination Log. When we plant seeds, we record the date, plant name, and date of germination. We soon produced so many types of plants by seed that I had to segregate the germination logs by plant type (*i.e.*, vegetables were divided into four categories: tomatoes, greens, lettuce, and miscellaneous).

Date:	Plant:	288	OT	Other	Germ Date
2/15/2000	Burbank	2	___	___	2/20/2000
" /11/ "	Lillian's Yellow Heirloom	1	___	___	2/21/2000
2/16/2000	Peacevine Cherry	2	___	___	2/22/2000

Individual Plant Logs. These logs are kept by category. Record the individual plant name (*i.e.*, Burbank tomato), container size, and date planted with the number of flats or containers planted. Each time a new batch of Burbank tomatoes is germinated, go back to that entry and record the date and number of flats.

Type __Tomato Burbank__ Size ___ 4" (no flats) ___ 6" (no ea) __6 pack__ other (6 per flat)

2 /30/00 (14.5) __/__/__ ( ) __/__/__ ( ) __/__/__ ( )
3 /15/ 00 (7) __/__/__ ( ) __/__/__ ( ) __/__/__ ( )
__/__/__ ( ) __/__/__ ( ) __/__/__ ( ) __/__/__ ( )

Rooted Plant Material. When new cuttings are put into rooting medium log the name of the plant, source of the cuttings, type of rooting medium, date plant was placed in the medium, and number planted. There is also a place to note the condition of the cuttings or anything else that might affect the rooting process.

Plant Name: __Rosemary - Upright__ **Date Cut:** __11__/__13__/__98__
Source of Plant: __✓__MHF Stock Plants ____ Field Cuttings ____Other
Rooting Material Used: __25%__Vermiculite __25%__Perlite __50%__Peat ____Coir
Date Planted: __11__/__13__/__98__ **# Planted:** ____Flats ____Cells __350__Open Tray
Notes: __Rained the day before — Beautiful, hydrated cuttings__

Daily Note. This is a generic monthly page I use (large calendars are also good for this purpose) to remind myself of things that need to get done, bug scouting reports, brief observations of activities, or anything that does not need a journal's worth of space.

Month __April__   **Year** __1999__

NOTE

SUN ___ _____
MON ___ _____
TUE ___ _____
WED ___
THU _1_ Call Johnny's Seeds re order — Have Susan read orientation manual
FRI _2_ Grow IT Nursery calling about tomatoes — Out right now — will have 'em later
SAT _3_ Order, Fish Emulsion & Peat Moss

SUN _4_ Need to do some more sw basil !!
MON _5_ TDA inspection today — Fertilized ½ greenhouse
TUE _6_ Fertilized rest of plants — Did some 'basil plugs
WED _7_ Big week — lots of orders
THU _8_ Deliv. — Austin   Grow IT called again while I was out.
FRI _9_ Deliv. — San Antonio
SAT _10_ Need to take the plastic off the GH — Order more flats

Handwritten Invoice. A simple invoice that meets your individual needs can be created on a word processor. Just print out multiple copies and use carbon paper between two of them so you have a copy to give the customer and one for your records. Just be sure to keep track of invoice numbers so they match the order in which they were written. In other words, if the last invoice you created in your program was #134, then you need to start your handwritten invoices with #135.

Invoice # *135*

The Name of your Business
Your Address
PH & FAX
Email address (optional)

Sold To
Grow Green Nursery
9999 Randy Road
Best Town, Texas

Phone: *666-6666*

Invoice Date *10 , 10 , 00*
Ordered By *Grantus Green*
Sold By *LP*
P O #

# of Flats	Pot Size	Pack Qty.	# of Plants	Description	Unit Cost	Totals	
2	4 "	18		*Sweet Basil*	12.60	25.20	
2	4 "	18		*Apple Mint*	12.60	25.20	
5	6 pk	6		*1 flat ea of all the lettuce varieties*	10.00	50.00	
				Total		100.40	

Received By *G. Green*   Date *10 10 00*

Sample Availability List. This is an example of a list one might send out to potential wholesale customers. Note that is has all the information I listed in the discussion in the *Marketing and Merchandising* chapter.

Date___/___/___

Wellgrown Plant Nursery
1234 Country Lane
Best Town, Anywhere

Ph: (333) 555-6666
Fax: (333) 555-7777

All Plants Certified Organically Grown

Availability for 3/3/99			A=annual P=perennial B=biennial	
Order	Description	Avail	Comments	A/P/B
	Herbs		**4 inch, 18 count flat - $12.60/flat**	A/P/B
	Sweet Basil, Compact Genovese	6	Medium green, deeply scented. Excellent for pesto.	A
	Thyme, German Winter	4	Sturdy plant. Classic, spicy flavor.	P
	Rosemary, Upright	4	Beautiful, dark green bushy plant. Strong flavor. To 5' x 4-5'.	P
	Spearmint	7	Classic tea mint, like grandma had in her garden.	P
	Apple Mint	4	Mild, fruity mint with heavenly scent.	P
	Orange Mint	4	Strong, bergamot flavor. Good for fruit salads.	P
	Lemon Balm	3	Sprawling shrub w/light green, lemon scented & flavored leaves.	P
	Peppers		**4 inch, 18 count flat - $10.00/flat**	
	Bell, "Yankee Bell"	8	Open pollenated. Sturdy. Medium size, green-to-red sweet peppers.	A
	Cayenne	8	Long slender pods from green to red. Very hot.	A/P
	Jalapeno	6	Non-hybrid. Lots of medium green to red pods. 1" x 2". Hot, good flavor.	A/P
	Bolivian Rainbow Pepper (Orn)	5	Shrub to 3' with loads of 1" hot peppers ranging from purple to tan to orange to red.	A/P
	Vegetables		**6 packs, 6 count flat - $10.00/flat**	
	Lettuce, "Vulcan"	7	Beautiful, sl frilly, light green lettuce with pink to reddish blush. Mild flavor.	A
	Lettuce, "Black Seeded Simpson"	7	Light green, sl frilly, mild flavor.	A
	Lettuce, "Rouge D'Hiver"	6	Medium size, red tinged romaine. Good flavor.	A
	Lettuce, Red Oakleaf	4	Deep red leaves shaped like Spanish oaks. Mild flavor. Beautiful in salads.	A
	Lettuce, Green Oakleaf	5	Same as the red, only a medium green and a sl stronger flavor.	A
	Mustard Green, "Osaka Purple"	6	Spicy, med-to-large leaves with almost irridescent purple/red color. My favorite mustard.	A
	Mustard Green, Mizuna	8	Mildly spicy, medium green with sharply pointed, lobed leaves. Good salad green.	A
	Mustard Green, "Tatsoi"	5	Mild, deep green, sm to med leaves turned under like a spoon. Beautiful rosette growth.	A

Ordered by:_____

Weekly Wholesale Inventory. This is used to keep track of what has been sold and what is still available. Orders are marked as received (by phone or by fax) so that current availability is at your fingertips at all times until delivery day. The total number available at the beginning of the week is typed in directly under each plant name. Using sweet basil as an example, the beginning count was six flats. Grow More Nursery ordered two flats which left me with four (circled). Green Things Nursery didn't order any basil, but Plants R Us ordered two flats which left me with two (circled). By circling the number left over, it makes it easier to see when you enter the next order. At the end of the week, having this in front of you when you create your invoices makes it a cinch to figure out who ordered what.

Circling the number left after the current order makes it easier to see as you work your way down the page.

CUSTOMER	Sw Basil 6	Thyme 4	Rosemary 4	Spearmint 7	Apple Mint 4	OrangeMint 4	LemnBalm 3		Ppr Bell 8	Ppr Cayenne 8	Ppr Jalep 6
Grow More	2	4	1	3	2	2	2	5				2	1		2	6	1	7	1	5
Green Things											1	5	1	6	1	4
Plants R Us	2	2	2	1	2	0	2	3	2	2	2	2	2	-1		1	4	1	4	1	3

CUSTOMER	Ppr BRB 5	Ltc Vulcan 7	Ltc BSS 7	Ltc RDvh 6	Ltc RdOak 4	Ltc GrOak 6		Osaka Pur 6	Mizuna 8	Tatsoi 5
Grow More	2	3	1	4	1	6	1	5	1	3	1	4		1	5	1	7	1	4
Green Things	1	2	1	5	1	5	1	4	1	2	1	3		1	4	1	6	1	3
Plants R Us	1	1	1	4	1	9	1	3	1	1	1	2		1	3	1	4	1	2

PLANT ACTIVITY LOG

___/___/___ Plant:_____ Root Condition: ___Weak ___Strong ___Thick ___Thin

From: ___PT ___2" ___4" ___Qt ___6" ___Gal ___ Other_____ Plants per pot: _____

To: ___6 Pk ___2" ___4" ___Qt ___6" ___Gal ___2 Gal ___3 Gal ___HB 8" ___HB 10" ___Planter (___")

Planted:_____ Note: _____

___/___/___ Plant:_____ Root Condition: ___Weak ___Strong ___Thick ___Thin

From: ___PT ___2" ___4" ___Qt ___6" ___Gal ___ Other_____ Plants per pot: _____

To: ___6 Pk ___2" ___4" ___Qt ___6" ___Gal ___2 Gal ___3 Gal ___HB 8" ___HB 10" ___Planter (___")

Planted:_____ Note: _____

___/___/___ Plant:_____ Root Condition: ___Weak ___Strong ___Thick ___Thin

From: ___PT ___2" ___4" ___Qt ___6" ___Gal ___ Other_____ Plants per pot: _____

To: ___6 Pk ___2" ___4" ___Qt ___6" ___Gal ___2 Gal ___3 Gal ___HB 8" ___HB 10" ___Planter (___")

Planted:_____ Note: _____

___/___/___ Plant:_____ Root Condition: ___Weak ___Strong ___Thick ___Thin

From: ___PT ___2" ___4" ___Qt ___6" ___Gal ___ Other_____ Plants per pot: _____

To: ___6 Pk ___2" ___4" ___Qt ___6" ___Gal ___2 Gal ___3 Gal ___HB 8" ___HB 10" ___Planter (___")

Planted:_____ Note: _____

___/___/___ Plant:_____ Root Condition: ___Weak ___Strong ___Thick ___Thin

From: ___PT ___2" ___4" ___Qt ___6" ___Gal ___ Other_____ Plants per pot: _____

To: ___6 Pk ___2" ___4" ___Qt ___6" ___Gal ___2 Gal ___3 Gal ___HB 8" ___HB 10" ___Planter (___")

Planted:_____ Note: _____

___/___/___ Plant:_____ Root Condition: ___Weak ___Strong ___Thick ___Thin

From: ___PT ___2" ___4" ___Qt ___6" ___Gal ___ Other_____ Plants per pot: _____

To: ___6 Pk ___2" ___4" ___Qt ___6" ___Gal ___2 Gal ___3 Gal ___HB 8" ___HB 10" ___Planter (___")

Planted:_____ Note: _____

GERMINATION LOG

Date:	Plant:	288	OT	Other	Germ Date
__/__/__	_____	___	___	___	__/__/__
__/__/__	_____	___	___	___	__/__/__
__/__/__	_____	___	___	___	__/__/__
__/__/__	_____	___	___	___	__/__/__
__/__/__	_____	___	___	___	__/__/__
__/__/__	_____	___	___	___	__/__/__
__/__/__	_____	___	___	___	__/__/__
__/__/__	_____	___	___	___	__/__/__
__/__/__	_____	___	___	___	__/__/__
__/__/__	_____	___	___	___	__/__/__
__/__/__	_____	___	___	___	__/__/__
__/__/__	_____	___	___	___	__/__/__
__/__/__	_____	___	___	___	__/__/__
__/__/__	_____	___	___	___	__/__/__
__/__/__	_____	___	___	___	__/__/__
__/__/__	_____	___	___	___	__/__/__
__/__/__	_____	___	___	___	__/__/__
__/__/__	_____	___	___	___	__/__/__
__/__/__	_____	___	___	___	__/__/__
__/__/__	_____	___	___	___	__/__/__
__/__/__	_____	___	___	___	__/__/__
__/__/__	_____	___	___	___	__/__/__
__/__/__	_____	___	___	___	__/__/__
__/__/__	_____	___	___	___	__/__/__
__/__/__	_____	___	___	___	__/__/__
__/__/__	_____	___	___	___	__/__/__
__/__/__	_____	___	___	___	__/__/__
__/__/__	_____	___	___	___	__/__/__
__/__/__	_____	___	___	___	__/__/__
__/__/__	_____	___	___	___	__/__/__
__/__/__	_____	___	___	___	__/__/__
__/__/__	_____	___	___	___	__/__/__
__/__/__	_____	___	___	___	__/__/__
__/__/__	_____	___	___	___	__/__/__
__/__/__	_____	___	___	___	__/__/__
__/__/__	_____	___	___	___	__/__/__
__/__/__	_____	___	___	___	__/__/__
__/__/__	_____	___	___	___	__/__/__
__/__/__	_____	___	___	___	__/__/__
__/__/__	_____	___	___	___	__/__/__
__/__/__	_____	___	___	___	__/__/__
__/__/__	_____	___	___	___	__/__/__
__/__/__	_____	___	___	___	__/__/__

Individual Plant Log

Type: _____ Size: ___4" (# flats) ___6-pk (# flats) _____Other (# flats or ea)

___/___/___ (   )   ___/___/___ (   )   ___/___/___ (   )   ___/___/___ (   )
___/___/___ (   )   ___/___/___ (   )   ___/___/___ (   )   ___/___/___ (   )
___/___/___ (   )   ___/___/___ (   )   ___/___/___ (   )   ___/___/___ (   )
___/___/___ (   )   ___/___/___ (   )   ___/___/___ (   )   ___/___/___ (   )

Type: _____ Size: ___4" (# flats) ___6-pk (# flats) _____Other (# flats or ea)

___/___/___ (   )   ___/___/___ (   )   ___/___/___ (   )   ___/___/___ (   )
___/___/___ (   )   ___/___/___ (   )   ___/___/___ (   )   ___/___/___ (   )
___/___/___ (   )   ___/___/___ (   )   ___/___/___ (   )   ___/___/___ (   )
___/___/___ (   )   ___/___/___ (   )   ___/___/___ (   )   ___/___/___ (   )

Type: _____ Size: ___4" (# flats) ___6-pk (# flats) _____Other (# flats or ea)

___/___/___ (   )   ___/___/___ (   )   ___/___/___ (   )   ___/___/___ (   )
___/___/___ (   )   ___/___/___ (   )   ___/___/___ (   )   ___/___/___ (   )
___/___/___ (   )   ___/___/___ (   )   ___/___/___ (   )   ___/___/___ (   )
___/___/___ (   )   ___/___/___ (   )   ___/___/___ (   )   ___/___/___ (   )

Type: _____ Size: ___4" (# flats) ___6-pk (# flats) _____Other (# flats or ea)

___/___/___ (   )   ___/___/___ (   )   ___/___/___ (   )   ___/___/___ (   )
___/___/___ (   )   ___/___/___ (   )   ___/___/___ (   )   ___/___/___ (   )
___/___/___ (   )   ___/___/___ (   )   ___/___/___ (   )   ___/___/___ (   )
___/___/___ (   )   ___/___/___ (   )   ___/___/___ (   )   ___/___/___ (   )

Type: _____ Size: ___4" (# flats) ___6-pk (# flats) _____Other (# flats or ea)

___/___/___ (   )   ___/___/___ (   )   ___/___/___ (   )   ___/___/___ (   )
___/___/___ (   )   ___/___/___ (   )   ___/___/___ (   )   ___/___/___ (   )
___/___/___ (   )   ___/___/___ (   )   ___/___/___ (   )   ___/___/___ (   )
___/___/___ (   )   ___/___/___ (   )   ___/___/___ (   )   ___/___/___ (   )

Type: _____ Size: ___4" (# flats) ___6-pk (# flats) _____Other (# flats or ea)

___/___/___ (   )   ___/___/___ (   )   ___/___/___ (   )   ___/___/___ (   )
___/___/___ (   )   ___/___/___ (   )   ___/___/___ (   )   ___/___/___ (   )
___/___/___ (   )   ___/___/___ (   )   ___/___/___ (   )   ___/___/___ (   )
___/___/___ (   )   ___/___/___ (   )   ___/___/___ (   )   ___/___/___ (   )

Type: _____ Size: ___4" (# flats) ___6-pk (# flats) _____Other (# flats or ea)

___/___/___ (   )   ___/___/___ (   )   ___/___/___ (   )   ___/___/___ (   )
___/___/___ (   )   ___/___/___ (   )   ___/___/___ (   )   ___/___/___ (   )
___/___/___ (   )   ___/___/___ (   )   ___/___/___ (   )   ___/___/___ (   )
___/___/___ (   )   ___/___/___ (   )   ___/___/___ (   )   ___/___/___ (   )

Rooted Plant Material

Plant Name:_____ Date Cut: ___/___/___
Source of Plant Material: ____Stock Plants ____Field Cuttings _____Other
Rooting Material Used: %____Vermiculite %____ Perlite %____Peat %____Coir ____Other
Date Planted: ___/___/___ # Cuttings:___ Put In: ____Flats ____Cells ____Open Tray
Notes:_____

Plant Name:_____ Date Cut: ___/___/___
Source of Plant Material: ____Stock Plants ____Field Cuttings _____Other
Rooting Material Used: %____Vermiculite %____ Perlite %____Peat %____Coir ____Other
Date Planted: ___/___/___ # Cuttings:___ Put In: ____Flats ____Cells ____Open Tray
Notes:_____

Plant Name:_____ Date Cut: ___/___/___
Source of Plant Material: ____Stock Plants ____Field Cuttings _____Other
Rooting Material Used: %____Vermiculite %____ Perlite %____Peat %____Coir ____Other
Date Planted: ___/___/___ # Cuttings:___ Put In: ____Flats ____Cells ____Open Tray
Notes:_____

Plant Name:_____ Date Cut: ___/___/___
Source of Plant Material: ____Stock Plants ____Field Cuttings _____Other
Rooting Material Used: %____Vermiculite %____ Perlite %____Peat %____Coir ____Other
Date Planted: ___/___/___ # Cuttings:___ Put In: ____Flats ____Cells ____Open Tray
Notes:_____

Plant Name:_____ Date Cut: ___/___/___
Source of Plant Material: ____Stock Plants ____Field Cuttings _____Other
Rooting Material Used: %____Vermiculite %____ Perlite %____Peat %____Coir ____Other
Date Planted: ___/___/___ # Cuttings:___ Put In: ____Flats ____Cells ____Open Tray
Notes:_____

Plant Name:_____ Date Cut: ___/___/___
Source of Plant Material: ____Stock Plants ____Field Cuttings _____Other
Rooting Material Used: %____Vermiculite %____ Perlite %____Peat %____Coir ____Other
Date Planted: ___/___/___ # Cuttings:___ Put In: ____Flats ____Cells ____Open Tray
Notes:_____

Plant Name:_____ Date Cut: ___/___/___
Source of Plant Material: ____Stock Plants ____Field Cuttings _____Other
Rooting Material Used: %____Vermiculite %____ Perlite %____Peat %____Coir ____Other
Date Planted: ___/___/___ # Cuttings:___ Put In: ____Flats ____Cells ____Open Tray
Notes:_____

Plant Name:_____ Date Cut: ___/___/___
Source of Plant Material: ____Stock Plants ____Field Cuttings _____Other
Rooting Material Used: %____Vermiculite %____ Perlite %____Peat %____Coir ____Other
Date Planted: ___/___/___ # Cuttings:___ Put In: ____Flats ____Cells ____Open Tray
Notes:_____

Month_____   **Year**_____

Daily Note

SUN ___ _____
MON ___ _____
TUE ___ _____
WED ___ _____
THU ___ _____
FRI ___ _____
SAT ___ _____

SUN ___ _____
MON ___ _____
TUE ___ _____
WED ___ _____
THU ___ _____
FRI ___ _____
SAT ___ _____

SUN ___ _____
MON ___ _____
TUE ___ _____
WED ___ _____
THU ___ _____
FRI ___ _____
SAT ___ _____

SUN ___ _____
MON ___ _____
TUE ___ _____
WED ___ _____
THU ___ _____
FRI ___ _____
SAT ___ _____

SUN ___ _____
MON ___ _____
TUE ___ _____
WED ___ _____
THU ___ _____
FRI ___ _____
SAT ___ _____

Goals:_____
_____

Appendix B
Employee Orientation/Procedures

Who Are You Working for?

Misty Hill Farm is a producer of certified organic herb, vegetable and ornamental plants. Organic certification is through the Texas Department of Agriculture as is the license to sell nursery and floral plants. Organic certification means that all plants grown by Misty Hill Farm, from seed or cutting to finished plant, have not been exposed to any chemical fertilizers, herbicides, fungicides or pesticides. All fertilizers are earth-based and natural. Pest control is primarily preventative, using close observation and beneficial insects such as ladybeetles and lacewings as a first line of defense. If pest insect populations become too high then soap and/or botanical insecticides are used to bring the levels down. Disease is controlled primarily by keeping the environment clean; *i.e.,* debris and dead or diseased plants are removed from the growing area as soon as discovered.

By law, a product (such as a plant) cannot be labeled "organic" unless the producer has met standards set forth by the Texas Department of Agriculture and the producer has been annually inspected for compliance. This and a yearly fee paid by the grower keep certification current.

Mixing Soil

6 cu. ft. (3 bags)	Composted Pine Bark (Most companies call it "soil conditioner")
3 cu. ft.	Peat Moss (loose)
1 cu. ft.	Extra Coarse Vermiculite
1 cu. ft.	Coarse Vermiculite
1 cu. ft.	Perlite
1.5 cu. ft. (1 bag)	Back-to-Earth Fine Screened Soil Conditioner (non-defoliated cotton burr compost)
5 gal. (40-50 lbs.)	Knippa Basalt or Decomposed Granite Sand (these come in bulk)

| 2-2½ gal. | Bat Guano (about 6-7 lbs.) |
| 2 cans (28-30oz) | Soft Rock Phosphate (cans are like from canned tomatoes or some other vegetable) |

• Components spread in even layers are easier to mix.
• Peat moss must be broken up (loosened) before mixing in.
• Cotton burr compost must sometimes be broken-up before mixing in.
• Wear a mask when measuring out the perlite and vermiculite and when mixing the soil.
• Use flat blade shovel to check sides, corners and bottom of bin for "pockets" of individual soil components.
• Keep soil covered with plastic when not using to retain moisture.
• Use cart to carry soil components to the bin. Do not carry them yourself from the shed!

Working With Plugs

Plug Trays are the molded plastic trays that are seeded using a vacuum seeder, or by hand (in the case of large seeds). They produce small plants that are easier to handle and allow more uniformity for a better-looking end product. The plug trays we use have 288 individual cells that are filled with a special plug soil that allows the tiny roots to move and grow easily.

Germination of the seed is when the embryonic leaves called cotyledons appear just above the soil surface. These are not real leaves but a temporary food storage system that keep the plant going until the "true" leaves appear and start manufacturing food. The time it takes a seed to germinate varies according to plant genes and specific seed requirements such as light, day/night length, soil temperature or moisture levels. From the time seeds are planted in the trays, a record is kept of when they germinate, to when they are planted. Plug trays must never be allowed to dry out, especially before and during germination. When these tiny, delicate plugs become dry it produces stress in the plant that it may never overcome. Often, a "stressed" plug becomes a stunted, yellow, struggling plant.

Guidelines for Planting Plugs:

• A plug is ready to be planted when it has at least one full set of "true" leaves (the leaves that appear following the cotyledon). Some plants need two sets. If you are not sure, check the root system. If the root fills the cell, then it is time.

• Have your soil-filled containers in flats ready ahead of time so plants can go right into the pot after being removed from the plug tray. This means you need to know what size container the plugs are going into, which is usually a six-pack or four-inch. Sometimes they go into hanging baskets. If you are not sure, ask.

• Removal of the plug from the plug tray is called "popping." The plugs are punched or popped out from the bottom of the plug tray with a plug popper. The popper is generally a rounded stick that fits into the drain hole on the bottom of the tray, and pushed gently upward until the plug eases out of the cell.

• The popped plug is then inspected and placed into a holding dish or tray. Unless all the plugs are the same size, grade the plugs by placing into three categories: small, medium and large. By doing this, you keep plants of similar size and development together in the same flat to minimize bench sorting later.

• Often the soil surface of plugs develops a greenish crust. This is moss and must be removed before planting the plug. If not removed, the moss will spread to the surface of the pot, blocking water and oxygen to the root. Even if there is no visible moss, remove the top layer of soil, to eliminate any insect eggs, bacteria and fungi that may be present.

• The tiny roots of the plug are delicate, so disturb them as little as possible. Avoid mashing roots into the soil when planting the plugs. This disrupts the microscopic root hairs that are necessary for maintaining the viability of the plant while it makes it's transition from plug tray to pot. Gently "guide" them into the soil with a tool that works best for you. The less you shock them, the faster they will adjust to their new pot and begin active growth again.

• Generally plugs should be buried deeply. Bottom leaves should be close to the soil surface. This keeps them from getting too tall in the pot before they are mature enough to leave the greenhouse. Tall does not necessarily mean ready.

Repotting Plants

Repotting is done when a plant of any size needs a larger size pot. How you do this depends on the type of plant and the extent and health of it's root system. The following are things to consider when working on a project of this nature.

Stepping Up

A plant is put into a larger pot when it is too big or mature for the pot its currently in. This may be indicated by a potted plant that falls over due to top-heavy growth or roots that have filled the pot and need more room for further growth.

• Take a 1/4"- 1/2" layer of top surface soil off all plants to be repotted as this may harbor insect eggs, plant debris, bacteria, moss, etc.

• Check new pots before using to be sure all drain holes are open. If not, they need to be popped or cut out. Proper drainage depends on drainage holes that are not blocked.

• Before repotting, examine the roots. Healthy roots are generally white or (in certain plants) pink, moderately thick, well branched, and should have molded slightly to the shape of the pot.

• If roots are especially thick, loosen by gently squeezing the root ball and, if necessary, de-tangle the roots by combing your fingers downward through them until they are loose and free.

• If the root ball cannot be easily penetrated with your finger then it is "pot-" or "root-bound." A root ball this thick needs pruning and loosening to encourage it to form healthy new roots in the larger container. The easiest way to do this is to slice four evenly spaced vertical slits from the top of the root ball to the bottom, and then peel or carve 1/2"-1" off the bottom. If roots are too tight and formed you may need to slice off the bottom half of the root ball and continue trying to comb out the roots.

• If roots are weak and spindly, remove only a little of the surface soil and plant the root ball intact.

• If brown roots are present along with the white ones, try cleaning these away until the white, healthy roots are visible and dominant.

- If you are not sure how to approach the plants you are repotting, ask for help.
- As you re-pot any plant, examine the top and undersides of the leaves. Report any discoloration of the leaves or insect infestation immediately.

A rule of thumb for stepping up a plant is to place it into a new pot no more than two inches in diameter larger than the old pot. Many plants, because they grow very slowly, must be stepped up gradually, and will not tolerate going into a new pot too big for it's root system. If the container is too big, then there is more soil than root, potentially causing the root ball to be exposed to excess moisture when the soil is watered. This may cause the root to die before it has a chance to grow into the new environment. However, there are exceptions. Many annuals and fast-growing perennials can adapt rapidly to a much larger pot because the rate of growth allows the root system to fill the new space quickly.

Insect/Disease Control

Scouting (plant inspection) should be done daily as infestations of "bad bugs" can literally happen overnight. However, do not kill anything unless you have made a positive identification of the pest. Many ominous-looking eggs, larvae, pupae, crawlers and fliers are beneficial. We do not kill spiders, as they are voracious predators of many insects we would rather not have around. Generally though, if the plant is damaged (holes, discoloration, curling, withering, etc.), and there are large numbers of some kind of insect covering the underside of the leaves, you can be reasonably sure that it is an undesirable guest.

After positive identification of the pest insect you then have to decide on the most reasonable course of action. If it is just a few pests on the leaves then mashing the insects with your fingers is fine as long as you are not damaging the plant. If it is a moderate to severe infestation, then the plants may have to be washed outside or in the sink with a strong spray of water to reduce the number ("load") of insects. Then, if there is a possibility of residual adults or eggs, spraying with a solution of soap and/or pyrethrum or neem oil may be necessary. If washing the plant would be difficult (as is often the case with leafy, vegetable six-packs), then spraying might be the only solution. In either case, when spraying, be sure to cover all surfaces of the plant. Wear gloves and pick up the leaves to make sure the underside of all the leaves and the leaf buds are coated.

When scouting, report any plants that have discolored, wilted or mottled leaves. Also report plants with dying leaf buds. Brown, gray, black, yellow or white spots or areas may indicate viral, bacterial or fungal disease. Chewing and sucking insects often carry these diseases with them from other plants outside and transfer them to the plants inside the greenhouse. In the case of bacteria and fungus, spores are frequently on plant debris or are blown in from outside. Keeping discarded trimmings and dead plant material picked up decreases plant exposure to many pathologic organisms. Pick off any leaves that are infected if only a few show signs of a problem. If the whole plant is infected it may need to be burned or tossed into the compost pile.

Preparing Plants for Delivery

A day or two prior, plants will need to be readied for delivery to the customers. This involves several steps:

• Plants will need to be inspected for problems. Look thoroughly for insects, or diseases that make the plant unsuitable for delivery. Trim off dead leaves, clean off the soil surface, and add extra soil if necessary. Do whatever is needed to make the plants attractive and presentable.

• After plants have been checked, they then need to be graded for size and quality. For instance, if you have seven flats of sweet basil to be delivered, look through the flats for any plants that are poor quality and replace them with plants that reflect the quality of the rest of the flat. Put plants of equal size together in flats. If the flats are six-packs of vegetables or flowers, then check the individual cells in the pack for dead plants, poor growth or any other inconsistency. Replace the individual cells of defective plants with good plants (there will always be extras), matching the quality of the rest of the plants in the pack. All the flats or individual container plants going out the door should be of the best and most consistent quality.

• If individual plants do not have labels, either tag them as you are grading or after the flat or individual containers are ready.

Plant tags must be upright in the container and placed in a consistent pattern in each plant in the flat. For instance, if you place the tag centered in front or in back of the four-inch plant, do the whole flat the same way. Six-packs get one tag per pack. All other individual containers get one each.

• When the plants are all ready, they must then be placed on the holding bench according to individual orders. For example if A+ Nursery ordered two flats of Basil, one flat of Oregano, two flats of Calendula and six gallons of Rosemary, then those plants will be "pulled" and placed on the holding bench together as an order. The first nursery to order gets the first and best plants. All orders must be pulled and placed on the holding bench. If there are salable plants left, and if the person delivering has room to take extra plants for sale, then those plants must be segregated on their original benches so it is clear which ones are available for sale this week.

• When it is time to load the delivery van or truck, the orders will be placed on the vehicle in the opposite order of delivery. For instance, if A+ Nursery is the last delivery of the day, then their order will be placed on the truck or van first, etc.

Routine Activities

A few activities are done on a regular basis, regardless of individual projects. Some are done on a specific day and some should be done anytime they are needed.

• Once per week, the greenhouse growing area will be swept and cleared of clutter. Used containers will be stacked and put away. Stray tools (scissors, clippers, trimmers, etc.) will be gathered and placed in their appropriate containers. Puddles will be mopped, benches cleared of leaf litter, and litter buckets emptied. This activity is usually done on Friday.

• Whenever the need is observed, consolidate and grade flats, cull out dead plants, trim away unruly foliage, pull off dead leaves, and scout for bugs.

• If the walkways are getting cluttered, take time out to clear them. Remove and/or put away used pots, folding stools, large tools, mops, brooms, flats or plants that make movement through the paths unsafe. If things are put away as you work, this won't need to be done so often.

• Clean work surfaces and areas after projects. This saves you time with the start of your next task by not having to tidy up before you begin work. Sweep up spilled soil, wipe work surface clean, stack used pots, and put planting tools in their proper containers.

• Clean tools between projects and at the end of each day. Clean metal blades of any trimming or cutting tool with scrubber and soapy water with bleach. (Solution should be one part bleach to ten parts soapy water.)

• When time allows, used gallon, six-inch and quart containers may be rinsed and washed for future use. Wash thoroughly in soapy water (as above with bleach), and rinse in vinegar water (about one cup of nine percent vinegar to five gallons of water). The vinegar removes soap and bleach residue as well as calcium deposits from the water. Drain on an empty bench, and then stack and put away.

• It is everyone's responsibility to watch the level of soil in the soil bin. If it is almost empty, collect supplies from the shed and have ready to mix a new batch right away. If everyone is working together, this can be done quickly and efficiently to decrease the pause in planting.

Watering the Plants

Watering the plants inside and outside must be done by hand with a hose and watering wand. Water only plants that need it. If the soil is wet below the surface, then do not water that plant. Sometimes plants look dry on the surface but are wet or even soggy underneath. If you have a question about it, stick your finger into the soil, at least an inch down, to determine moisture need. If you can't tell, bring the moisture meter with you and compare the reading on the meter to what you feel with your finger. This will help you determine if water is needed.

• Water in the morning when temperatures are still cool.

• Drench each container thoroughly to make sure the entire root system gets water. Shallow watering leads to thick, matted roots near the surface of the soil that eventually prevents water from reaching the rest of the container.

- During the hot months, you might water plants that are slightly moist in the morning, because they will likely be dry by afternoon.
- Also during the hot months, small plants (four-inch, six-packs, etc.) could need to be watered twice during the day, once in the morning and once in the afternoon as needed.
- Thoroughly water the plug trays with a mister/fogger as needed. If the weather is cloudy and humid, they might not need as much water as days when it is hot and dry. Check frequently and never let the plants in the trays dry out completely. Young seedlings die quickly when deprived of water.
- Water all newly potted plants immediately and thoroughly.

Telephone Courtesy

When answering the phone, say, "Misty Hill Farm, this is ___ (Marilyn, Kathy, Leslie, etc.)." No matter how busy you are, do not make the caller feel that you are inconvenienced by his/her call. Wear a "smile" in your voice. Answer questions if you are able, and if not, take a message and tell them Louise will return their call. Be courteous. Make sure they know their inquiry or request is important.

Resolving Conflict With Other Employees

All employees must remember that successful completion of tasks in horticulture depends on people working together as a team. Even if you are working alone on one aspect of a task, others depend on you to do it well and in a timely manner in order for the job to be completed. If you have a conflict with another employee or are having trouble with the task you have been assigned, my employees are told, you must immediately let Louise know. Gossip regarding another employee will not be tolerated. Problems must be addressed immediately in order to keep them from interfering with everyone else's work. If you feel comfortable talking a problem out with the conflicting person, then do so. Remove yourselves from the work area and talk it out. *Do not,* however, let it become a shouting match. If the conflict has elevated to that level, it must be presented to Louise. All problems have solutions and must be addressed promptly to avoid further stress.

Appendix C
Soil Texture Analysis

Supplies

Quart jar with straight sides and a lid.

Teaspoon of plain Calgon (yes, the stuff you put in your bath).

Enough soil to fill the jar 2/3 full. Take an even sample that goes down at least 6-8 inches. Mix thoroughly before putting into the jar. (Before mixing, sift the material to get rid of rocks or large organic debris. If all the material is approximately the same size, then your measurements will be more accurate.)

Water.

Method

Fill the quart jar 2/3 full of soil and the rest of the way with water. Add the Calgon, put the lid on and shake vigorously until everything is thoroughly mixed. Let settle for one hour. Shake the jar again and let sit for 24 hours undisturbed.

At the end of 24 hours you will see that the soil has settled into distinct layers. If organic matter is present, it will be the very top layer. Then the layers will descend from clay to silt to sand. Measure the distance from the very bottom of the jar to the top of the clay layer and record that number. Then measure each separate layer individually and record as you measure. The percent of each is calculated by dividing the depth of each layer by the total depth of all the layers. (See example next page.)

Total soil measurement = 5 inches

Clay layer = 1 inch (1 inch divided by 5 inches = .02, which is 20%)

Silt layer = .75 inch (.75 inch divided by 5 inches = .15, which is 15%)

Sand layer = 3.25 inches (3.25 inches divided by 5 inches = .65, which is 65%)

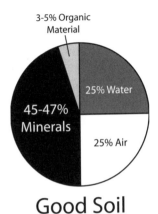

3-5% Organic Material

25% Water

45-47% Minerals

25% Air

Good Soil

The above calculations give you a general idea of what kind of soil you have. To be more specific, you can apply these percentages to the Soil Texture Guide published by the USDA. By charting your calculations on the triangle, you will have a more definitive analysis of your soil.

If you want to know what percentage of organic matter you have in your soil then measure the very top layer and add that to your previous total soil measurement for the clay, silt and sand. Then divide your organic matter calculation from the new total soil measurement and you will know what percent of organic material you have in your soil. If we use the example I gave above, it might look something like this:

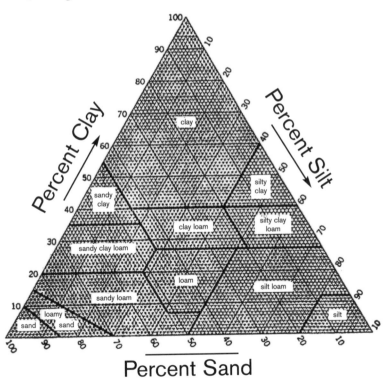

Percent Clay

Percent Silt

Percent Sand

Organic Matter layer = .25 inch.

Previous Total Soil Measurement = 5 inches + .25 inch
= New total Soil Measurement of 5.25 inches.

.25-inch divided by 5.25 inches = .048, which is 4.8%.

Healthy soil contains approximately 50% solid material and 50% pore space. The solid material is subdivided into about 45-47% minerals (clay, silt and sand) and about 3-5% organic matter, which includes living microorganisms. The pore space (between all the solid material pieces) should be balanced with about 25% air and 25% water.

To figure out what kind of soil you have, apply the information you have gathered to the soil chart. Simply find the percentage of each element on the respective side and draw a straight line from that point to the other side. At some point, the lines will intersect and that place will indicate what kind of soil you have.

Resources

My Favorite Books

Be aware that some of these books might have newer, revised editions. My goal is to guide you to authors and publishers who have provided consistently good reference material for me. There are lots of great books out there.

Basics

Botany for Gardeners, An Introduction and Guide. Brian Capon. Timber Press, Inc., Portland, OR, 1990. ISBN 0-88192-163-7 (hardcover), ISBN 0-88192-258-7 (softcover). This is a great book for beginning amateur botanists or for those of you who have forgotten your high school or college botany lessons. It is technical enough to give you a good botanical foundation, but written in an easy-to-understand format.

Howard Garrett's Organic Manual. Howard Garrett. The Summit Group, Ft. Worth, TX, 1993. ISBN 1-56530-082-3. Good basic primer on organic principles and organic garden placement and maintenance. Howard has an easy style and passion for the subject, which makes this a great read. Should be on the shelf of every organic grower.

Howard Garrett's Texas Organic Gardening Book. Howard Garrett. Gulf Publishing Co., Houston, 1993. ISBN 0-88415-038-0. Much of the same information as in the *Organic Manual,* but has lots of nice photographs and is very attractively formatted. Emphasis on Texas hardy plants.

Pay Dirt, Farming and Gardening with Composts. J.I. Rodale. The Devin-Adair Company, New York, 1946. How easy it is to forget that the alarms went off over 60 years ago about the potential problems associated with growing food plants with man-made chemicals. J.I. Rodale was among a handful of outspoken proponents of keeping farming and gardening simple and basic to preserve the integrity of the precious topsoil and prevent pollution of ground water and soil. If you can find this book (I lucked into it back in the '70s at a garage sale), read it. It will astound and amaze your earthly heart. It's free to read online.

Plants Plus, A Comprehensive Guide to Successful Propagation of House and Garden Plants. George Seddon and Andrew Bicknell. Rodale Press, Inc., Emmaus, PA, 1987. ISBN 0-87857-717-3. Although this book is written for the backyard gardener, it has very good information on basic propagation techniques from seeds to cuttings. The book is divided into different categories of plants with specific examples of how those plants would best be propagated. I recommend it for anyone who will be propagating their own plant material.

Texas Native Plants

Native Texas Plants, Landscaping Region by Region. Sally Wasowski with Andy Wasowski. Gulf Publishing Co., Houston, 1988, 1991. ISBN 0-87719-201-4. I believe there has been a revision since this edition but this is one of my dog-eared favorites. Could be helpful for folks who have just moved to Texas and don't have a clue how to landscape for their area. Excellent descriptions of plants with reasonably good pictures to help you identify (and hopefully use) the natives in your own back yard.

Trees, Shrubs, and Woody Vines of the Southwest. Robert A. Vines. University of Texas Press, Austin, TX, 1986. ISBN 0-292-73414-X. I'm not sure how the creased and torn paper jacket is still cradling this hardcover tome of mine. I have used this book many times for field identification of plants. Very detailed descriptions of native plants with accurate black and white illustrations. Also has historical information about how it got its name, if it has traditional medicinal uses, who or what generally forages this plant, and what common names are associated with this plant.

Neil Sperry's Complete Guide to Texas Gardening. Taylor Publishing Co., Dallas, 1991. ISBN 0-87833-799-7. Although I have a different comfort level with horticultural chemicals than Neil, I have to recommend this book as an all-around gardening primer. He has lots of basic information about creating gardens and planting. His plant recommendations go beyond natives into other "introduced" or hybrid varieties that are generally well adapted for Texas. Descriptions are brief but succinct. Nice illustrations and photographs. Another good one for those who don't know how to garden in Texas.

How to Grow Native Plants of Texas and the Southwest. Jill Nokes. Gulf Publishing Co., Houston, 1986. ISBN 0-87719-034-8. For growers who want to commercially propagate native plants, this is the book for you. Not only does she go into basic propagation techniques (with beautiful illustrations to complement the descriptions), but she gives very detailed explanations of how to handle wild-harvested plants, how to reproduce them via seed collection and germination, and where and when to get cuttings. Although all native plants are not covered, there is a wide enough range of families and species that one could feel confident getting results on any plant with this book as a guide.

J. Howard Garrett's Plants of Texas ID Swatcher. Howard Garrett. The Summit Group, Ft. Worth, TX, 1993. ISBN 1-56530-083-1. This is just like any swatcher only it has pictures of plants and their descriptions instead of paint colors or fabrics. Intended for landscape planning, I have found it convenient to take with me when visiting arboretums or plant shows and nurseries to identify plants I'm not familiar with. Many of the plants are not natives but are Texas hardy. Natives are identified at the top with the name. Handy learning tool.

Herbs

There are thousands (or more) herb books available. These are some that proved most useful to me as a grower. Each had pieces of the "herb puzzle" that helped me learn to grow the plants and put together accurate information for the customer. Although I also used the Internet, these books were my bibles.

The Encyclopedia of Medicinal Plants. Andrew Chevallier. D.K. Publishing Inc., New York, 1996. ISBN 0-7894-0672. This is one of the most comprehensive books on medicinal plants I have seen. He talks extensively about the traditional forms of healing around the world and the herbs and methods used. He takes you into a magical world of healing plants with photos, illustrations and in-depth descriptions of each plant including origin, morphology and habitat, related species, biochemical constituents, key actions, research that has been done, traditional and current usage, parts used and how it is best prepared. The back is full of lessons on preparing home remedies and suggestions regarding herbs for specific ailments. A great reference book.

Rodale's Illustrated Encyclopedia of Herbs. Rodale Press, Emmaus, PA, 1987. ISBN 0-87857-699-1. Without preamble this book digs right in to herb descriptions giving you history, uses and cultivation for each, with simple, black-and-white illustrations of each plant. Interspersed throughout the book are individual sections describing the many uses including bathing, dying, cooking, gardening (growing), healing, botany, history and lotions with herbs. I found "pearls" in this book that I couldn't find anywhere else. It is definitely a good foundational reference.

The Random House Book of Herbs. Roger Phillips and Nicky Foy. Random House Inc., New York, 1990. ISBN 0-679-73213-6. This book is one I refer new herb gardeners to all the time. It has beautiful photographs of the plants in-ground and some similar groups (like mint) arranged on a page, close-up, for proper identification. The book is divided into herb categories (culinary, salad, vegetable, berries, teas, scented, strewing, dyeing and medicinal) for those interested in putting in theme gardens. Each plant has a description of the history and traditional and current uses and growing recommendations. This is definitely one of my favorites.

Park's Success with Herbs. Gertrude B. Foster and Rosemary F. Louden. G.W. Park Seed Co. Inc., Greenwood, SC, 1980. I can't remember where I got this book (probably from the Park Seed Company), but it was one of the first books on herb growing I bought. I have referred to it often over the years because I enjoy the way these two ladies (mother and daughter) describe the plants (mostly culinary). The descriptions are primarily horticultural, giving the reader an in-depth understanding of the nature of the plant and the best way to propagate it and includes a photo of the seedling for identification. There are also brief descriptions of uses with occasional recipes. Good basic primer for new commercial herb growers.

Reader's Digest Magic and Medicine of Plants. The Reader's Digest Association, Inc., Pleasantville, NY, 1989. ISBN 0-89577-221-3. My mom gave me this book around the time I first started thinking about growing herbs for a living. It is one of the best overall botanical references I have found for field identification of many wild and some cultivated herbs. The pictures are exquisitely drawn, color plates of each plant, many incorporating the root, and all including the flowers and seeds. When referencing the history of a plant, I often turned to this book for unusual stories relating to the traditional use of the herb. It is a beautiful and interesting reference on the history of medicine, basic botanical/chemical information, myths (and magic), finding plants in the wild, making your own herbarium, nomenclature and basic information on a plethora of wonderful plants.

Herb Gardening in Texas. Sol Meltzer. Gulf Publishing Company, Houston, 1992. ISBN 0-88415-043-7. This book is a must for anyone in Texas that wants to grow herbs. Sol is knowledgeable, funny, interesting and informative. He writes what he knows and wants you to know too. Down-to-earth Texas primer.

Culpepper's Color Herbal. Sterling Publishing Co., Inc., New York, 1983. ISBN 0-8069-8568-2. This book is just interesting. It has nice color illustrations of the plants and their blooms and astrological associations of the herb as well as snippets of Culpepper's descriptions regarding the uses and value of the plant and descriptions of modern uses. This is a nice book to look at and it is always interesting to "hear" what the early herbalists said about our beloved herbs.

The Complete Medicinal Herbal. Penelope Ody. Dorling Kindersley, Inc., New York, 1993. ISBN 1-56485-187-X. I had actually gotten this book before the Andrew Chevallier volume, and though it is not as comprehensive by less than half the entries of the other, it does have its value. First of all, it's very visual with lots of nice photographs and illustrations. Ody also describes the history of medicine as Chevallier does but she adds her own special view and ideas. She also has (as does Chevallier) a large section in the back with "ailment guides" and a descriptive section on preparing home remedies.

Rodale's Successful Organic Gardening: Herbs. Patricia S. Michalak. Rodale Press, Emmaus, PA, 1993. ISBN 0-87596-557-1 (hardcover), 0-87596-558-X (softcover). This is one of a series of books by Rodale Press on various aspects of gardening. This one focuses on gardening with herbs. Two-thirds of the book is spent on the actual propagation and cultivation of herbs. Very graphic and descriptive, and an excellent guide for those who are new to growing herbs. The actual herb section is descriptive but limited to a few of the best-known and most popular herbs.

Scented Geraniums, Knowing, Growing and Enjoying Scented Pelargoniums. Jim Becker and Faye Brawner. Interweave Press, Loveland, CO, 1996. ISBN 1-883010-18-7. Growing scented pelargoniums (geraniums) has become almost as popular in the herb world as roses have become to home gardeners. This tiny little book (96 pages) is packed with information on propagating, growing and using these distinctive plants. If you want to expand your plant repertoire to include scented geraniums, then I recommend this book.

Herbs for Texas. Howard Garrett. University of Texas Press, Austin, TX, 2001. ISBN 0-292-72830-1 (softcover), 0-292-78173-3 (hardcover). Howard's herb book gives people in Texas a starting place for growing herbs in their gardens. He gives his usual information on organic growing and recipes and then alphabetically lists herbs that do well in Texas. Good book for people coming to Texas from other parts of the country who need some guidance.

Peppers

The Pepper Garden. Dave DeWitt and Paul W. Bosland. Ten Speed Press, Berkeley, CA, 1993. ISBN 0-89815-554-1 (softcover). This book has been my pepper-growing bible. It has everything you ever wanted to know about the history, types, pests, and growing requirements of peppers. They even give you candid advice on the idea of growing peppers for a living. Good primer.

Peppers of the World. Dave DeWitt and Paul W. Bosland. Ten Speed Press, Berkeley, CA, 1996. ISBN 0-89815-840-0. Again the dynamic duo comes through. Wonderful photographs along with very descriptive text takes you through the world of chile breeding and identification of the major peppers of the world. It is absolutely fascinating if you like peppers and want to learn to properly identify them. It can be very confusing if you aren't careful.

The Great Chile Book. Mark Miller. Ten Speed Press, Berkeley, CA, 1991. ISBN 0-89815-428-6. Written by the celebrated anthropologist-turned-chef of Coyote Cafe fame, this book not only gives you some interesting history and facts about chiles, but actual-size photographs of each of the pepper pods described. Includes some recipes in the back from the restaurant. Nice complement to the famous chile posters.

Pests and Pestilence

Rodale's Successful Organic Gardening: Controlling Pests and Diseases. Patricia Michalak and Linda A. Gilkeson. Rodale Press, Emmaus, PA, 1994. ISBN 0-87596-611-X (hardcover), 0-87596-612-8 (softcover). Another of the gardening series by Rodale Press, this book concentrates on identifying pests (including the four-legged kind) and diseases and getting to know the beneficial insects that can give you a hand and gentle solutions to insect pests. Good photographs along with descriptive text guide you well through the major problems you might face as a grower. There is a big emphasis on prevention.

The Organic Gardener's Handbook of Natural Insect and Disease Control. Edited by Barbara W. Ellis and Fern Marshal Bradley. Rodale Press, Emmaus, PA, 1992. ISBN 0-87596-124-X. Similar emphasis as the previous book but much more comprehensive. Although the photographs tend to be a bit small, the text makes up for any questions one might have. Every grower should have this book on their shelf.

Rodale's Garden Insect, Disease and Weed Identification Guide. Miranda Smith and Anna Carr. Rodale Press, Emmaus, PA, 1988. ISBN 0-87857-758-0 (hardcover), 0-87857-759-9 (softcover). I include this book because it has really detailed, black-and-white illustrations of insects and plants. The section on weed identification is great if you plan to put in a garden for demonstration or personal purposes. There is also a section in the back with good photographs of insects and plants already described. This one is a keeper.

Texas Bug Book. C. Malcolm Beck and J. Howard Garrett. University of Texas Press, Austin, TX, 1999. ISBN 0-292-70869-6. The minute you look at the cover of this book you can tell it's going to be good. Full of great photos and insightful anecdotes, this is a reference that should be on any grower's shelf. For each insect (good, bad or neutral) they give the common names, scientific name, size, identifying marks, life cycle, habitat, feeding habits, natural control, organic control (if needed) and descriptions of any economic damage it may incur (if any). Howard also includes his famous formulas for insect control and fertilizing and some suggestions for growing roses, pecan and fruit trees without chemicals.

A Field Guide to Texas Snakes. Alan Tennant. Gulf Publishing, Houston, 1998. ISBN 0-88719-277-4. This is the best field guide for identifying snakes in Texas, and would probably be helpful no matter where in the country you lived. Great photographs and very detailed descriptions about their habitat, normal prey, reproduction, behavior, coloring and shape, how common they are, and what snakes they look similar to. I read this book from cover to cover. Fascinating.

Seed/Plant/Fertilizer Suppliers

I have placed an asterisk (*) next to the companies that I have had personal experience with. There are a lot of suppliers out there. You just have to find the ones you like and trust. (Abbreviations: HL=Heirloom OP=Open Pollinated Hyb=Hybrid OG=Organic)

The Chile Woman. 1704 Weimer Rd., Bloomington, IN 47403. (812) 332-8494. Chile/Pepper Seeds. *www.thechilewoman.com.*

Companion Plants. 7247 N. Coolville Ridge Road, Athens, OH 45701. (740) 592-4643. Contains a good variety of herb plants and seed. *www.companionplants.com.* E-mail complants@frognet.net.

Cook's Garden. P.O. Box 535, Londonderry, VT 05148. (800) 457-9703. Seeds: (OG, HL, Hyb) vegetables, herbs, flowers. *www.cooks garden.com.*

Dwyer Greens. 4730 Co. Rd. 335, P.O. Box 975, New Castle, CO 81647. (970) 984-0967. Seeds/plants: herbs, flowers, vegetables. *www.dwyergreens.com.*

Eden Organic Nursery Services, Inc. P.O. Box 4604, Hallandale, FL 33008. (954) 455-0229. Seeds: (OP, OG, Hyb) peppers, tobacco, herbs, vegetables. Insect/pest control, gardening supplies. *www.eonseed.com.* E-mail info@eonseed.com.

Elixir Farm Botanicals. 1316 N. Benton Avenue, Spingfield, MO 65802. (417) 261-2353. Medicinal herbs: plants, roots, seeds. *www.elixir farm.com.*

Enchanted Seeds. P.O. Box 6087, Las Cruces, NM 88006. (505) 523-6058. Pepper/chile seeds. *www.enchantedseeds.com.*

Goodwin Creek Gardens. P.O. Box 83, Williams, OR 97544. (800) 846-7356. Good variety of perennial plants and seeds, many native. *www.goodwincreekgardens.com.*

Harmony Farm Supply and Nursery. 3244 Hwy 116 H, Sebastopol, CA 95472. (707) 823-9125. Seeds: (OP. HL). Beneficial insects, tools, irrigation supplies, fertilizers, etc. *www.harmonyfarm.com.*

Heirloom Seeds. P.O. Box 245, West Elizabeth, PA 15088. (412) 384-0852. Seeds: (OP, OG, HL, untreated) vegetable, herb, flower. *www.heirloomseeds.com.* E-mail mail@heirloomseeds.com.

Home Harvest Garden Supply Online. 3807 Bank St., Baltimore, MD 21224. (800) 348-4769. Seeds: (OG, HL, Hyb) Vegetable, Herb, Flower. Organic fertilizers, natural pest/disease control. *www.garden ingcatalog.com.*

Horizon Herbs.* LLC, P.O. box 69, Williams, OR 97544. (541) 846-6704. Organic, Medicinal Herb Seeds, Plants, and Live Roots. *www.horizonherbs.com.* E-mail herbseed@chatlink.com.

High Country Gardens. 2902 Rufina St., Santa Fe, NM 87505. (800) 925-9387. Perennial plants that grow well in most parts of the U.S, Many are Native and/or Xeric. Organic fertilizers. A lot of information on xeriscaping and gardening with native plants. *www.high countrygardens.com.* E-mail plants@highcountrygardens.com.

Johnny's Selected Seeds.* 955 Benton Avenue, Winslow, ME 04901. Commercial line: (207) 861-3900. Seeds: (OP, HL, OG, Hyb) vegetables, herbs, flowers, grasses, legumes/cover crops, grains. Gardening/growing supplies. *www.johnnyseeds.com.* E-mail info @johnnyseeds.com.

Jon's Heirloom Plants. P.O. Box 54, Mansfield, MO 65704. (870) 404-4771. Plants: (HL, OG), *www.jonsplants.net.* E-mail jonsplants @yahoo.com.

Lingle's Herbs. 2055 N. Lomina Ave., Long Beach, CA 90815. (562) 598-4372, (800) 708-0633. Organic herb plants. *www.linglesherbs .com*. E-mail info@linglesherbs.com.

Mountain Valley Growers, Inc. Certified Organic Herbs and Perennials, 38325 Pepperweed Road, Squaw Valley, CA 93675. (559) 338-2775. *www.mountainvalleygrowers.com*. E-mail customerservice@mountainvalleygrowers.com.

Native Seeds/SEARCH.* 526 N 4th Ave., Tucson, AZ 85705. (520) 622-5561. Heirloom seeds, native crafts/gifts and food from the Southwest. *www.nativeseeds.org*.

North Country Organics. P.O. Box 372, Depot St., Bradford, VT 05033. (802) 222-4277. Links to wholesale distributors for their organic products such as fertilizers, soil amendments, compost, pest controls, soil testing, etc. *www.norganics.com*. E-mail ncoin fo@norganics.com.

Peaceful Valley Farm Supply. P.O. Box 2209, Grass Valley, CA 95945. (888) 784-1722. Seeds: (OG, OP). Beneficial insects, tools, growing supplies, organic fertilizers, etc. *www.groworganic.com*.

The Pepper Gal. P.O. Box 23006, Ft. Lauderdale, FL 33307. (954) 537-5540. All kinds of pepper/chile seeds. E-mail peppergal@pepper gal.com.

Planet Natural. 1612 Gold Avenue, Bozeman, MT 59715. (800) 289-6656 (orders only), (406) 587-5891. Natural products for home, lawn and garden. *www.planetnatural.com*. E-mail info@planetnat ural.com.

R.H. Shumway's Catalog Fulfillment Center. 334 W. Shroud St., Randolph, WI 53956. (800) 342-9461. All heirloom seeds/plants. Growing/gardening supplies. *www.rhshumway.com*.

Reimer Seeds. P.O. Box 236, Mt. Holly, NC 28120. Seeds: (HL) pepper, vegetable, herb, flower. *www.reimerseeds.com*. E-mail mail@reimer seeds.com.

Richters Herb Specialists.* 361 Hwy 47, Goodwood, Ontario, L0C 1A0, Canada. (905) 640-6677, (800) 668-4372. Huge variety of herb seeds, plug trays and plants. Not certified organic, but use earth-friendly methods to grow their plant stock. *www.richters.com.*

San Jacinto Environmental Supplies. 2221-A West 34th Street, Houston, TX 77018. (713) 957-0909. Complete organic/sustainable horticultural and agricultural supplier. Manufacturer of organic fertilizers.

Seed Saver's Exchange. 3076 N. Winn Road, Decorah, IA 52101. (319) 382- 5990. Seeds: (OG, HL) vegetable, herb, bulbs, flowers, garlic. *www.seedsavers.org.*

Seeds of Change.* P.O. Box 15700, Santa Fe, NM 87506. (888) 762-7333. Completely organic. Seeds: (HL, OP, rare seeds) Vegetable, herb, flower, garlic, grains and some fruit trees. Some bulk seeds available. Also food and gardening supplies. *www.seedsofchange.com.*

Seeds for the South. 410 Whaley Pond Road, Graniteville, SC 29829. Seeds: (Hyb, OP, HL) vegetable, herb. *www.seedsforthesouth.com.*

Seeds of Texas Seed Exchange. P.O. Box 730, Sapello, NM 87745. An organization whose mission is to save our seed heritage. *csf.colorado.edu/perma/stse/.*

Sow Organic Seed. P.O. Box 527, Williams, OR 97544. (888) 709-7333. Seeds: (OP, OG) vegetable, herb, flower. *www.organicseed.com* E-mail organic@organicseed.com.

Tao Herb Farm. P.O. Box 327, Salmo, BC, VOG 170 Canada. (250) 357-2550. Seeds: (OG, HL) vegetable, herb. *www.taoherb farm.com.* E-mail taoherbfarm@netidea.com.

Territorial Seed Company. P.O. Box 158, Cottage Grove, OR 97424. (541) 942-9547. Seeds/plants: (OP, HL, Hyb) vegetable, herb, flower. Gardening supplies, organic fertilizer, beneficial insects, organic pest control. *www.territorial-seed.com.*

Tinmouth Channel Farm. 148 Channel Rd., Tinmouth, VT 05773. (802) 446-2812. Entire catalog is organic herb plants and seed.

Totally Tomatoes.* P.O. Box 1626, Augusta, GA 30903. (803) 663-0016. Incredible variety of heirloom and hybrid tomato and pepper seeds. *www.totallytomato.com.*

Vermont Bean Seed Company. 334 W. Stroud St., Randolph, WI 53956. (800) 349-1071. Untreated seeds: (HL, Hyb) vegetable (some very unusual), flower. Gardening supplies. *www.vermont bean.com.*

Wholesale Perennial Sources-Links. Links to companies that sell perennial plants and related products. *www.uvm.edu/~pass/perry/linkswn.html.*

World Wide Seed Company. 7111 W. 151st St., P.M.B. 177, Overland Park, KS 66223. Fax (913) 814-0177. Amazing diversity of seeds, unusual categories. E-mail worldwideseed@aol.com.

Beneficial Insects

This list was supplemented with sources from the following website, which can be accessed for additional information on each company: *www.cdpr.ca.gov/docs/ipminov/ben_supp/contents.htm.*

A-1 Unique Insect Control. 5504 Sperry Dr., Citrus Heights, CA 95621. (916) 961-7945. *www.a-1unique.com.*

Activated Biological Control, LLC. P.O. Box 394, Elk Grove, CA 95759. (408) 469-7833.

American Insectaries, Inc. 30805 Rodriquez Rd., Escondido, CA 92026. (760) 751-1436. E-mail jdavis@mailhost2.csusm.edu.

Applied Bio-Control. P.O. Box 118, Waterford, CA 95386. (209) 874-1862.

Applied Bio Pest. 3310 Net Place, Oxnard, CA 93035. (805) 984-9224, (800) 787-BUGS (outside CA). E-mail biopest@jetlink.net.

Arizona Biological Control Inc. (ARBICO). P.O. Box 4247, Cty. Rd. B, Tucson, AZ 85738. (520) 825-9785.

Beneficial Insectary. 9664 Tanqueray Ct., Redding, CA 96003. (530) 226-6300 or (800) 477-3715. *www.insectary.com.*

Beneficial Insect Company. P.O. Box 119, Glendale Springs, NC 28629. (336) 973-8490.

Better Yield Insects. 44 Bristol Road, Narragansett, RI 02882. (401) 792-3416.

Bio Ag Services. 4218 W. Muscat, Fresno, CA 93706. (559) 268-2835.

Bio Ag Supply. 710 South Columbia, Plainview, TX 79072. (806) 293-5861 or (800) 746-9900. E-mail wwinters@texasonline.net.

BioLogic Company. Springtown Road, P.O. Box 177, Willow Hill, PA 17271. (717) 349-2789.

BioSmith Pest Management Service. 385 West Shaw Ave. #121, Fresno, CA 93704. (209) 265-0266.

Biotactics, Inc. 20780 Warren Rd., Perris, CA 92570. (909) 320-1366. *www.benemite.com.* E-mail sales@benemite.com.

Bowen Biosystems. Bo-Biotrol, Inc., 2875 Arden Ln., Merced, CA 95340. (209) 384-2130 or (800) 900-0246.

Buena Biosystems. P.O. Box 4008, Ventura, CA 93007. (805) 525-2525. *www.buenabiosystems.com.*

BugLogical Control Systems. P.O. Box 32046, Tucson, AZ 85751. (520) 298-4400. *www.buglogical.com.*

The Bug Store. 113 West Argonne, St. Louis, MO 63122. (800) 455-2847, (314) 966-2287. *www.bugstore.com.* E-mail bugstore@mo.net.

California Bio-Works. 33016 Road 204, Woodlake, CA 93286. (209) 564-2620

EcoSolutions, Inc. 334 East Lake Road, Ste. 196, Palm Harbor, FL 34685. (813) 787-3669.

Foothill Ag Research (FAR), Inc. 510½ Foothill Parkway, Corona, CA 91720. (909) 371-0120.

Good Bugs Insectary. 30761A Road 216, Exeter, CA 93221. (209) 592-1681, (209) 897-0891, (209) 637-3115. E-mail bugman@light speed.net.

Greenfire Inc. 347 Nord Avenue #1, Chico, CA 95926. (800) 895-8307, (916) 895- 8301.

The Green Spot. Department of Bio-Ingenuity, 93 Priest Road, Nottingham, NH 03290-6204. (603) 942-8925 (main number), (603) 942-5027 (24 hr. voice mail).

Gulf Coast Biological Controls. 366 FM 2550, Huntsville, TX 77340. (800) 524-1958 (orders only), (409) 291-2302 (free consulting).

Hydro-Gardens, Inc. (HGI Worldwide Inc.), P.O. Box 25845, Colorado Springs, CO 80936. (719) 495-2266, (800) 634-6362. E-mail hgi@usa.net.

Integrated BioControl Systems, Inc. P.O. Box 96, Aurora, IN 47001. (812) 537-8673. E-mail goodbug@seidata.com.

Integrated Fertility Management (IFM). 333 Ohme Gardens Rd., Wenatchee, WA 98801. (509) 662-3179, (800) 332-3179. E-mail philn@televar.com.

Integrated Pest Insectary, LLC. 2228 North Ila Avenue, Fresno, CA 93705. (209) 456-0990.

International Technology Services. P.O. Box 19227, Boulder, CO 80308. (303) 473-9141.

IPM Laboratories, Inc. Main Street, Locke, NY 13092. (315) 497-2063. E-mail ipmlabs@baldcom.net.

Koppert Biological Systems. 2856 South Main, Ann Arbor, MI 48103. (313) 998- 5589.

Kunafin "The Insectary." Rt. 1, Box 39, Quemado, TX 78877. (800) 832-1113, (210) 757-1181.

The Ladybug Company. P.O. Box 329, Berry Creek, CA 95916. (530) 589-5227.

Ladybug Farms. 4012 Stephen Drive, North Highlands, CA 95660. (916) 348-1917.

Ladybug Sales. P.O. Box 903, Gridley, CA 95948. (916) 868-5059, (916) 868-1627.

M&R Durango, Inc. P.O. Box 886, Bayfield, CO 81122. (970) 259-3521. E-mail sales@goodbug.com.

Natural Pest Control. 8864 Little Creek Dr., Orangeville, CA 95662. (916) 726-0855, (916) 923-3353.

Nature's Control. P.O. Box 35, Medford, OR 97501. (541) 899-8318. E-mail bugsnc@teleport.com.

Novartis BCM North America. P.O. Box 2430, Oxnard, CA 93034. (805) 986-8265.

N-Viro Products Ltd. 610 Walnut Avenue, Bohemia, NY 11716. (516) 567-2628

Oxnard Pest Control Association. 666 Pacific Avenue, P.O. Box 1187, Oxnard, CA 93032. (805) 483-1024.

Pest Management Supply Inc. P.O. Box 938, Amherst, MA 01004. (800) 272-7672.

Plant Sciences, Inc. 342 Green Valley Road, Watsonville, CA 95076. (408) 728-7771.

PNE, Inc. 2900A Longmire Drive, College Station, TX 77845. (409) 693-5801.

Praxis. 2723 116th Ave., Allegan, MI, 49010. (616) 673-2793. *www. datawise.net*, E-mail praxis@datawise.net.

Rincon-Vitova Insectaries, Inc. P.O. Box 1555, Ventura, CA 93002. (805) 643-5407, (800) 248-BUGS(2847). E-mail bugnet@west.net.

Sierra Ag. 2749 E. Malaga Ave., Fresno, CA 93725. (209) 233-0585. *www.agrobiologicals.com/companyC/1267.htm*. E-mail IPM@Sierra Ag.com.

Stanley Gardens. P.O. Box 913, 295 Jackson Street, Belchertown, MA 01007. (413) 323-6196. *www.agrobiologicals.com/companyC/ 1268.htm*.

Sweetbriar Development, Inc. 1767 San Juan Road, Watsonville, CA 95076. (408) 722-5577. *www.agrobiologicals.com/company/ C321.htm.*

Thermo Trilogy Corporation. 9145 Guildford Rd., Suite 175, Columbia, MD 21046. (301) 483-4984.

Tip Top Bio-Control. P.O. Box 7614, Westlake Village, CA 91359. (805) 375-1382.

Visalia Insectary Inc. P.O. Box 3205, Visalia, CA 93278. (209) 732-6249. E-mail sailmax@aol.com.

Horticultural Distributors

Texas:

Adams Wholesale Supply, Inc. 1434 E. Bitters Road, San Antonio, TX 78216. (210) 822-3141, (800) 788-9581.

BWI Companies, Inc. P.O. Box 990, Nash, TX 75569. (903) 838-8561. *www.bwicompanies.com.* This is the largest horticultural distributor in Texas and they have distribution centers in other states (MS, TN, MO, FL, SC, LA, AL, KS). To find the one closest to you call the above number or peruse the website.

Gard'n-Wise Distributors, Inc. 1400 E. Loop 289, Rt. 1 Box 900, Lubbock, TX 79401. (806) 744-8894. *www.gardenwise.com.*

Kinney Bonded Warehouse, Inc. 102 North 13th St., Donna, TX 78537. (800) 292-7547, (956) 464-4491. E-mail: sales@kinney bonded.com.

Natural Industries, Inc. 6223 Theall Rd., Houston, TX 77066. (888) 261-4731. *www.naturalindustries.com.*

Rabbit Hill Farm. 288 SW Cty. Rd. 0020, Corsicana, TX 75110. (903) 872-4289. *www.aogc.org/pages/rhf.* E-mail rhf@airmail.net.

Other States:

Agri-Growth International, Inc. 11040 N. 28 Drive, Unit 327, Phoenix, AZ 85029. (602) 942-4493. E-mail herb@agriorganics .com.

Association of Natural Biocontrol Producers. *www.anbp.org.*

North American Horticultural Supply Association. 1900 Arch St., Philadelphia, PA 19103. (215) 564-3484. E-mail nahsa@fernley .com.

Agriculture Contacts

Texas Department of Agriculture. P.O. Box 12847, Austin, TX 78711. (512) 463-7476. *www.agr.state.tx.us.*

U.S. Department of Agriculture. *www.usda.gov.*

Appropriate Technology Transfer for Rural Areas (ATTRA). P.O. Box 3657, Fayetteville, AR 72702. (800) 346-9140. This site lists national and international organic certifying agencies. *www.attra.org.*

Labels and Labeling Equipment

Checkpoint. (800) 874-4465. Tags, printers, software. *www.economy label.com.*

Gardenware. P.O. Box 130, 139 E. Dawes, Cannon Beach, OR 97110. (503) 436-0612. Custom labels, software. *www.gardenware.com.* E-mail info@gardenware.com.

Integra Color Horticultural Printers. 3638 Executive Blvd., Mesquite, TX 75149. (972) 289-0705, (800) 933-9511. Full service, custom and preprinted tags. *www.integracolor.com.* E-mail web master@integracolor.com.

The John Henry Company. 5800 W. Grand River Ave., Lansing, MI 48906. (800) 748-0517. Pre-printed and custom tags. *www.thejohn henrycompany.com.*

JVK USA. P.O. Box 662, Lewiston, NY 14902. (905) 641-5599, (800) 665-1642. Custom tags, printers, software. *www.jvk.net.* E-mail info@jvk.net.

Label It, Inc. 10100 N.W. 116 Way, Ste 1, Miami, FL 33178. (305) 887-4949. Labels, software, printers. *www.labelit.com*. E-mail sales@label-it.com.

Associations

American Botanical Council. P.O. Box 144345, Austin, TX, 78714. (512) 926-4900. *www.herbalgram.org*, E-mai abc@herbal gram.org. Publication: *Herbalgram*.

American Horticultural Society. 7931 E. Boulevard Dr., Alexandria, VA 22308. (703) 768-5700. *www.ahs.org*. Publication: *The American Gardener*.

Herb Growing and Marketing Network. P.O. Box 245, Silver Springs, PA 17575. (717) 393-3295. *www.herbworld.com*. E-mail herbworld @aol.com.

Herb Society of America. 9019 Kirtland Chardon Rd., Kirtland OH 44094. (440) 256-0514. *www.herbsociety.org*. E-mail herbs@herb society.org.

Native Plant Society of Texas. P.O. Box 891, Georgetown, TX 78627. *www.npsot.org*. E-mail coordinator@npsot.org. *Note:* There is a native plant society in many U.S. states; to do a search, enter the name of your state and Native Plant Society.

Organic Trade Association. P.O. Box 547, Greenfield, MA 01302. (413) 774-7511. *www.ota.com*. E-mail info@ota.com.

Texas Nursery and Landscape Association. 7730 S. IH 35, Austin, TX 78745. (512) 280-5182. *www.txnla.org*. E-mail info@txnla.org.

Texas Organic Growers Association (TOGA). P.O. Box 15211, Austin, TX 78761. (877) 326-5175. *www.texasorganicgrowers.org*.

Publications

Acres U.S.A. P.O. Box 91299, Austin, TX 78709. (800) 355-5313, (512) 892-4400. A monthly guide to sustainable agriculture. The latest techniques for growing organic/sustainable crops and livestock. Offers many books of interest to organic grower. *www.acresusa. com*.

Greenhouse Product News. Scranton Gillette Communications, 380 E. Northwest Hwy., Des Plaines, IL, 60016. This is a free publication for people in the business of growing plants. It is loaded with advertisements but all are products used in the horticulture business. There are also many well-written articles about the industry.

Green Prints, "The Weeders Digest." P.O. Box 1355, Fairview, NC 28730. (800) 569-0602. *www.gardennet.com/greenprints.* Sharing "the human side of gardening."

The Herb Quarterly. P.O. Box 689, San Anselmo, CA 94979. *www.herbquarterly.com.* E-mail may@herbquarterly.com.

Organic Gardening. 33 E. Minor St., Emmaus, PA 18098. (610) 967-5171, (800) 666-2206. *www.organicgardening.com.* E-mail organicgardening@rodale.com.

Texas Gardener. P.O. Box 9005, 10566 North River Crossing, Waco, TX 76712, (254) 848-9393, (800) 727-9020. *www.texasgardener .com.* E-mail suntex@calpha.com.

Informal Education

Master Gardener Classes. These classes are widely available from state universities. Check with your local university to learn what is available near you. In Texas classes are offered through Texas A&M University. *mastergardener.tamu.edu.*

Glossary

After-Ripening: The maturation process needed by most seeds in order to be viable (able to germinate).

Allelopathy: This is where a plant inhibits growth and/or germination of other plants by releasing chemicals from twigs, leaves and sometimes roots into the surrounding soil. The word allelopathy means "mutual suffering."

Alfalfa Meal: A perennial legume used as fodder for animals, green manure for crops and, when cut, dried and ground into a meal is useful as a soil amendment providing nitrogen, phosphorus, potassium, calcium, magnesium, trace minerals, triacontanol (a growth stimulant), sugars, starches and amino acids.

Angiosperms: A class of plants that produces flowers (with reproductive capability) and then fruit with seeds.

Annual: A plant whose entire life cycle (germination, growth, fruiting, death) is completed in the timespan of one growing season.

Axil: The angular space between the stem and the upper surface of the attached leaf.

Axillary Bud: A bud located in the leaf axil that will produce a new side shoot (stem) when the chemical message is given to do so.

Bacillus thuringiensis (Bt): A rod-shaped bacterium harmless to humans but deadly to larval forms of butterflies and moths.

Biennial: Plants that complete their life cycle in the span of two growing seasons.

Binomial Nomenclature: The two-part naming system developed by a Swedish naturalist Carolus Linnaeus in the 18th century.

Blood Meal: Dried, slaughterhouse blood. Used as a high-nitrogen soil amendment.

Bolting: Unusually rapid growth of an annual plant with premature flowering.

Bone Meal: A by-product of the meat industry, bone meal is animal bones that have been pasteurized, dried and ground into a powder. Used as a calcium and phosphorus soil amendment.

Bract: Modified leaf found below a (often insignificant looking) flower or inflorescence. The best example is the red leaf bracts of Poinsettias and Bougainvilleas.

Calcium Sulfate: Gypsum, as it is commonly called, is a mined or industrial by-product material used to correct calcium deficiency, especially in alkaline soils, and to loosen tight clay soils, allowing better drainage.

Callus: The tough, hardened tissue that covers a wounded area of a plant. Some stem cuttings must be allowed to callus to prevent rotting when placed in soil to root.

Calyx: The usually green whorl of sepals that cover and protect a flower bud until it opens.

Chloroplasts: These are the specialized cellular bodies located primarily in leaves where light energy is converted into food by the pigment chlorophyll.

Chlorosis: A condition of a plant producing yellowing of the leaves, which decreases photosynthesis and therefore food production.

Citrus Oil (d-limonene): Oil from the skins of citrus fruit (oranges, grapefruit, lemons, etc.), used to repel and even kill some pest insects.

Clay: An inorganic component of soil with individual particles sized less than 0.002 mm.

Coir: The fibrous, outside hull of the coconut, chopped finely and used as a substitute for peat moss in the horticulture industry.

Cold-Hardening: In preparation of freezing winter temperatures, the cells of deciduous plants change structure and function slightly to prevent the fatal formation of ice crystals.

Colloidal Phosphate: Often referred to as soft rock phosphate, this is mined, crushed phosphate that has been suspended in clay. Used as a calcium and phosphorus soil amendment.

Compost Tea: A liquid infusion made from compost and water. Used as a fertilizer drench or mixed with molasses and seaweed and applied as a foliar spray.

Compound Leaves: Multiple leaves (leaflets) attached to the petiole in various patterns.

Corolla: All the layers of petals of a flower. The design and color is developed by the species to attract specific pollinators.

Cotton Burr Compost: Cotton burrs are the wickedly sharp calyx of the cotton flower in which the cotton boll rests. This by-product of the cotton industry is composted and used as a soil amendment providing nitrogen, phosphorus and potassium.

Cottonseed Meal: A by-product of cotton ginning, the seed is ground into a meal and used as a soil amendment providing nitrogen, phosphorus and potassium.

Cotyledon: Embryonic food storage unit sometimes called "seed leaves" or "milk leaves" that emerge after germination along with the embryonic root (radicle).

Cultivar: A specific, named variety of a certain species of plant, carefully cultivated to retain its desirable characteristics.

Cuticle: The waxy, protective coating on leaves and stems formed by a substance called cutin that primarily keeps the plant from losing too much water.

Damping Off: Seedlings dying from pathogenic soil fungi such as Pithium, Fusarium and Rhizoctonia.

Day-Neutral Plant: A plant whose flowering response does not depend on maximum or minimum day length.

Deciduous: Refers to perennial plants that lose their leaves in the autumn as they become dormant for the winter.

Determinate Growth: Generally refers to fruiting annuals that produce only one or two (often large) flushes of fruit.

Diatomaceous Earth (D.E.): Soft, powdery substance that is the crushed skeletal remains of single-celled diatoms from ancient oceans. Used against specific insect pests.

Diffuse Root System: This is the finely branched root system that maintains itself closer to the soil surface in order to take advantage of surface moisture and topsoil nutrients.

Dormancy: The state of a plant when growing (cellular activity) has slowed or stopped due to heat and/or drought or cold temperatures.

Dormant Oil: A petroleum-based oil used in the winter or early spring on trees and shrubs to treat over wintering pest eggs or insects.

Drip Zone (Drip Line): The area of soil directly under the outer tips of the branches of trees and shrubs (perimeter) that often has root tips waiting for water to drip off the leaves.

Earthworm Castings: Earthworm excrement that is finely digested organic matter. Used as a soil amendment.

Evergreen: Perennial plants that stay green throughout the year, even in times of dormancy.

Family: This is a group of plants of various genera with broad similarities. According to the International Code of Botanical Nomenclature, all family names end in –*aceae*.

Fish Emulsion: Emulsified fish by-products in a concentrated, liquid form used as fertilizer.

Foliage: The collection of leaves associated with above-ground stems/branches of a plant.

Forcing: A process implemented by commercial growers utilizing artificial light, temperatures and/or specific hormones to cause a plant to grow in a controlled manner.

Genes: The molecular-sized hereditary units attached to chromosomes in the nucleus of all cells that dictate the inheritable characteristics of an organism.

Genotype: Gene composition that creates the visible characteristics.

Genus: A taxonomic (scientific classification) subdivision of families that, in turn, contains a number of related species.

Germination: The miraculous process in which a seed takes in (imbibes) water, and with light and temperature requirements met, will send chemical messages to the embryonic plant inside the seed to begin growing.

Granite: Coarse-grained, light-colored, hard igneous rock, crushed and used as mulch in garden paths and as sand or meal in soil as a source of potassium and other trace minerals. Has paramagnetic properties.

Greensand: A silica-based material mined from ancient ocean beds. Officially called glauconite, this greenish colored sand is used as a soil amendment for potassium and iron.

Guano: Aged, dried excrement from bats and sea birds. Used as a high nitrogen soil amendment.

Gypsum: See *Calcium Sulfate*.

Hardening Off: The process of gradually exposing young plants to outdoor conditions to that they are well adapted by the time they are expected to be planted.

Hardiness Zone: The geographical (zonal) guidelines set up by the U.S. Department of Agriculture (USDA) that indicate average winter and, in some cases, summer temperatures.

Hardy Plants: Native or non-native plants that survive the challenging environmental stresses of your region, from extreme cold and/or heat, to drought, humidity, rainfall and specific soil conditions.

Heirloom: Plants with enduring lineage whose characteristics are the result of natural selection rather than hybrid gene mixing.

Herbaceous: Plants that have soft, flexible, green stems and leaves, with limited woody-type tissue.

Herbicide: Chemicals that have selective or broad-spectrum plant killing properties.

Hormone: Organic chemicals produced by all parts of plants that "excite" or catalyze biochemical activities affecting growth and development of the plant.

Horticultural Oils: Various grades of petroleum-based oils on the market for insecticidal use.

Horticulture: The activity of growing flowers, fruits, vegetables, tropical, native and other ornamental plants, or the science or art of cultivating a garden. It also refers to the businesses involved in the propagation, growing and selling of plant material in containers.

Host: Plants used by parasites as a source of nourishment.

Humus: The organic component of soil derived from decomposed plants and animals.

Hybrid: Often designated in seed catalogs as F1, meaning the plant will be an offspring of two related species of plants, each of which contributes specific, desirable characteristics to the genes of the hybrid plant.

Imbibition: The absorption of water by a dry substance or structure causing softening, swelling and increased volume. Seeds imbibe water during the process of germination.

Indeterminate Growth: Annual plants that fruit continuously and whose growth patterns and production are primarily influenced by soil, water and nutritional factors.

Inflorescence: A cluster of flowers at the end of a stalk. The following are some types:

> **Composite Head:** Classic example is the sunflower with a tight, central cluster of small disc flowers surrounded by larger petals from ray flowers.

> **Spike:** Flowers that are attached directly to the stem such as many Salvias.

> **Raceme:** Flowers that are attached to the stem by a short stalk on plants like Baptisia, Cassia and Penstemon.

> **Panicle:** Flowers that are attached to well-branched stems. Examples would be Begonia, Dianthus and Impatiens.

> **Umbel:** Flowers attached to a group of flower stalks originating from one point at the top of the stem. Examples would be Fennel, Dill and the Alliums.

Inorganic: As a rule, substances not containing carbon as an essential element.

Insecticidal Soap: Potassium salts from natural plant oils and animal fats, used as a non-toxic pesticide.

Internode: The stem space between nodes that varies widely depending on species and genus.

Latex: Latin for "fluid." This is the sticky, most often white (but may be opaque or clear) substance that oozes from breaks along the stems and roots of certain plants (most notably Euphorbias).

Lava Sand: A combination of crushed volcanic rock often including basalt. Used as a soil amendment for drainage, minerals and paramagnetic properties.

Leaf: The primary site for manufacture of food for the plant via photosynthesis. Commonly called the leaf blade because of its flattened shape designed to more easily capture light

Leaf Scar: The healed scar left on the stem where a leaf has been broken off or fallen off from age.

Lenticel: Often looking like scale insects or scars, these are actually pores seen on the smooth stems of woody plants that allow the passing of gases (including oxygen) between living cells of the inner bark.

Lime: A general term referring to the various white, powdery materials containing a substantial amount of calcium carbonate.

Loam: Technically, the native inorganic compounds sand, silt and clay in varying percentages. Some believe that the word loam indicates that the soil also has humus.

Macronutrients: Mineral elements used in small amounts by plants for healthy growth and development. These are: carbon (C), hydrogen (H), oxygen (O), nitrogen (N), phosphorus (P), potassium (K), sulfur (S) and calcium (Ca).

Meristem: The area in plants where active cell division (mitosis) is occurring.

> **Apical** meristems are found at the root and growing tips.
>
> **Lateral** meristems are located along the inside of the stem and roots.
>
> **Intercalary** meristems between the blade and the stem enabling grasses to continue growing despite being nipped off by teeth or mowers.

Mycorrhizae: Specific soil fungi creating a beneficial relationship with the young root systems of many species of plants.

Micronutrients: Mineral elements used in small-to-tiny amounts by plants for healthy growth and development. These are: magnesium (Mg), iron (Fe), copper (Cu), zinc (Zn), manganese (Mn), molybdenum (Mo) and boron (B).

Molasses: A very sweet, thick, black syrup which is a by-product of the cane sugar industry. Contains iron, sulfur, potassium and other trace elements.

Native Plants: Plants that are indigenous to a specific region.

Naturalized Plants: Non-native plants that have been introduced to a region by wind, animals or humans and are uniquely suited to the area to the point of growing as well or better than the native plants.

Necrosis: Death of a stem, roots and/or leaves often caused by calcium deficiency because of its importance in the synthesis of pectin, which is what holds cell walls together.

Neem Oil: An oil used as a botanical insecticide extracted from a tall, native East Indian tree (*Azadirachta indica*) which is cultivated in tropical Asia.

Nodes: The segment of a stem from which leaves and axillary buds originate.

Non-Hybrid: Refers to plant species and varieties that have not been interbred.

NPK: Nitrogen, phosphorus and potassium and their relative amounts in a fertilizer or soil sample. All three are fundamentally important to normal, healthy plant growth.

Open-Pollinated: Non-hybrid plants that are wind, insect- or self-pollinated and are capable of cross-pollinating with other plants of similar species.

Organic: Broad term referring to anything on earth (or beyond!) containing carbon (and hydrogen), the inference being "living organisms." Also refers to the avoidance of laboratory-produced chemical fertilizers and pesticides and emphasis on earth-generated ("organic") fertilizers and plant-based pesticides

Parasite: Specific fungi, bacteria, viruses and some plants that are unable to manufacture their own food and so must attach themselves to a "host" plant and invade the root or ariel (above-ground) tissue in order to procure enough nourishment to live out their life cycle, which includes reproduction.

Peat Moss: The partially decomposed (carbonized) remains of any of various mosses of the genus sphagnum.

Perennial: Plants that have an indefinite lifespan.

Perlite: A natural glass-like material heated to very high temperatures which pops it into a light, porous material.

Petiole: The leaf stalk which attaches many leaves to the stem of the plant.

pH: A scale from 1 to 14 assigning numbers to soil indicating relative acidity or alkalinity, 1 being extremely acid, 14 extremely alkaline, and 7 being essentially neutral.

Phenotype: This is the apparent or visible expression of a genetic characteristic such as leaf shape, height, width, color, etc.

Photoperiodism: Refers to the day length required by certain plants for the development of flowers.

Photosynthesis: A process where a green chemical in leaves (chlorophyll) uses light energy, carbon dioxide (CO_2) and water (H_2O) to create food for the plant.

Phototropism: Caused by the plant hormone auxin, this is the growth movement of plants to a source of light.

Phytotoxin: Poisonous chemicals (predominantly alkaloids) produced and stored by plants causing symptoms in humans from mild rashes to death.

Phytotoxicity: Refers to the damaging effect of chemicals applied to plants resulting in stress or even death of the plant.

Pine Bark: A by-product of the lumber milling industry where bark is removed from trees, sent through chopping blades, and graded by particle size for use in the horticulture industry.

Plug: A small starter plant grown in the cell of a tray with compact, well established roots generally formed in the shape of the cell it is grown in.

Pyrethrin: A viscous, liquid ester extracted from white, daisy-like flowers of certain Chrysanthemum family members. Used as a botanical insecticide.

Pyrethroids: Laboratory-produced, synthetic compounds that have similar effects of the natural substances *Pyrethrum* and *Pyrethrin*. Cannot be used in an organic program.

Pyrethrum: A powder made from the crushed, white, daisy-like flowers of certain Chrysanthemum family members. Used as a botanical insecticide.

Radicle: The tiny, embryonic root inside a seed that is attached to the cotyledon (food source) and a pair of embryonic leaves (see *Cotyledon*).

Rhizome: Horizontal stems growing below the soil level which are capable of developing roots and new shoots from nodes and axillary buds.

Root: Underground portion of a plant which serves to anchor the plant in place and absorb water and nutrients from the soil.

Root Cap: Protective covering on the tips of roots that protect them from sharp or hard substances as they work their way through the soil.

Root Hair: Tiny, almost microscopic projection from root epidermal (outer layer) cells. Important in the uptake of water.

Root Pressure: The pressure produced within the cells in roots that forces water and nutrients up the stem to all areas of the plant as needed.

Rotenone: A white, crystalline compound derived from the roots of either derris (a woody vine of tropical Asia) or cube' (a woody plant in the pea family found in tropical America). Used as a botanical insecticide.

Runner: Stem growing along the surface of the soil (horizontally) planting itself as it goes by producing roots at nodes or at the growing tip.

Sabadilla: The powdered seed of *Schoenocaulon officinale* (a member of the lily family) found in Central America and Mexico. Used as a botanical insecticide.

Sand: An inorganic component of soil with individual particles sized between 0.02–2 mm.

Scarify: The process of breaking through the tough outer coat of some seeds by scratching or etching with a knife, file or sandpaper to improve uptake of water.

Seaweed: Kelp that is ecologically harvested, dried and ground into a powder. It comes in either powder or liquid concentrate and is used as fertilizer.

Seed: The dormant reproductive package produced by fruiting plants and containing an embryo and stored food.

Seed Coat: Protective outer covering on seeds that must be penetrated in order for water to get into the seed.

Selected Variety: Variety of a species bred through natural genetic selection from growing the plant out over time and selecting progeny with desirable characteristics, rather than gene mixing via intentional cross-pollination.

Sessile Leaf: A leaf blade that is attached directly to the stem.

Shrub: Generally a woody plant with many, branching stems close to the ground.

Silt: An inorganic component of soil with individual particles sized between 0.002-0.02 mm.

Simple Leaf: A single leaf blade attached to a petiole (petiolate leaf) or directly to the stem (sessile leaf).

Soil: The combination of native sand, silt and clay present in varying percentages with, most often, one or two components dominating. It can also contain moderate to large amounts of various types of rock and/or humus.

Species: A (often large) sub-group of a genus with primary, genetic characteristics similar enough to be identifiable, and whose individual members are able to interbreed freely.

Stem: This is the phenomenally complicated "shoot system" of a plant which consists of primary and secondary branching, with attached leaves (for food) and flowers (for reproduction).

Sticky Traps: Yellow or blue colored cards covered with a sticky substance that traps pest insects as they fly to the color that attracts them most.

Stolons: Often called "runners," these are stems that originate near the parent plant and root easily when the growing tip touches the soil.

Stoma: Microscopic openings in the leaf surface allowing transfer of light, water (in and out) and carbon dioxide to the chloroplasts for photosynthesis to occur (plural: *stomata*).

Stretching: Temporary elongation of the internodal space due to low light levels creating a weak, spindly and often pale plant.

Stunting: Plants with abnormally short stems, small, often deformed leaves, and overall poor color and performance.

Sucker: A vegetative shoot arising from an underground root attached to a parent plant. Often removed, as it saps energy (nutrients and water) from the primary plant.

Sulfur: Yellow, natural mineral powder that binds with calcium in garden soil to bring an alkaline pH down. Often called elemental sulfur or flower (flour) of sulfur.

Summer Oil: A petroleum-based oil (sometimes just referred to as horticultural oil) that is lighter than the dormant oil and used primarily during the warmer times of the year against specific insect pests.

Symbiosis: When plants have a mutually beneficial relationship with another species such as insects that feed on the nectar and spread pollen and birds that eat the fruit and drop the indigestible seed.

Tap Root System: A system of one or more large roots growing vertically down to find deep water sources and mineral deposits.

Taxonomist: Plant scientists that give plants their internationally recognized scientific names.

Trace Nutrients: Mineral elements used in tiny amounts by specific plants for healthy growth and development. These are: chlorine (Cl), aluminum (Al), sodium (Na), silicon (Si) and cobalt (Co).

Transpiration: Water vapor lost from stomatal openings during normal metabolic processes.

Tree: A plant with one or two main stems or "trunks" supporting a large crown of foliage.

True Leaves: The leaves that emerge from a seedling after the cotyledon has given the tiny plant the food needed to begin real growth.

Turgid: The state of a plant when cells are adequately hydrated and are therefore fully "inflated." The plant appears upright, firm and perky.

Variegation: Even or uneven color patterns found in leaves or flowers of plants that is mostly an inherited genetic trait. Probably adaptive, but may also be induced by viral genetic meddling.

Vascular Plant: Any plant containing water- and food-carrying tissues like the xylem and phloem, not unlike the arteries and veins in animals.

Vein: The "vascular" part of the leaf, xylem and phloem. A midrib is the large vein that runs down the middle of the leaf from which all the other smaller veins originate.

Vermiculite: A micaceous, hydrated silicate mineral heated to very high temperatures expanding it into a light, puffy material used in many commercial potting mixes to lighten and retain moisture.

Viability: The state of a seed that is capable of germination if all conditions necessary are met.

Water Holding Capacity: The amount of water held in a soil after normal, gravitational runoff.

Whorled: Flowers, petals or leaves arranged in a ring around the stalk or stem. An example of flowers arranged this way is the Monarda family (horse mint, bee balm).

Wood: The dense, internal tissue developed by mature plants that aids in supporting the trunk, stem and/or branch as it lengthens and expands.

Xeric: Of or characterized by conditions requiring very little water to survive.

Xeriscape: A form of landscaping using xeric plants (those needing little water to survive) to conserve dwindling groundwater and aquifers in regions where this is a concern.

Index

horticultural oils, for pest control, 158
horticulture, defined, 79
host, 82
hybrid, 84
hydration, 215-216

indeterminate growth, 82
inflorescence, 73
information, for consumers, 178-180
insect stings, 213-214
insecticidal soap, for pest control, 159
intercalary meristem, 65
Internal Revenue Service, 3
internode, 57-58
interview, of potential employees, 192-194

labels, 176-178
lateral meristem, 62
latex, 59
lava sand, 118
leaf, arrangements of, 67
leaf axil, 59
leaf blade, 64
leaf, 63-70; compound, 65; margins, 66; palmately compound, 66; pinnately compound, 66; scar, 58; sessile, 64; simple, 65
lenticel, 59
license, nursery/floral, 14
light, for seed germination, 49
lime, 118
Linnaeus, Carolus, 85
lung care, 216-217

macronutrients, 86
managing employees, 196-200
manure, 118
market certificate, 14-15
market research, 10-11
marketing, 171-175
McKenzie, Robin, 208
merchandising, 176-189
mesophile microorganisms, 143
mesophyll, 67-68
mice, in greenhouse, 104-105
micronutrients, 86

microorganisms, 143-144
midrib, 64
miscellaneous forms, 227-237
misting systems, for propagation, 37-38
Misty Hill Farm, xi-xii
moisture, in compost, 144; requirements for seed germination, 49-50
molasses, 118
monocots, 45
mulch, 168-169
multiple fruit, 78-79
mycorrhizae, 56

NPK, 86, 114
National Organic Standards, 16
native plants, 82
naturalized plants, 82-83
necrosis, 83
nectar, 76
nectaries, 76
neem oil, for pest control, 159
nitrogen, in compost, 145
node, 57-58
nomenclature, 180-181
non-hybrid, 84

open-pollinated, 85
organic certification, 15-19
organic, defined, 79-80
organic horticulture, defined, 80
organization, of sales area, 184-185
osmosis, 52
ovary, 73
ovules, 73
oxygen, in compost, 144

panicle, 73
paramagnetism, 98-99
parasite, 83
parenchyma, 61
particle size, in compost, 146
payroll, liabilities and taxes, 200-202
peat moss, 95
pedicel, 71
perennial, 83
perianth, 72